Transport Law in Germany

Transport Law in Germany

Dieter Schwampe

This book was originally published as a monograph in the International Encyclopaedia of Laws/Transport Law.

Founding Editor: Roger Blanpain
General Editor: Frank Hendrickx
Volume Editor: Eric Van Hooydonk

Wolters Kluwer

Published by:
Kluwer Law International B.V.
PO Box 316
2400 AH Alphen aan den Rijn
The Netherlands
E-mail: international-sales@wolterskluwer.com
Website: lrus.wolterskluwer.com

Sold and distributed in North, Central and South America by:
Wolters Kluwer Legal & Regulatory U.S.
7201 McKinney Circle
Frederick, MD 21704
United States of America
Email: customer.service@wolterskluwer.com

Sold and distributed in all other countries by:
Air Business Subscriptions
Rockwood House
Haywards Heath
West Sussex
RH16 3DH
United Kingdom
Email: international-customerservice@wolterskluwer.com

Printed on acid-free paper

ISBN 978-94-035-0315-8

e-Book: ISBN 978-94-035-0203-8
web-PDF: ISBN 978-94-035-0240-3

Printed in the United Kingdom.

The Author

Dieter Schwampe, admitted to the Hamburg Bar in 1985, has been practising law in Germany for thirty-three years. Since twenty-nine years he is a partner of the law firm Dabelstein & Passehl, which after a recent merger is now called Arnecke Sibeth Dabelstein, one of the largest German firms in the areas of maritime, aviation, logistics and transport. Dieter Schwampe specializes in maritime law, general transportation law and marine insurance law. In his career, he has published dozens of books and articles on the mentioned subjects. He is the current President of the German Maritime Law Association (*Deutscher Verein für Internationales Seerecht*), a member of the Executive Council of the Hamburg Association on Insurance Science (*Hamburger Verein für Versicherungswissenschaft*) and a past member of the Executive Council of the Transport and Forwarding Law Committee of the German Lawyers Association. He is also member of the Executive Board of the Comité Maritime International (CMI), Vice Chairman of the Association International de Droit des Assurance (AIDA) and a member of the Legal & Liability Committee of the International Union of Marine Insurance (IUMI). He is also a member of the German Maritime Arbitrators Association (GMAA) and is regularly appointed as arbitrator. Finally, he is teaching general transport law, maritime transport and marine insurance law at the University of Hamburg, which appointed him as Professor of Law in 2013.

The Author

Table of Contents

Table of Contents

List of Abbreviations

ADN	European Agreement concerning the International Carriage of Dangerous Goods by Inland Waterways
ADS	Allgemeine Deutsche Seeversicherungsbedingungen (German General Rules of Marine Insurance)
ADSp	Allgemeine Deutsche Spediteurs-bedingungen (General German Forwarders Conditions)
AEG	Allgemeines Eisenbahngesetz (General Railway Act)
AG	Aktiengesellschaft (Stock Corporation)
ALV	Allgemeine Lotsverordnung (General Pilotage Ordinance)
AtomG	Atomgesetz (Nuclear Act)
BGB	Bürgerliches Gesetzbuch (Civil Code)
BG Verkehr	Berufsgenossenschaft für Transport und Verkehrswirtschaft (Employers Mutual Insurance Association for the Transport and Traffic Industry)
BinSchLV	Verordnung über die Lade- und Löschzeiten sowie das Liegegeld in der Binnenschifffahrt (Ordinance on Loading and Discharging Times and Demurrage in Inland Navigation)
BNatSchG	Bundesnaturschutzgesetz (Federal Act on the Protection of Nature)
BSchG	Binnenschifffahrtsgesetz (Inland Navigation Act)
CMNI	Budapest Convention on the Contract for the Carriage of Goods by Inland Waterways
CLC	International Convention on Civil Liability for Oil Pollution Damage
CLNI	Strasbourg Convention on the Limitation of Liability in Inland Navigation
EEZ	Exclusive Economic Zone
EGBGB	Einführungsgesetz zum BGB (Introductory Code to the Civil Code)
EGHGB	Einführungsgesetz zum Handels-gesetzbuch (Introductory Code to the Commercial Code)

EVO	Eisenbahnverkehrsordnung (Railway Traffic Ordinance)
FamFG	Gesetz über das Verfahren in Familiensachen und in den Angelegenheiten der freiwilligenGerichtsbarkeit (Act on Procedure in Family and Voluntary Matters)
FlaggRG	Flaggenrechtsgesetz (Law oft he Flagg Act)
GewO	Gewerbeordnung (Trade Regulation Code)
GGVSEB	Gefahrgutverordnung Straße, Eisenbahn und Binnenschifffahrt (Dangerous Goods Ordinance on Road, Railway and Inland Navigation)
GmbH	Gesellschaft mit beschränkter Haftung (Company with limited liability)
GVG	Gerichtsverfassungsgesetz (Constitution of Courts Act)
HGB	Handelsgesetzbuch (Commercial Code)
InsO	Insolvenzordnung (Insolvency Code)
IOPC-Fund	International Oil Pollution Compensation Fund
LLMC	Convention on Limitation of Liability for Maritime Claims
LuftVG	Luftverkehrsgesetz (Air Traffic Act)
LuftVZO	Luftverkehrszulassungsordnung (Air Traffic Licensing Ordinance)
MARPOL	International Convention for the Prevention of Marine Pollution from Ships
ÖlSG	Ölschadengesetz (Oil Damage Act)
OSPAR	Convention for the Protection of the Marine Environment of the North-East Atlantic
PBefG	Personenbeförderungsgesetz (Passenger Carriage Act)
SchBesV	Schiffsbesetzungsverordnung (Ship Manning Ordinance)
SchRG	Schiffsrechte Gesetz (Ship Rights Act)
SchRegO	Schiffsregisterordnung (Ship Register Ordinance)
SeeArbG	Seearbeitsgesetz (Maritime Labor Act)
See-BV	Seeleute-Befähigungsverordnung (Crew Qualification Ordinance)
SeeLG	Seelotsgesetz (Maritime Pilotage Act)
SeeFSichV	Verordnung über die Sicherung der Seefahrt (Ordinance for the Safety of Ocean-Shipping)
SeeSchStrO	Seeschifffahrtstraßenordnung (Traffic Regulations for Navigable Maritime Waterways)

List of Abbreviations

SeeStrO	Verordnung zu den Internationalen Regeln von 1972 zur Verhütung von Zusammenstößen auf See (;) (Ordinance on the International Rules of 1972 for the Prevention of Collisions at Sea)
StGB	Strafgesetzbuch (Criminal Code)
StVG	Straßenverkehrsgesetz (Road Traffic Act)
SvertO	Schifffahrtsrechtliche Verteilungs-ordnung (Shipping Law Limitation Procedure Ordinance)
USchadG	Umweltschadengesetz (Environmental Damage Act)
VVG	Versicherungsvertragsgesetz (Insurance Contract Act)
WaStrG	Bundeswasserstraßengesetz (Federal Waterways Act)
WHG	Wasserhaushaltsgesetz (Water Managment Act)
WSA	Wasser- und Schifffahrtsamt (Water and Shipping Office)
WSD	Wasser- und Schifffahrtsdirektion (Water and Shipping Directorate)
ZPO	Zivilprozessordnung (Civil Procedure Code)
ZVG	Zwangsversteigerungsgesetz (Enforced Sales Act)

List of Abbreviations

General Introduction

§1. Geography

1. Germany is a north-western European country stretching 886 km from the North Sea and Baltic Sea in the north to the Alps in the south, and 632 km from the Rhine in the west to the Oder in the east. It has a border length of 3,757 km that is shared with nine other European countries, eight of which belonging to the European Union (EU): Denmark (68 km), Poland (449 km), Czech Republic (812 km), Austria (817 km), Switzerland (316 km), France (455 km), Luxembourg (136 km), Belgium (157 km) and the Netherlands (576 km). The country stretches between 47°16′15″ and 55°03′33″ latitude and 5°52′01″ und 15°02′37″ longitude. In the North Sea there are two sets of islands in coastal waters, the East Frisian and North Frisian islands, as well as one high sea Island, Helgoland. The main islands in the Baltic Sea are Fehmarn, Rügen and Usedom. The German North Sea Coast is a Wadden Sea coast, an intertidal zone characterized by tidal floods and wetlands with an extremely rich biosphere.

The country has a territory of 367,168 km^2. It is spread over sixteen federal states, Baden-Württemberg, Bavaria, Berlin, Brandenburg, Bremen, Hamburg, Hesse, Lower Saxony, Mecklenburg-West Pomerania, North Rhine-Westphalia, Rhineland-Palatinate, Saarland, Saxony, Saxony-Anhalt, Schleswig-Holstein and Thuringia.

The four major rivers are Rhine (865 km in Germany), Weser (744 km), Elbe (727 km) and Danube (647 km). The largest lake is Lake Constance in the south (536 km^2), with borders to Germany, Austria and Switzerland.

The lowest place in Germany is located in Schleswig-Holstein at – 3.54 m below sea level, the highest point the *Zugspitze* mountain in Bavaria at 2.962 m above sea level.

§2. Demography

2. Germany has a population of 82.67 million. (2016) and a population density of 226 inhabitants per km^2. Leaving aside Berlin, Hamburg and Bremen, which are cities and at the same time federal states, the federal state with the highest density is North Rhine-Westphalia with 524 inhabitants per km^2, the federal state with the lowest density is Mecklenburg-West Pomerania with 69 inhabitants per km^2. Around 89.6% of the population have a German passport; the number of people with migration background living in Germany is about 19%. Germany has immigrants from 192 countries, the main group being of Turkish origin (around 1.49 million), followed by Polish origin (around 0.78 million), Syrian origin (0.637 million) and Italian Origin

(0.61 million, all figures as of 2016). About 2.4 million people living in Germany are nationals of other EU Member States. The birth rate in 2014 was relatively low with 1.47 children per female (8.8 births per 1,000 inhabitants). In every year since 1972 more people have died than were born. In 2015, 20.2% of the inhabitants were below 20 years of age, 24.1% between 20 and 40 years, 30.3 between 40 and 60 years, 21.8% between 60 and 80 years and 5.6% older than 80 years. Germany has the second oldest population in the world after Japan.

§3. Information on the Political and Legal System of the Country: Form of Government

3. Germany is a federal republic consisting of sixteen states. The capital is Berlin, which is also one of the sixteen states. The state form is a parliamentary republic with two chambers, the *Bundestag*, the federal parliament, consisting of 630 members, and the *Bundesrat*, consisting of representatives appointed by the *Länder*. Acts are passed with the majority vote of the *Bundestag* and require the involvement and approval of the *Bundesrat* where the Constitution (*Grundgesetz*), which was adopted in 1949, expressly provides so. The highest political rank is that of the President (*Bundespräsident*). Although he has to sign every law passed by the legislative, he has mainly a representative and ceremonial position. He is not directly elected by the people, but by the Federal Assembly (*Bundesversammlung*). The most powerful position is that of the Chancellor (*Bundeskanzler*). Also the Chancellor is not directly elected, but elected by the members of Parliament. Ministers are chosen by the Chancellor and appointed by the President. The German parliamentary democracy is greatly influenced by political parties, which have a special protection under the Constitution. There are mainly two larger parties, the Social Democratic Party and the Christ democratic Union, with some smaller parties like the Free Democratic Party, the Greens, the lefts or the right-wing Alternative for Germany. A political party needs to acquire 5% of the votes in order to be represented in Parliament.

Germany is a member of the EU and the NATO

4. The German judiciary system is a four tier system. There are two different courts available as first instance courts. Their jurisdiction depends on the claim amount. The court in charge for claims with a value of up to EUR 5,000 is the Local Court (*Amtsgericht*). Any party can represent itself in proceedings in the Local Court. There are 639 Local Courts in Germany (2016). A Local Court consists of one professional and a legally trained judge. If the claim value exceeds EUR 5,000, the court in charge is the Regional Court (*Landgericht*). Regional Courts consist of Chambers, the Chambers for Civil Matters and Special Chambers for Commercial Matters. The Chamber for Civil Matters consists of three professionals and legally trained judges; Chamber for Commercial Matters consists of one professional, a legally trained judge and two commercial judges, who may be legal laymen. The Regional Courts are not only first instance courts for claims with a value of more than EUR 5,000, but also hear appeals from Local Courts. Time for an appeal is one month after the service of the judgment. Generally there is no further appeal from an appeal decision of a regional court. There are 115 Regional Courts in Germany (2016).

5. Appeals from a Regional Court are heard by the Court of Appeal (*Oberlandesgericht*). Courts of Appeal consist of Senates. A Senate consists of three legally trained judges. An appeal against a Regional Court decision is admissible if it burdens the appellant with more than EUR 600. There are currently twenty-four Courts of Appeal. Appeals from the Courts of Appeal are heard by the Federal Court (*Bundesgerichtshof*). The Federal Court consists of Senates, each Senate sitting with five professionals and legally trained judges. A further appeal from an Appeal Court (*Revision*) requires permission, which may have been given either by the Court of Appeal or by the Federal court itself, if the Court of Appeal has denied it. Claim values, which had been relevant in the past, have no relevance anymore. A further appeal shall be allowed if the case is of principal interest, or if is required for the further development of the law or in order to secure a consistent jurisprudence. A judgment of the Federal Court is final and binding.

6. If in any of the courts a party pleads that a statutory provision is in breach of the German Constitution, all courts have the power to consider this. All courts may hold that the statutory provision is not in breach of the constitution. If they intend holding that there is a breach of the Constitution, they have no power to decide this but have to refer the matter to the Constitutional Court. The Constitutional Court as such is not part of the civil courts system. It only hears complaints for breach of the constitution. It may become involved if, after a final decision of the Federal Court, a party complains that its constitutional right to be heard in court has been breached.

There are about 14,900 judges active in all German civil courts, of which there are about 43% female (2016).

The language in court is German, which requires that generally all documents submitted must be accompanied by a translation in German. But many courts familiar with transport matters meanwhile accept documentation in the English language, if neither party protests. A law is in preparation which will allow courts to hold proceedings completely in English.

§4. General Introduction Relating to Transportation

7. Given its central European location, Germany has always been a transit country from the Scandinavian countries in the North to Switzerland and Austria and the Mediterranean countries in the South, and from France and the Benelux countries in the West to Poland, the Baltic states and Russia in the East. Germany has a well-developed highway and railroad system, which, however, is reaching its capacity limits due to the ever increasing traffic. The river Rhine is a very important inland waterway for cargo carriage, to a lesser extent also the rivers Elbe and Danube. The major German rivers are connected with a system of well-maintained canals. Germany has two major ports, Hamburg and Bremen/Bremerhaven, with access to the North Sea and various ports on the Baltic Sea, including Kiel, Lübeck and Rostock.

§5. Inland Waterways and Ports

8. Transportation on inland waterways is, even in times of increasing use of trucks for cargo transportation, an important part of transportation in Germany. Given the congestion of roads and the environmental impact of road transport, transport by inland vessels could play a much more relevant role, but despite political support did not make real progress in the last forty years. Transportation by inland craft is done on the rivers Rhine, Main, Danube, Mosel, Neckar, Weser, Elbe, Oder and Havel, which are connected by a system of canals, the major ones being the *Mittelland* canal, the *Elbe-Havel* canal, the *Elbe* side canal, the *Main-Danube* canal, the *Oder-Havel* canal, the *Rhine-Herne* canal, the *Dortmund-Ems* canal, the *Datteln-Hamm* canal and the *Wesel-Datteln* canal. The total volume of cargo carried on all inland waterways amounted in 2016 to 221 million tons. This means that the cargo volume on inland waterways is practically stagnating since the 1970s, fluctuating between 220 and 240 million tons. But carriage of containers had a steady growth from 2015 to 2016 by 2.5% to a total of 2.5 million TEU. Almost 60% of the cargo carried consists of coal, ores and oil and its products. In 2015 there were 1,999 German inland cargo ships with a total capacity of 2,585,236 tons, 411 tug and push boats, 983 day trip passenger ships and 60 inland cruise vessels.

9. The major German ports are those which are both sea and inland craft ports, i.e., Hamburg and Bremen/Bremerhaven. Hamburg is the largest German port and ranks third in Europe after Rotterdam and Antwerp, and nineteenth in the world (2016). It is located 110 km away from the North Sea on River Elbe. The port covers an area of about 80 km^2. It has four container terminals with twenty-two berths with about 7.500 m quay length. There was a total cargo volume of 138.2 million tons and container through-put of 8.9 million in 2016, less than in previous years as a consequence of the sanctions imposed against Russia. More than 10,000 vessels call the port every year. The port of Hamburg is a major feeder port for Scandinavian ports and all Baltic states. The ports of Bremen and Bremerhaven rank second in Germany with major container turnover in Bremerhaven. Germany opened its first and only deep-water port, the Jade-Weser-Port, directly on the North Sea coast in 2012.

§6. Railroads

10. The first German railway line with steam locomotives was opened between the cities of Nürnberg and Fürth in 1835. In 1837 the first long distance line between Leipzig and Dresden (120 km) followed. Railway lines were originally developed by private enterprises but soon the then kingdoms took control and administration of many lines. After World War I, pursuant to the Weimar Constitution, the state-owned and/or run regional railways were taken over by the German Reich. The first railway covering all of Germany, *Deutsche Reichsbahn*, was founded not but before 1924. It provided all railways services until the end of World War II. It was nationalized in East Germany and operated the east German railway system under its original name in what later became the German Democratic Republic (GDR). In West Germany, after the end of World War II the remainders of *Deutsche Reichsbahn* in the western zones were controlled by the allied forces and put together as *Deutsche Bundesbahn* upon formation of the Federal Republic of Germany in 1949. In the course of the reunification of Germany in 1989 both railways were put together. Since 1994 the national German railway is registered as an *Aktiengesellschaft* (stock corporation) in the company register of Berlin-Charlottenburg under the name *Deutsche Bahn*. All shares are in the hands of the state. Also in 1994 the German laws on railways were reformed, since then distinguishing between railway infrastructure companies and railway operating companies. Around 87.5% of the German railway net is operated by one railway infrastructure company, namely *DB Netz*, a subsidiary of *Deutsche Bahn*. Next to *Deutsche Bahn* there is meanwhile a great variety of private railway operating companies both in the carriage of passengers and of cargo. The German railway system has a length of around 42,000 km and as such ranks sixth worldwide by net length and fourth by net length in relation to territory. Passenger trains and cargo trains generally use the same infrastructure, subject to certain tracks reserved for the Intercity Express high-speed passenger trains introduced in 1989.

§7. Road Systems

11. Germany has a highly developed road system, the highest categories being *Autobahnen* (motorways) and *Bundesstraßen* (national highways). The total length of the road net is about 650,000 km, out of which about 12,900 km are motorways, making Germany holding the sixth longest net of motorways worldwide. Due to its location in central Europe the German road net is used for transit purposes by many neighbouring countries. The use of roads is free for passenger cars, but a toll is levied for cargo vehicles on motorways. A toll also for passenger cars is in discussion since years. Speed is limited to 50 km/h within settlements and 100 km/h outside on all roads which are not designated motorways. There is no general speed limit on motorways, but many parts of the German motorway net are subject to speed limits.

§8. Airports and Airlines

12. Germany has a total of thirty-nine commercial airports, many of which have regional character only, but sixteen being classified as international airports. The largest airports by passenger numbers (2016) are Frankfurt (60.7 million), Munich (42.2 million), Dusseldorf (23.5 million), Berlin (21.3 million) and Hamburg (16.2 million). The largest cargo airports by freight tons are Frankfurt (2.15 million), Leipzig (1.05 million) and Köln/Bonn (0.78 million). The first airport opened in Germany was the Hamburg airport in 1911.

13. The major German airline is Lufthansa Group, which carried 109.7 million passengers with 700 planes in 2016, followed by Air Berlin, who filed for insolvency in August 2017 (28.9 million; 144 planes), TUI (8.55 million; 27 planes), Germanwings (7.78 million; 59 planes) and Condor/Thomas Cook (6.73 million; 38 planes).

§9. Pipelines

14. Germany is a large consumer for oil and gas but has only little own production. Oil and gas are imported and carried into the country by tank vessels and pipelines. Pipelines are also used for national distribution. There are eight oil pipeline operators active in Germany operating pipelines with a length of 2,400 km, which supplies 80% of the German refineries with crude oil. Their business is regulated by a special Act, the *Rohrfernleitungsverordnung* (Long Distance Pipeline Ordinance). The longest pipeline connection is the South European Pipeline, an international pipeline linking Lavera-Fos in France with the MIRO refinery in Karlsruhe. It has a length of 770 km and a capacity of 35 million tons. Gas is delivered by pipelines from Norway (Europipe I).

§10. Important Data Relating to Transport Activity

15. Below are some important transport data (*source*: Statistical Yearbook 2016):

- About 2.1 million people working in transport industry are employed in about 91,000 companies.
- The annual turnover of the transport industry is EUR 291 billion.
- 79% of all goods are carried on roads.
- A total of 4,547 billion tons of cargo were carried, of which 3,572 million were carried by road, 367 million tons by rail, 292 million tons by seagoing ships, 221 million tons by inland navigation, 91 million tons by pipelines and 4.4 million tons by air.

§11. Ministry or Department Responsible for Transport Policy

16. Under the German Constitution (*Grundgesetz*), the Federation has the exclusive legislative power for, *inter alia*, treatise on trade and navigation, for air transport, for rail transport as far as carried out by railways owned by the Federation. There are concurrent legislative powers between the Federation and the *Länder* (Federal States), *inter alia*, for ocean and coastal shipping and inland navigation, road transport, rail transport to the extent not performed by railroads owned by the Federation. Concurrent legislative power means that the *Länder* (Federal Sates) have legislative powers as long as and to the extent that the Federation has not exercised its legislative power by enacting a law.

17. The federal motorways and the federal waterways are owned by the Federation. While the Federation carries out the administration of the federal waterways through its own offices, the administration of the federal motorways is done by the *Länder* (Federal States) on federal commission.

18. On federal level, the Ministry in charge of transport is the *Bundesministerium für Verkehr und digitale Infrastruktur*, the Federal Ministry of Traffic and Digital Infrastructure, with offices in Berlin and Bonn. It administrates federal transport policies through a number of Federal Offices, including the *Luftfahrtbundesamt* (Federal Office for Air Traffic), *Bundesaufsichtsamt für Flugsicherung* (Federal Office for the Supervision Air Security), *Bundesamt für Güterverkehr* (Federal Office for Cargo Traffic), *Bundesanstalt für Straßenwesen (Federal Road Research Institute), Bundesanstalt für Wasserbau* (Federal Office for Water Infrastructure), *Bundesamt für Seeschifffahrt und Hydrographie* (Federal Office for Ocean shipping and Hydrography) and *Wasser- und Schifffahrtsverwaltung des Bundes* (Federal Water and Shipping Administration).

19. The *Länder* all have their own Ministries of Traffic, administrating transport issues either on state level to the extent that the Federation has not exercised its concurrent legislative powers or administrating federal powers on federal commission.

20. Private maritime law is handled by the Federal Ministry of Justice, while the Ministry of Traffic and Digital Infrastructure is, through the Federal Office for Ocean Shipping and Hydrography, in charge of flag state and ship registration matters, licensing of seamen. Security on the ocean, including safe manning aspects, and port state control is dealt with and exercised by a Social Security Association, namely the *Berufsgenossenschaft für Transport und Verkehrswirtschaft* (Employers Mutual Insurance Association for the Transport and Traffic Industry), acting through its Ship Safety Division.

Part I. Introduction

Chapter 1. Definitions, Notionsand Delineations

§1. Law of the Sea

21. The Law of the Sea is a part of the Law of Nations. As such, under the German Constitution (Article 26), the general rules of the international Law of the Seas form part of the German Federal Law. Apart from that, Germany has ratified many Conventions in the area of the Law of the Sea, foremost the Convention on the International Maritime Organization, 1948 and the United Nations Convention on the Law of the Sea, 1982. Hamburg is the seat of the International Tribunal for the Law of the Sea (ITLOS).

§2. Maritime Law, Transport Law and Civil Law

22. In the broader sense, transport law is part of the civil law. The general civil law is contained in the *Bürgerliches Gesetzbuch* (BGB; Civil Code). While a contract for transport is generally seen as a particular form of a contract for works, which is contained in §§ 631 et seq. BGB, transport law has traditionally not been dealt with in the BGB. The basic provisions on contracts of carriage have always been in the *Handelsgesetzbuch* (HGB; Commercial Code). But traditionally German law had special laws in place for the various modes of transport. Since 1986 the private transport law only distinguishes between general transport and ocean transport, the former being dealt with by the Fourth Book of the Commercial Code, the latter by its Fifth Book. Multimodal transport is dealt with in the Fourth Book. As a matter of principle, general transport law will apply to multimodal transport, safe for the application of maritime law if loss of or damage to goods was caused on the sea leg of the carriage.

23. The relationship between transport law and general civil law is complex and difficult. The reason for this is that the BGB contains numerous provisions which regulate non-performance or bad performance of obligations. In contrast, transport law has its own provisions dealing with non-performance or bad performance, mostly in respect of the carrier's obligations. With § 280 BGB it also contains the basic course of action for breach of contract: 'If the obligor breaches a duty arising from the obligation, the obligee may demand damages for the damage caused thereby. This does not apply if the obligor is not responsible for the breach of duty.' Obviously, transport law has its own provisions in respect of damages. The question arises, therefore, to what extent general civil law as contained applies next to the special provisions of the transport law or whether transport law sets aside general civil law. Unfortunately, there is no clear and general answer to these questions. There exist many court decisions and the legal literature is full of comments on which general provisions of the BGB apply next to transport law in what situation. This outline of transport law is not the proper place to set out what has been decided and argued in this respect, but the reader must be aware of the difficulties and the need of in-depth studies for individual factual settings.

§3. Law on Standard Business Terms

24. There is one area of civil law; however, the relevance of which for transport law cannot be overestimated. These are the provisions on standard business terms as contained in §§ 305 et seq. BGB. According to § 305 (1) BGB standard business terms are defined as all contract terms pre-formulated for more than two contracts which one party to the contract, which the law refers to as the 'user', presents to the other party upon entering into the contract. The relevance of this area of law is obvious when bearing in mind that transport agreements are widely based on pre-formulated standard clauses. Such standard causes may either be prepared by industry associations, like BIMCO in the maritime field, IATA in aviation, or by national forwarders associations. Or they may be developed by individual companies, and as such are met in Germany both as standard terms of shippers and of carriers or forwarders.

25. While German law generally is characterized by freedom of contract, this is significantly reduced where standard clauses form part of the contract. §§ 305 et seq. BGB insofar aims to protect what the law calls 'the other party', this being the party to the contract which is confronted with standard clauses by his contractual opponent, the user of the standard clauses. Comparable legislation exists also in other jurisdiction, but there this legislation is limited to the consumer area and does not extend to commercial contracts. This is different in Germany. The scope of application of the provisions is dealt with in § 310 BGB. By excluding only a part of the provisions for contracts with entrepreneurs and by stipulating that in respect of certain other provisions, reasonable account shall be taken of the practices and customs that apply in business dealings, it is obvious that otherwise the law applies also to standard business of and between partners of commercial contracts, including commercial contracts of carriage.

This is not the place to go into details of the law on standard business terms. A concise overlook must be sufficient.

26. First, the law deals with requirements according to which standard business terms become part of a contract at all. This is an area which is of less relevance for commercial contracts, as the relevant statutory provisions are declared inapplicable in contracts with entrepreneurs. For consumer contracts, § 305 BGB contains some significant requirements for standard business terms to be included, but for commercial contracts it is sufficient that the parties either expressly or even impliedly agreed on their application. In particular, it is not necessary that the other party receives the terms or is aware of its content at the time of conclusion of the contract.

27. While it may be treated as natural that in case of dispute whether standard business terms have found their way into a contract this question must be finally determined by the court, it may seem more unusual what role the courts play in respect of standard business terms which the courts find to have been agreed upon by the parties. This starts with the possibility for a court to hold that one or more of the terms are so unusual that the other party to the contract did not need to expect to encounter them. If this is so held, according to § 305c (1) BGB, such terms do not form part of the contract – despite the fact that the court, before reaching such conclusion, must have first found that the terms as such had been agreed upon by the parties. In a way, thus, the courts have the power to hold that something has not been agreed simply because it was, in the words of the heading of § 305c BGB, a 'surprising' term.

This protection obviously is not available to the user of the standard business terms, but to the other party which has been confronted with the terms by the user. This demonstrates how important it is to identify who was the user of the terms. This may be particularly difficult if the terms are standard contract forms which may have been referred to by either party so that it may be somewhat of a chance who had been the first to refer to them. Actually, this is one area of continuous criticism of the law, and there are still strong views supporting that the law should be changed in this respect of commercial contracts, as the results may seem to be arbitrary.

28. If none of the terms is in this sense surprising, it may be that the court finds that a term can have different meanings. The test applied in this respect is different from the usual test of interpreting contractual agreements. Usually the courts have to determine the true intention of the parties, taking into account all relevant circumstances, to which not only belong the negotiations leading to the contract, but also the way the parties have actually executed their contract after conclusion. The test for interpreting standard business terms is different. Here it is not relevant what the parties to the contract may have intended with the term, but what an average party would objectively have understood it to mean. It is open to either party to demonstrate that the parties had a joint different understanding. If so this would be treated as an individual agreement which has priority over any construction of a standard term (§ 305b BGB). But in the absence of such joint different understanding, the construction will be an objective one. If such construction leads to two or more possible results, then § 305c (2) BGB stipulates that the resulting doubts are resolved against the user. In practice this means that the court has to adopt such interpretation of the term which is most favourable for the other party. Again this shows how important it is to determine who the user of the terms is.

29. But the law does not only confer on the courts the task to find whether terms have been validly agreed on and what they actually mean, but it confers on the courts also the task to examine the content of the terms and to decide whether, even if agreed on by the parties and being effective parts of the contract, they are nevertheless invalid. In this respect § 307 (1) 1 BGB stipulates that provisions in standard business terms are ineffective if, contrary to the requirement of good faith, they unreasonably disadvantage the other party to the contract with the user. The broad language gives an idea of how much influence the courts do have under German law to determine what is and what is not an effective part of a contract. But the lawmaker has given some guidance what might be contrary to good faith.

First and foremost, an unreasonable disadvantage may arise from the provision not being clear and comprehensible (§ 307 (1) 2 BGB). This so-called transparency requirement plays an important role particularly in consumer contracts, and there in particular in respect of insurance conditions, but the principle as such applies also for commercial contracts.

Second, § 307 (2) BGB contains a legal presumption: in case of doubt an unreasonable disadvantage is to be assumed to exist if a provision is not compatible with essential principles of the statutory provision from which it deviates, or if it limits essential rights or duties inherent in the nature of the contract to such an extent that attainment of the purpose of the contract is jeopardized. Again, the law gives the courts far-reaching possibilities to interfere with the content of what has been agreed by the broad concepts of 'incompatibility' with 'essential principles' and 'essential' rights, 'nature of the contract' and 'jeopardy' of the 'purpose' of the contract.

It cannot come as surprise that views can very much differ on whether a standard business term survives those tests. This explains the great number of decisions rendered in this area of law year by year.

Chapter 2. Main Sources of Transport Law

§1. Maritime Law

I. Treaties

30. Germany has ratified a significant number of international conventions regulating maritime law. They are in force either by enforcing the text of the convention as German law or they are incorporated into an existing German law as such. Difficulties arise in the area of the Hague and Hague-Visby Rules. Germany is a Hague rules country, and as such bound to apply the Hague Rules in relation to other Hague Rules countries. The Visby Protocol was never ratified by Germany, but the main provisions incorporated into the German Commercial Code in 1986. During the preparatory work leading to the new German maritime law of 2013, it was debated whether Germany should terminate the Hague Rules. This was actually suggested by an expert commission, which had been established by the Ministry of Justice and which prepared the first draft of the new law. At the end, Germany remained a Hague Rules country, with the new law containing elements of the Visby Protocol and the Rotterdam Rules, making it again necessary to provide for the application of the Hague Rules in relation to other Hague Rules countries:

- International Convention for the Unification of Certain Rules of Law Relating to Collision Between Vessels, 1910.
- International Convention for the Unification of Certain Rules Relating to Civil Jurisdiction in Matters of Collision, 1952.
- International Convention for the Unification of Certain Rules of Law Relating to Bills of Lading, 1924.
- International Convention for the Unification of Certain Rules Concerning the Immunity of State-Owned Ships, 1926 and the additional Protocol of 1934.
- International Convention for the Unification of Certain Rules Relating to the Arrest of Sea Going Ships, 1952.
- Convention on Facilitation of International Maritime Traffic, 1965.
- International Convention on Civil Liability for Oil Pollution Damage, 1969 as modified by the amending Protocol of 1992 (CLC 1992).
- International Convention on the Establishment of an International Fund for Compensation for Oil Pollution Damage, Brussels 1971 as modified by the amending Protocol of 1992 (Fund Convention 1992) and the additional Protocol of 2003.
- International Convention on Oil Pollution Preparedness, Response and Co-operation, 1990, and Protocol on Preparedness, Response and Co-operation to Pollution Incidents by Hazardous and Noxious Substances, 2000 (OPRC-HNS Protocol).

- Convention Relating to Civil Liability in the Field of Maritime Carriage of Nuclear Material, 1971 (Nuclear Material 1971).
- Convention on the International Regulations for Preventing Collisions at Sea, 1972 as amended (COLREG 1972).
- International Convention for the Prevention of Pollution from Ships, 1973 as modified by the amending Protocols of 1978 and 1997 (MARPOL 1978/97).
- International Convention for the Safety of Life at Sea, London 1974 as amended (SOLAS 1974) and the additional Protocols of 1978 and 1988 and the Agreement 1996.
- Convention on the International Maritime Satellite Organization, 1976 with Amendments.
- Convention on Limitation of Liability for Maritime Claims, 1976 as modified by the amending Protocol of 1996.
- International Convention on Load Lines, 1966 with Protocol of 1988.
- International Convention on Tonnage Measurement of Ships, 1969.
- International Convention for Safe Containers (CSC), 1972.
- Protocol 1993 relating to the Torremolinos International Convention for the Safety of Fishing Vessels, 1977.
- International Convention on Standards of Training, Certification and Watchkeeping for Seafarers, 1978 and Amendments.
- Convention for the Suppression of Unlawful Acts against the Safety of Maritime Navigation, 1988 and the Protocol of 1988.
- International Convention on Salvage, 1989.
- International Convention on Civil Liability for Bunker Oil Pollution Damage, 2001 (Bunker Convention).
- Athens Convention relating to the Carriage of Passengers and their Baggage by Sea, 1974 with Protocol of 2002.
- International Convention on the Control of Harmful Anti-fouling Systems on Ships, 2001.
- International Convention for the Control and Management of Ships Ballast Water and Sediments, 2004.
- Maritime Labor Convention, 2006.
- Nairobi International Convention on the Removal of Wrecks, 2007.

Germany has also signed, but not ratified, the International Convention for the Unification of Certain Rules relating to Maritime Liens and Mortgages, 1967, which has not come into force. Germany has incorporated its provisions into its national law. Germany also signed the International Convention on Maritime Liens and Mortgages, 1993, but decided not to change its national law to bring it in line with this convention when reforming the national maritime law in 2013.

II. National Legislation

31. The German private maritime law is contained in the Fifth Book of the *Handelsgesetzbuch* (HGB; Commercial Code). Law reform in the maritime field is traditionally slow and scarce in Germany. Since the enactment of the Commercial Code in 1898, the maritime law as contained in the Fifth Book was amended only a few times, namely for the incorporation of the Hague Rules, the Limitation Conventions and the Salvage Convention. In its current form it went into force on 26 April 2013.

Rights on ships, like ownership and mortgages, are dealt with in the *Schiffsrechtegesetz* (SchRG; Ship Rights Act).

The maritime labour law is contained in the *Seearbeitsgesetz* (SeearbG; Maritime Labor Act), which incorporates the Maritime Labor Convention.

§2. Inland Navigation

I. Treaties

32. Germany has ratified two conventions on inland navigation:

- The Budapest Convention on the Contract for the Carriage of Goods by Inland Waterways, 2003 (CMNI).
- Strasbourg Convention on the Limitation of Liability in Inland Navigation, 1988 and 2012 (CLNI).

II. National Legislation

33. The national inland navigation is split between the *Handelsgesetzbuch* (HGB; Commercial Code), which contains inland navigation law on contracts of affreightment and bills of lading, and the *Binnenschiffahrtsgesetz* (BSchG; Inland Navigation Act), which deals with all other matters of inland navigation.

§3. Rail Transport

I. Treaties

34. In rail transport Germany has ratified the Convention concerning International Carriage by Rail, 1980 (COTIF) as amended by the Vilnius Protocol 1999.

II. National Legislation

35. Like in the area of inland navigation, contracts of carriage by rail are governed by the *Handelsgesetzbuch* (HGB; Commercial Code). There do exist further statutory regulations like the *Allgemeines Eisenbahngesetz* (AEG; General Railway Act), which deals with the safe operation of a railway, or the *Eisenbahnverkehrsordnung* (EVO;

Railway Traffic Ordinance) dealing with duties in respect of carriage of passengers and their baggage.

§4. Road Transport

I. Treaties

36. Germany has ratified the International Convention on the Contract for the International Carriage of Goods by Road, 1956 (CMR), including the additional Protocol of 1978.

II. National Legislation

37. Contractual road carriage is subject to the general transport law as contained in the Fourth Book of the *Handelsgesetzbuch* (Commercial Code). These statutory provisions are modelled after the CMR, though they have kept the structure of the German transport law. Outside contract, road traffic is governed by the *Straßenverkehrsgesetz* (StVG; Road Traffic Act), which provides, *inter alia*, for a no-fault liability for traffic accidents.

§5. Air Transport

I. Treaties

38. Germany has ratified the Chicago Convention on International Aviation, the International Air Service Transit Agreement and the International Air Transport Agreement, all of 1944.

As to private air transport law, Germany has ratified the Convention for the Unification of Certain Rules for International Carriage by Air (Montreal Convention), 1999.

II. National Legislation

39. National air carriage is subject to the general transport law as contained in the Fourth Book of the *Handelsgetzbuch* (HGB; Commercial Code). Non-contractual air transport law and passenger transport law are dealt with in the *Luftverkehrsgesetz* (LuftVG; Air Traffic Act), which provides for no-fault liability with a limitation depending on the weight of the aircraft.

§6. Multimodal Transportation

I. Treaties

40. There is no multimodal convention in force up to now. Germany has neither ratified nor signed the United Nations Convention on International Multimodal Transport of Goods, 1980. But some of the international conventions ratified by Germany contain provisions on multimodal transport, such as Article 2 CMR for multimodal road, rail and sea transport; Article 48 CIM for multimodal rail and sea carriage; Article 38 Montreal Convention for multimodal transport by air and any other kind of transport mode; Article 2 CMNI for multimodal inland navigation and sea transport.

II. National Legislation

41. Multimodal transport is dealt with the Commercial Code in §§ 452 et seq. HGB as part of the general transport law. These provisions give preference to multimodal provision in international conventions (*see* above).

Chapter 3. Jurisdiction and Courts

42. Germany being a federal republic, the court system distinguishes between courts of the federal states, the *Länder*, and federal courts. For civil matters there is a four-tier system. The lowest court in the system is the *Amtsgericht*, the Local Court. It sits with one judge and is in charge of disputes of values up to EUR 5,000. These courts are meant to be close to the people and the public, so there is a huge number of 650 all over Germany. If the value of the dispute exceeds EUR 5,000, the Court of First Instance, which is also an appeal court for the Local Courts, is the *Landgericht*, the Regional Court. There are 115 Regional Courts in Germany. Regional Courts sit with three professional judges in ordinary civil matters, but all Regional Courts also have special Chambers for Commercial Matters. These also consist of three judges, but here only one is a legally trained judge by profession, the other two being commercial men. Commercial matters are all disputes between merchants. Disputes in maritime law are commercial matters regardless of whether merchants are involved on both sides. An appeal against a decision of a Regional court is lodged with the *Oberlandesgericht*, the Higher Regional Court. Most of the *Länder* have one Higher Regional Court only, but Baden-Württemberg and Rhineland-Palatinate have two each, and Bavaria, Lower Saxony and North Rhine-Westphalia have three each. Higher Regional Courts sit with three professional judges. These were the courts of the *Länder*. The court of last instance in civil matters is the *Bundesgerichtshof*, the Federal Court of Justice. It is a federal court and sits with five professional judges. Separate from the general court system, finally, is the *Bundesverfassungsgericht*, the Federal Constitutional Court. It is only in charge of alleged breach of the German Constitution and as such not a final instance for civil matters.

43. Thy system does not have special Admiralty Courts, but there are special departments for maritime matters at the Local Courts. The Regional Court of Hamburg, which is dealing with most of the German maritime disputes, has two specialized Chambers for Commercial Matters which deal with all collision cases. In the Appeal divisions, there are particular Senates, which deal with all transport matters. Limitation proceedings in maritime matters are dealt with exclusively by the Local Court of Hamburg.

44. Courts have jurisdiction for all defendants resident in their regional areas. For transport matters, there are special jurisdiction rules. According to § 30 *Zivilprozessordnung* (ZPO; Civil Procedure Code) those Courts have additional (not exclusive) jurisdiction, in whose geographical area the agreed place of acceptance of the cargo by the carrier or the agreed place of delivery is located. This applies to all kinds of contracts of transport of cargo. § 31 ZPO contains a special rule for salvage: if the defendant has no seat within Germany, the court at the seat of claimant has jurisdiction, if the claimant has a seat in Germany. This is an exception to the rule that jurisdiction of the courts is dependent on the seat of the defendant, not of the claimant.

Chapter 4. State Immunity and Transport Law

45. Foreign states have immunity under the general principle of the law of the nations, which have the force of German law according to Article 26 of the German Constitution. Foreign states have no immunity for their non-sovereign acts, when they participate in the general trade and commerce. The same applies if a state participates through a state-owned company. For Member States of the International Convention for the Unification of Certain Rules Concerning the Immunity of State-Owned Ship of 1926, such as Germany, Article 1 provides that seagoing ships owned or operated by States, cargoes owned by them, and cargoes and passengers carried on State-owned ships, as well as the States which own or operate such ships and own such cargoes shall be subject, as regards claims in respect of the operation of such ships or in respect of the carriage of such cargoes, to the same rules of liability and the same obligations as those applicable in the case of privately owned ships, cargoes and equipment.

Chapter 5. Transport Intermediaries

46. Modern transport involves a number of service providers who are governed by special sets of rules. Liner operators usually act through agents. There is no special law for agents in the shipping or transport area. They are subject to the general rules of *Handelsvertreter* (Commercial Agents) as contained in §§ 84 et seq. *Handelsgesetzbuch* (HGB; Commercial Code). The task of the liner agent is generally to accept bookings for cargo, to arrange taking over and delivery of cargo and the clearance of incoming and outgoing vessels. German courts have held that a liner agent, when accepting booking of cargo, act on behalf of the line and not in their own name, even if they do not expressly say so.

Shipbrokers act as intermediaries between those who provide transport capacity (shipowners, charterers) and cargo owners. They are regulated by the general provisions on *Handelsmakler* as contained in §§ 93 et seq. HGB. They owe duties to both parties. Shipbrokers earn their remuneration only in case of a successful conclusion of the contract between their principals.

Forwarding agents play a vital role in transport. They are specially regulated in §§ 453 et seq. HGB. Forwarding agents generally only owe to their principals a duty of careful selection of the carrier. For three typical cases, however, the law stipulates that a forwarding agent has the rights and duties of a carrier: (a) if he performs the transport himself (§ 458 HGB); (b) if he has agreed with his principal a fixed amount as remuneration of his services (*Fixkostenspediteur* / Forwarding Agent on fixed Remuneration; § 459 HGB); (c) if he dispatches the goods of his principal together with goods of another principal as a collective consignment (§ 460 HGB). In Germany, forwarding agents usually carry out their business on basis of general terms and conditions. Most wider-spread are the *Allgemeine Deutsche Spediteursbedingungen* (ADSp; General German Forwarders Conditions)

Part II. Maritime Law

Chapter 1. The Vessel

§1. Definition and Legal Status of Vessels

47. The term *Schiff* (ship) is not legally defined in German law. It is settled by jurisprudence of the highest German civil court, the *Bundesgerichtshof* (Federal Court of Justice), that a ship is a vehicle of not only negligible size, which contains a hollow space but has the purpose and capability to carry goods or passengers on or under the water. It is irrelevant whether the vehicle as an engine or other means to move it, so that barges without engines are ships under German law. The requirement of a certain size excludes small vehicles like mall sailing boats, canoes or jet skis. The requirement of a hollow space excludes rafts, consisting of wood poles tied together, from ships. The requirements of the purpose and capability to carry, i.e., move from point to another, cargo or passengers excludes pontoon bridges, hotel or storage vessels and oil platforms. The requirement of carrying passengers or cargo on or under the water excludes hovercrafts, water planes and the so-called ground effect vehicles. Recently, wind farm construction vessels with jack-up facilities have come under discussion. The general view is that they qualify as ships as long as they are swimming but not anymore once they are jacked-up.

48. German law distinguishes between *Seeschiff* (seagoing ship) and *Binnenschiff* (inland navigation ship). The difference is not one of technical nature but of use of the vessel. In order to determine whether a ship is employed in ocean shipping, cf. § 476 *Handelsgesetzbuch* (HGB; Commercial Code), courts have held that this is the case if the ship is used on the ocean with certain regularity, even if the use on inland waters has been more often. What is not decisive for distinguishing a seagoing ship from and inland navigation ship is whether it has been entered into the Ship Register as one or the other ship. But according to § 6 *Schiffsregisterordnung* (SchRegO; Ship Register Ordinance), the owner of a ship registered as a seagoing ship cannot argue that his ship is an inland ship.

49. German law further distinguishes between commercial and non-commercial ships. The maritime law as contained in the HGB applies only to commercial ships. An exception is made by Article 7 of the Introductory Code to the Commercial Code, which stipulates that the Commercial Code provisions on the liability of the shipowner for persons on board the ship, on collision of ships, on salvage and on limitation of liability apply also to non-commercial ships.

50. German law also distinguishes between a ship and a ship under construction (new building). They are registered in different parts of the Register of Ships, and hypothecation of a new building is separately dealt with in the law (for both *see* below). For civil law matters it must be decided from which moment on a ship under construction is legally treated as a ship, giving potential rise to a shipowner's liability. Unfortunately, the dividing line is not completely clear. There exists one decision of the Federal Court of Justice according to which a new building is a ship at least from the moment on in which it is in the water. Whether this excludes a legal quality as a ship for all earlier moments is not yet decided.

§2. Registration and Nationality of Ocean-Going Ships

51. According to Article 91 of the United Nations Convention on the Law of the Sea every State shall fix the conditions for the grant of its nationality to ships, for the registration of ships in its territory, and for the right to fly its flag. It is further stipulated that ships have the nationality of the State whose flag they are entitled to fly. This nationality as well as the registration of the vessel are subject to the *Flaggenrechtsgesetz* (FlaggRG; Law of the Flag Act) and the *Schiffsregisterordnung* (SchRegO; Ship Register Ordinance). According to § 3 SchRegO a commercial ship can be registered in the Register of Ships, if it may or has to fly the German flag. Commercial ships owned by German nationals must fly the German flag. The same applies to unlimited or limited partnerships or juridical persons with seats in Germany, if there is a majority of German nationals as personally liable partners and as partners generally, or as board members (§ 1 FlaggRG). Such ships are generally not allowed to fly a foreign flag (§ 6 FlaggRG), but may be allowed according to § 7 FlaggRG to do so, if they fulfil certain requirements in respect of training and education under German regulations of certain seamen. Such ships remain registered in the German Register of Ships. In order to cope with the commercial pressure on traditional shipping nations, such as Germany, Germany has introduced an International Register of Ships, which is dealt with by § 12 FlaggRG. A ship qualifies for this Register (which is administered by the Federal Ministry of Traffic), if it fulfils the requirements of international ocean-going traffic according to the income tax law.

52. The Register of Ships is not one single register, but there are seventeen different registers administrated by Local Courts. Most of these registers are in coastal cities (Brake, Cuxhaven, Emden, Kiel, Rostock, Wilhelmshaven) or such with seaborne trade and ports (Bremen, Duisburg, Hamburg, Rostock, Stade), but there are also registers in landlocked cities with rivers (Berlin, Mannheim,. Regensburg, Saarbrücken, St. Goar, Wiesbaden, Würzburg), but ships registered there are almost exclusively inland ships.

53. Ships flying the German flag are, once in international waters, treated as part of the German territory, so that all German laws apply.

§3. Registration of Ships under Construction

54. Ships cannot only be registered once they are ships in the legal sense, but they already are registered during the time they are under construction. Every Register of Ships contains as a special section a Register of New-Buildings. The law deals with them in §§ 65 et seq. *Schiffsregisterordnung* (SchRegO; Ship Register Ordinance). The reason for allowing registration of a new building is to enable registration of a mortgage on a new building as a security for loans granted for the purpose of building a ship. Actually, mortgaging of a new building is a requirement for registration of the new building as such. According to § 66 SchRegO a new building will only be registered, if there is simultaneous registration of a mortgage on the new building (leaving aside the other option of an enforced sale of the new building, which also allows registration of the new building for the purposes of the enforced sale).

§4. Acquisition and Ownership

55. In respect of acquisition, German law distinguishes between the law of contract and the law of ownership. There are no limitations under German law for entering into a contract for the sale and purchase of a ship or for acquiring ownership of a ship. A foreigner may acquire ownership of a German ship just as a German may acquire ownership of a foreign ship.

There do not exist special provisions for the sale and purchase of a vessel, so that the general provisions of §§ 433 et seq. *Bürgerliches Gesetzbuch* (BGB; Civil Code) apply (§ 452 BGB), or the provisions of the United Nations Convention on Contracts for the International Sale of Goods, CISG, which has been ratified by Germany.

While Germans treat ships in many respects more similar to real estate, ships are movables, and the acquisition and transfer of ownership are even easier than that of any other movable. Transfer of ownership of ships registered is regulated in the *Schiffsrechtegesetz* (SchRG; Ship Rights Act). According to § 2 SchRG all what is required is that the seller and the buyer agree that ownership shall pass. Although no special form is required for the agreement to transfer title, in practice a written contract will be issued, mostly in internationally widely used forms as the Norwegian Saleform. There is no requirement of a notarial deed, but according to § 2 (2) either party may demand that such a deed is issued. It is noteworthy that title in a seagoing ship passes without any entry into the Register of Ships, while transfer of title of an inland ships requires entry of the transfer into the Register (§ 3 SchRG). Usually, however, the change of ownership will be entered into the Register of Ships, as § 15 (1) SchRG creates a legal assumption of ownership for the person registered as owner.

56. A ship can be owned by an individual, by an unlimited or limited partnership or by a juridical person. Under the Commercial Code all these different kinds of owners are called *Reeder* (§ 476 HGB). A personal owner has, subject to statutory provisions on limitation of liability, full liability for his own debts. In case of an unlimited partnership (*Offene Handelsgesellschaft)* all partners are jointly and severally liable for the debts of the company. In case of a limited partnership (*Kommanditgesellschaft)* only the personally liable partner (which can itself be a company with limited liability) is liable for the debts of the company, all other partners having no personal liability of the have paid in their shares into the company. In case of a juridical person, only such juridical person is liable for the debts of the company, not its directors or shareholders. Until the Maritime Law Reform of 2013 a ship could also be owned by a *Partenreederei*. This was a special company form which was available only to own a ship jointly with the specialty that all partners had an unlimited liability for the debts of the company, but this liability not being joint and several, but several exclusively and limited to the share of the respective partners in the company. This company form was abolished with the reform act, but existing companies continue to be governed by the old law regime.

Under the law an owner may own more than one ship. In practice, however, ships are owned by single ship companies as a way to manage liabilities.

Chapter 2. Maritime Liens and Mortgages

§1. Maritime Liens

I. General Concepts: Introduction

57. Under German law, a maritime lien (*Schiffsgläubigerrecht*) is a right on a ship, which secures a claim. The claims so secured are enumerated in the *Handelsgesetzbuch* (HGB; Commercial Code), and there are no other maritime liens on ships than those enumerated in the HGB. A maritime lien affords the lienor a statutory lien over the ship, which may be asserted against any party in possession of the ship (§ 597 (1) HGB). Maritime liens may come into conflict with mortgages registered on the vessel for financing the building or purchase of the vessel. The law must, therefore, clarify whether maritime liens have priority over mortgages or vice versa.

The German law on maritime liens is part of the HGB and contained in the Fifth Chapter of the Fifth Book, §§ 596–604 HGB. The provisions reflect the International Convention for the Unification of Certain Rules relating to Maritime Liens and Mortgages, 1967, which Germany has signed, though not ratified, and which has not come into force. Germany has also signed the International Convention on Maritime Liens and Mortgages, 1993, but decided in 2013 against incorporation of its provision into the new maritime law, despite the fact that this Convention meanwhile entered into force, the main reason being that with Estonia, Lithuania and Spain so far only three members of the EU have ratified the Convention.

58. Claims secured by a lien arise partly from contractual relationship and partly outside contractual relations. In both situations the debtor of the claim may be but is not necessarily the owner of the ship. But even if he is not, his property, the ship, will be burdened with the lien. A special situation arises if the ship is on a bareboat charter. Under German terminology a bareboat charterer is an *Ausrüster* which is only insufficiently translated as 'Operator'. § 477 (2) HGB provides that in relation to third parties, such an 'Operator' is regarded as being a shipowner. As a consequence, in such a scenario all liability vested by law in the shipowner is not the liability of the owner of the ship but that of its operator. Nevertheless the claimant, whose claim is secured by a maritime lien, is secured in the property of someone who is not his debtor.

59. The maritime lien is not limited to the claim itself but extends to statutory interest accruing on the claim and the costs for exercising the maritime lien (§ 597 (2) HGB).

60. A maritime lien does not exist forever but expires one year after the claim secured thereby has arisen (§ 600 (1) HGB). For the time the claimant is legally prevented from satisfying his claim from the ship, the time limit is prevented from running (§ 600 (3) HGB). The lien does not expire if the claimant arrests the ship on the basis of the lien within the one year time period, provided the ship is subsequently sold by way of execution of a judgment before the arrest in favour of the claimant has been lifted. Usually, arrests are lifted against the shipowner providing acceptable security. If this happens, the maritime lien will expire, the relevant time being either the one year after it came into existence, if the arrest is lifted prior to that year, or the moment of the lifting of the arrest. In such situation, the only security available for the claimant is the security provided by the shipowner. If, at the time of obtaining an executable judgment, the shipowner still owns the ship, the judgment can still be executed into the ship. But if the ship was sold, no execution of the judgment will be possible against the new owner.

61. The maritime lien extends to the ship's accessories, excepting those items forming part of the ship's accessories which did not become the property of the owner of the ship (§ 598 (1) HGB) and to any claim to compensation which the shipowner has against a third party for loss of, or damage to, the ship as well as to any general average allowances in respect of damage to the ship (§ 598 (2) HGB). What the lien does not extend to, however, is any claim under an insurance policy taken out for the ship by the shipowner (§ 598 (3) HGB).

II. Categories of Maritime Liens

62. Maritime liens are provided for by German law for the following claims:

- claims to wages due to the master and the other members of the ship's company (§ 596 (1) No. 1 HGB);
- claims to public charges such as vessel charges, port, canal and other waterway charges and pilotage charges (§ 596 (1) No. 2 HGB);
- personal injury, as well as from the loss of, or damage to property, occurring in direct connection with the operation of the ship; however, claims resulting from the loss of, or damage to property that are based on a contract or that could be derived from a contract shall be excluded (§ 596 (1) No. 3 HGB); but the aforementioned shall not apply to claims that derive from radioactive properties, or a combination of radioactive properties with toxic, explosive or other hazardous properties, of nuclear fuel or of radioactive product or waste (§ 596 (2) HGB);
- claims to a salvage reward, to special compensation, and to the costs of salvage; claims against the owner of the ship and against the creditor of the freight for contribution in general average; claims for wreck removal;
- claims of the social security authorities against the Shipowner, including unemployment insurance claims.

III. Enforcement of Maritime Liens

63. German procedural law generally distinguishes between proceedings leading to a judgment on the merits and the enforcement of such a judgment. This distinction also exists in respect of maritime liens. The claimant, thus, first has to obtain a judgment, alternatively a settlement agreement recorded in a court, confirming his lien and then enforce this judgment into the ship.

Judgments do not need to be final and binding, but executable. First instance judgments are executable against a security fixed by the court (usually covering the judgment debt plus costs for further proceedings). Judgments of the *Oberlandesgerichte* (Higher Regional Courts) are executable without a security. In both cases, however, the debtor can avoid execution if he provides security himself.

The judgment required is not one for payment, but one for the toleration of execution. Summary judgments issued in arrest proceedings are not sufficient, as they do not aim at satisfaction of a claim but only at security for the claim.

As it may in many cases be difficult to obtain such an executable judgment before expiry of the one year time limit, the claimant may be forced to start two proceedings, the substantive proceedings directed at obtaining a judgment against the shipowner to tolerate the execution of the lien, and arrest proceedings, which are the only way to avoid that the lien expires one year after the claim arose.

As it may be that not the claimant secured by a maritime lien starts proceedings for an enforced sale of the vessel, but another creditor of the shipowner, it is advisable for the lienor to notify his lien to the Register of Ships, in which the ship is registered. By this he secures that the register of ships will inform the court in charge of the enforced sale of the lien so notified, § 168b *Zwangsversteigerungsgesetz* (ZVG; Enforced Sales Act), so that the lien will be deemed to have been registered with such court.

64. The action for tolerance of execution of the maritime lien can be directed against the owner of the ship and, if the ship is on bareboat charter, also against the bareboat charterer, in German terminology the *Ausrüster* (§ 601 (2) HGB), only insufficiently translated with 'operator'. The reference to the owner or *Ausrüster* of the ship is a reference to the owner or *Ausrüster* of the ship at the time the maritime lien arose. If ownership or bareboat chart changed until the action shall be commenced, it can only be directed against the old owner or *Ausrüster*, but not against the new owner or *Ausrüster*. While § 597 (1) HGB provides that the lien may be asserted against any party in possession of the ship, this addresses only the exercise of the lien through execution of the judgment by way of enforced sale proceedings, but not the proper party for the proceedings.

In the proceedings the claimant will have to prove his claim. The existence of a maritime lien is a matter of law, not of fact. Once the claimant has proven his claim, it will be on the court to allow the maritime lien – if this exists for the claim pursued.

65. Despite the fact that German substantive law treats ships as movable and not immovable property, execution of judgments into ships follow the rules of execution of judgments into immovable property, § 864 *Zivilpozessordnung* (ZPO; Civil Procedure Code)). While the law allows to enter a mortgage into the Registers of Ships to secure the claim (§ 870a ZPO), this is no viable alternative, as by such a step the maritime lien would lose its priority. What is left is the enforced sale, which is carried out as provided for in the *Zwangsversteigerungsgesetz* (ZVG; Enforced Sales Act). The ZVG contains special provisions for the enforced sale of ships (§§ 162–170 ZVG), and even special provisions for ships not registered in a German Register of Ships (§ 171 ZVG), but unless the special provision stipulate otherwise, generally the procedure for an enforced sale follows the general rules which govern the enforced sale of immovable property (§ 162 ZVG).

66. The court in charge of the enforced sale, regardless whether the ship is registered in Germany or not, is the Local Court which has jurisdiction over the place where the vessel is (§ 163 ZVG). Usually this will be place where the ship had been arrested, so that the Local Court in charge of the enforced sale has already issued an arrest order in respect of that vessel. Together with the order of enforced sale, the court also has to make an order for protection and preserving of the ship (§ 165 ZVG), unless this has been done already in the context of the arrest.

67. The enforced sale is performed by the court making a respective order for such a sale (§ 15 ZVG). The order as such will be recorded in the Register of Ships (§ 19 ZVG). The order has, in respect of the claimant, the effect of an attachment (§ 20 ZVG) with the consequence that the owner cannot transfer ownership anymore (§ 23 ZVG).

68. The court will fix a date for the auctioning of the vessel (§ 35 ZVG). This date has to be published, next to the standard rules for publications, also in a suitable shipping newspaper (§ 168 ZVG). If the ship is registered in a foreign register of ships, the court shall inform the foreign register of the date of the auctioning (§ 170 (3) ZVG).

IV. Liens on Cargo

69. Maritime liens do not only exist on the ship for claims connected with the use on the ship, but they also exist for claims of the carrier on cargo in respect of his claims for freight and expenses. They are dealt with separate from the maritime liens and form part of the provision on the contract of carriage. Following the dichotomy of general transport law and maritime law, there are statutory provisions for liens on cargo both for maritime and for general transport, the latter applying also to multimodal transport. Both laws avail liens for the carrier over cargo carried under a contract of carriage in § 440 and § 495 *Handelsgesetzbuch* (HGB; Commercial Code). They protect freight, demurrage and expenses in respect of the cargo carried at that moment, and also any undisputed freight, demurrage or expenses carried by the same shipper under previous contracts. On principle, the liens are so-called possessory liens, i.e., they exist as long as the carrier has the cargo in possession, either his own direct possession, or indirect possession by a third party holding possession for the carrier, like a warehouse operator or a terminal. But they extend even after delivery, if the carrier pursues them by court proceedings within ten days after delivery, and if at the time the cargo is still in possession of the consignee. With expiry of the ten days period without commencement of court proceedings or prior transfer of possession from the consignee to a third party the lien extinguishes.

The law does not only avail liens on cargo to carriers, but also to forwarding agents, commission agents and warehouse keepers.

V. Ranking and Concurrent Claims

70. Maritime liens have priority over all other rights in the ship (§ 602 HGB), in particular also over rights created by fiscal law as security for tax or custom dues, and also over any mortgage registered on the vessel. A mortgagee, thus, always is exposed to the risk that maritime liens are created which have priority over their mortgage. A mortgage, thus, does not provide full security for a mortgagor. As regards ranking between maritime liens, according to § 603 HGB generally ranks follow the enumeration in § 596 HGB (*see* paragraph 62 above), but with some exceptions. Maritime liens as per § 593 (1) No. 4 HGB – maritime liens to secure claims to a salvage reward, to special compensation, and to the costs of salvage; claims against the owner of the ship and against the creditor of the freight for contribution in general average; claims for wreck removal – always have a ranking prior to any other maritime lien, even if such other maritime lien came into existence earlier. Within the same class of maritime liens, generally all maritime liens have the same ranking, regardless when they came into existence. Regarding claims for personal injury and loss of, or damage to property, occurring in direct connection with the operation of the ship (§ 596 (1) No. 3 HGB), however, liens securing personal injury claims have priority over liens securing property claims. And the maritime liens for salvage, general average, etc. as per § 596 (1) No. 4 HGB) have priority internally following the time they came into existence, with liens coming into existence at the same time having the same ranking.

71. As to the ranking of liens on cargo, liens in connection with the carriage of the cargo have priority over other liens. Apart from that, liens rank in order of time of their existence.

VI. Choice of Law

72. Property law not being harmonized by Regulations of the EU yet, the aspect is subject to the German international property law as contained in the *Einführungsgesetz zum Bürgerlichen Gesetzbuch* (EGBGB; Introductory Code to the Civil Code). Generally, under German property law it is not possible to agree on the applicable property law. This is correct also for maritime liens. The parties cannot agree separately on the law which shall apply to a maritime lien. According to Article 45 (2) 1 EGHGB the creation of statutory security interests in ships and other vehicles is subject to the law applicable to the underlying claim. This law is to be determined according to the provisions of the Rome Regulations. Indirectly the parties can influence the law applicable to a maritime claim, thus, by choosing the law applicable to the underlying claim. By choosing a law that either does or does not provide for a maritime claim, the parties can influence whether there will be a maritime lien or not. The ranking of maritime liens is not following the law of the underlying claim, but according to Article 45 (2) 2 *Einführungsgesetz zum Handelsgesetzbuch* (EGHGB; Introductory Code to the Commercial Code) the law of the country in which the property is situated. If maritime liens are pursued in a German court by arrests of a ship in a German port, thus, the court will determine the existence of the alleged maritime liens on basis of the law governing the underlying claims. If this leads to more than one maritime lien, the court will apply §§ 602–604 *Handelsgesetzbuch* (HGB; Commercial Code) to determine the ranking.

§2. Ship Mortgages

I. General Concepts

73. In modern times ship have become such high investments that they are paid only in absolutely rare cases with funds available to the buyer directly. In the vast majority of cases ships are financed through loans taken from banks. Banks require security for such loans. While also personal guarantees may play a role in this context, the typical security for a loan to finance a ship is a mortgage on the ship, in German legal terminology: a *Schiffshypothek*. The contractual framework of ship finance, thus, requires, *inter alia*, a loan agreement, an agreement to create a mortgage, and finally the creation of the mortgage itself. Further agreements come along with a standard ship finance, such as assignments of earnings and insurances and alike, but here we are looking on the mortgage to secure a loan.

74. German law deals with mortgages on ship in the *Schiffsrechtegesetz* (SchRG; Ship Rights Act). According to the legal definition in § 8 SchRG, a mortgage on a ship is an encumbrance on a ship securing a claim of a creditor allowing to seek satisfaction of his claim out of the ship. Mortgages can be created not only for existing claims, but also for future claims and conditional claims. The personal claim secured by the mortgage and the mortgage itself are separate rights, but they are invariably connected: the right of the mortgagee is determined exclusively by his claim.

As the mortgage is meant to secure the creditor, the claim is no better secured than by the value, and existence, of the ship. Should the ship be damaged, or lost, the security is reduced or vanishes. To enhance the security for a mortgagee, German law provides that the mortgage extends to the insurances of the ship (for details *see* below paragraph 87).

II. Creation of the Ship Mortgage

75. The creation of a mortgage on a ship is, first, subject to the general requirements under civil law. This means that the persons acting on behalf of the parties to the mortgage agreement must have proper authority to represent their principals. Due care must be applied to this requirement, in particular when parties involved are corporate parties, especially under foreign law, not registered in a German company register.

A mortgage cannot only be registered on the whole vessel as such but also on a fraction of the ship (§ 8 (3) SchRG). This was of little practical relevance even at times when ownership in a ship by fraction was possible by way of a so-called *Partenreederei*. This ancient company form lost its attraction over the years, as it exposes the part owners to liability for the company's debts, though only for the respective share of the part owner, but as such without limitation. The *Partenreederei* as a company form has been abolished in the course of the Maritime Law Reform of 2013. Existing *Partenreedereien* continue to exist, and fractional mortgages may be registered on such ships, but only for the share of a part owner. There is no requirement for consent by the other part owners.

76. Even without an express agreement between the parties, the mortgage on the ship extends to the ship's appurtenances (§ 31 SchRG), but only on those appurtenances which are owned by the owner of the ship. Appurtenances are released from the limitations by the mortgage on the ship if they are, not only temporarily, removed from the ship or if they are sold, if removal was done before the appurtenances were attached for the mortgagor. Though not expressly dealt with in the law it is settled that the mortgage extends also to such appurtenances which are brought on the ship only after the creation of the mortgage. The mortgage, thus, always extends to the present appurtenances, as long as these are owned by the shipowner. This is not the case if the seller of appurtenances reserves title until complete payment by the shipowner.

Even without an express agreement by the parties the mortgage does not only secure the debt for which it was agreed, but also statutory interest accruing on such debt and the costs for enforcing the mortgage (§ 29 SchRG).

77. A mortgage cannot only be registered on a single ship but, in the form of a *Gesamthypothek*, i.e., a collective mortgage, on a number of ships (§ 28 SchRG). In such a case the debt is secured for its full amount by all the ships on which the mortgage is registered. The mortgagee may allocate a certain part of the debt to a certain ship with the consequence that such ship only secures the respective part of the debt, but this allocation requires special registration in the register.

78. A mortgage can also be agreed as a *Höchstbetragshypothek*, i.e., a maximum amount mortgage (§ 75 SchRG). This is a mortgage for which, at the time of creation and registration, the debt is not finally determined. It comes into existence as a conditional mortgage only, which effectively becomes a mortgage at the time the debt is created, usually by agreement between the parties. One of the major differences to an ordinary mortgage is that the secured claim may be transferred subject to the rules applicable for the transfer of such claim, i.e., without observation of the special rules applicable for the transfer of a claim secured by a mortgage. If only the general provisions are observed, but not the special provisions for mortgages, a transfer of the maximum amount mortgage to the assignee, the new claimant, is impossible (§ 75 (3) SchRG).

79. Mortgages cannot only be agreed for ships but also for new buildings and floating docks. The latter had to be addressed separately from ships, as under German law a floating dock is not a ship itself (*see* above at paragraph 47). Under the law, a mortgage can be registered on a new building once the keel was laid and the new building was permanently marked by name or number until the time of launching (§ 76 SchRG). Modern shipbuilding, however, is mostly done by building in segments which are then connected to a building dock, which is flooded after completion. Mostly, thus, there is neither a traditional keel laying nor a launching in the old sense anymore. The law is, therefore, applied to the commencement of building of the first section and flooding of the building dock accordingly.

The mortgage on a new building extends to all appurtenances of the new building, but importantly also to all parts of the new building not yet built into the new building but already assigned for the new building and present on the yard, unless not owned by the owner of the new building (§ 79 SchRG).

A mortgage on a new building transforms into a mortgage on the finished ship. In practice, however, new buildings are deleted from the register of new buildings once they are finished and delivered to the buyer. Any mortgage on the new building had to be deleted prior to deletion of the ship from the register. Even if the mortgagor of the new building and the mortgagor of the delivered ship is the same, in practice a fresh mortgage securing a fresh loan agreement is agreed on and registered.

III. Formalities Relating to the Creation of Mortgage

A. Mortgage Deed

80. Different from mortgages on land, for which German law does provide for a mortgage deed in the sense that the mortgage can be validly transferred only by handover of the deed, there are no comparable mortgage deeds on ships.

B. Recording or Registration

81. A mortgage requires registration in the Register of Ships (§ 8 (2) SchRG). This is done by an agreement between the shipowner and the mortgagee that the ship shall be mortgaged and by registration of the mortgage in the register (§ 8 (2), 3 SchRG). The registration itself is done on basis of an *Eintragungsbewilligung*, a consent for entry into the register, which the mortgagor has to declare in a notarized form, § 37 *Schiffsregisterordnung* (SchRO; Ship Register Ordinance). The registration as such mentions the name of the mortgagor, the amount of the mortgage and the interest, if payable.

82. Once a mortgage is registered in the Register of Ships, this creates an assumption that the party registered as mortgagee actually is the mortgagee (§ 15 (2) SchRG). If a mortgage is deleted, there is a legal assumption that it does not exist anymore. Both assumptions are rebuttable.

IV. Ranking

83. The ranking of mortgages generally follows the sequence of registration (§ 25 (1) SchRG). But the ranking is subject to the agreement, which can also be found after a mortgage has been registered. A change in the ranking requires the consent of all mortgagees affected by the change in rank. If there are four mortgages on a ship and the ranks of the second and the third mortgage shall be switched, only the consent of those two mortgagees is required, as neither the first ranking nor the fourth ranking mortgagees are affected by this change. The consent has to be declared to the Register of Ships. It is irrevocable.

It must be noted, however, that maritime liens have priority over any mortgage (*see* above at paragraph 70).

V. Validity Period of Mortgage

84. There is no validity period for a mortgage as such in German law. As the mortgage is linked to the claim it secures, the mortgage will, however, cease to exist once the claim extinguishes. It can extinguish either by satisfaction or by waiver or by assignment to the debtor. Although of little practical relevance it should be added that the expiry of a prescription period, which the claim secured is subject to, does not affect the existence of the claim as such and, thus, does not lead to an extinction of the mortgage (*see also* paragraphs 94 et seq. below).

VI. Assignment of Mortgage

85. The mortgage extinguishes upon satisfaction of the claim. It cannot be transferred to a third party separately, but any transfer of the claim automatically has a transfer of the mortgage as a consequence.

VII. Extent of the Mortgage

86. According to § 29 SchRG, the mortgage automatically extends to statutory interest and the costs associated with the foreclosure and enforced sale.

Also without an express agreement between the parties, the mortgage on the ship extends to the ship's appurtenances (§ 31 SchRG), but only on those appurtenances which are owned by the owner of the ship. Appurtenances are released from the limitations by the mortgage on the ship if they are, not only temporarily, removed from the ship or if they are sold, if removal was done before the appurtenances were attached for the mortgagor. Though not expressly dealt with in the law it is settled that the mortgage also extends to such appurtenances which are brought on the ship only after creation of the mortgage. The mortgage, thus, always extends to the present appurtenances, as long as these are owned by the shipowner. This is not the case if the seller of appurtenances reserves title until complete payment by the shipowner.

87. Even more relevant, if there exists an insurance which is taken out for the ship, according to § 32 SchRG the mortgage extends to such insurance. Only insurances taken 'for the ship' qualify in this respect. This is the case for hull & machinery insurances and increased value insurances, but nor for, e.g., P&I insurances or loss of hire insurances. The effect of the extension is the same as a pledge of the insurance. In essence, the insurer can no more pay to the assured alone, but only jointly to the assured and the mortgagor. The SchRG contains a number of further provisions for the protection of the mortgagor. As regards the mortgagor, payments by the insurer to the assured under the policy are effective only if they are made for the repair of the ship and if such repairs are secured (§ 33 (1) SchRG). If the mortgagor has notified the insurer of the existence of the mortgage, the insurer must notify the mortgagor if premium has not been paid and this has been the reason for fixing a time limit for payment, or if the insurance contract has been terminated for unpaid premium (§ 34 (1) SchRG). A termination becomes effective, as regards the mortgagor, only two weeks after the insurer has notified the mortgagor of the effective termination (§ 33 (2) SchRG). Should the insurer be released from liability due to the behaviour of the assured, he remains generally under the obligation to make payment to the mortgagor (§ 36 (1) SchRG). Only in a few scenarios (§ 36 (2) SchRG) he is released also from liability towards the mortgagor: unpaid premium – here the mortgagor is protected by the notice according to § 33 SchRG, as it allows him to pay the premium himself with the two weeks' notice period; commencement of a voyage in unseaworthy condition; and deviation from the agreed or usual voyage – something of almost no relevance in a market, in which ships are no more insured for individual trips, but for a certain period, usually a year.

88. An insurer, which so pays to the mortgagor without having been obliged to make payment to the assured, effectively releases the assured from the obligation, which was secured by the mortgage, usually the ship finance loan. This leads, as between the assured and the insurer, to unjust enrichment of the assured with the consequence of a claim of the insurer against the assured for unjust enrichment according to § 812 *Bürgerliches Gesetzbuch* (BGB; Civil Code). According to § 37 SchRG, in case of payment by the insurer to the mortgagor, the mortgage passed from the mortgagor to the insurer and from then on secures the insurer's claim for unjust enrichment.

VIII. Enforcement of a Mortgage

89. An enforcement of the mortgage is only possible by enforced sale, § 47 (1) SchRG. Details of the enforcement procedure are contained in the *Zwangsversteigerungsgesetz* (ZVG; Act on Enforced Sale and Enforced Administration). This act governs the enforced sale of immovable property. Despite the fact that ships a (very) movable, the enforced sale follows the same procedure as laid down in this act, with only a few special rules contained in §§ 163–170 ZVG.

90. The court in charge of the sale is the court which has jurisdiction over the palace where the ship is located (§ 163 ZVG). Different from real estate, thus, the place of registration and the Register as such are not of relevance. Simultaneously with the order for an enforced sale the court has to order that the ship is guarded (§ 165 ZVG). The summons for a day at which the auction shall take place must also be published in a special shipping newspaper (§ 168 ZVG). There exist also special rules dealing with cases in which a mortgage is registered in a foreign currency (§ 168c ZVG). In view of the widespread practice of using the US dollar for ship finance, these provisions are of particular relevance. The summons for the hearing must contain a reference to the foreign currency. Upon commencement of the hearing the value of the foreign currency in Euros is determined and from this moment on stays fixed for the proceedings. Bids have to be made in Euros, and the distribution plan is prepared in euros also. If the mortgagor is not fully satisfied with the sales proceeds, the court fixes the unsatisfied balance in Euros, and the amount so fixed is decisive for the mortgagor's participation in possible insolvency proceedings. In all other respects the procedure is the same as for enforced sale of real estate. *See also* paragraph 96.

IX. Ship Mortgage and International Law

91. Mortgages on ships in international trade fulfil their purpose to secure loans given for the finance of the purchase of a ship only if they are internationally acknowledged. A mortgagor of a mortgage registered in Germany, thus, is dependent on foreign law accepting the existence and validity of the German mortgage and providing for procedures to protect the mortgage and allow an enforced sale, should there be a default under the finance contract allowing the foreclosure of the mortgage. Vice versa, the mortgagor of a mortgage registered in a foreign register needs protection in Germany, should he want to arrest the ship on basis of his mortgage, possibly in preparation for an enforced sale. German law provides such protection.

92. Arrests in ships are subject to the general provisions of §§ 916 et seq. of the *Zivilprozessordnung* (ZPO; Civil Procedure Code) and the 1952 Arrest Convention (*see* Chapter 15, paragraphs 365 et seq.). §§ 930, 931 ZPO distinguish between unregistered (§ 930 ZPO) and registered ships (§ 931 ZPO). The aspect of registration in this context refers to registration in a German register of ships (for details *see* paragraph 51). Ships carrying a foreign mortgage must necessarily be registered in a foreign register of ships, as in a German register of ships only a German mortgage can be registered. An arrest on basis of a foreign mortgage, thus, is subject to § 930 ZPO. The arrest is enforced by attachment and is subject to the general provisions on attachment of movable property. The difference to ships registered in Germany mainly consists of the lack of certain procedures on placer for the arrest of ships in German registered, such as the entry of a priority notice in the register of ships (§ 931 III ZPO), what the court obviously cannot achieve if the ship is not registered in Germany.

93. The arrest of a foreign ship on basis of a foreign mortgage only provides for security. Satisfaction in Germany can only be obtained if the mortgagor can, upon foreclosure of the mortgage, obtain an enforced sale in Germany. Enforced sales of ships are subject to the provisions of the *Zwangsversteigerungsgesetz* (ZVG; Act on Enforced Sale and Enforced Administration; for details *see* paragraph 96). § 171 ZVG contains particular provisions for the enforced sale of a foreign ship.

§3. Extinction of Ship Mortgage and Liens

I. Extinction of the Main Claim

94. The mortgage is an accessory right to the claim which it secures. The consequence is that with the extinction of the claim also the mortgage is extinguished. § 57 of the *Schiffsrechtegesetz* (SchRG, Ships Rights Act) expressly stipulates this. But there are two cases in which extinction of the underlying claim does not affect the existence of the mortgage. The first one is dealt with in § 59 SchRG and concerns the situation that the debtor is not the owner of the ship and that he can claim reimbursement of what he has paid from the shipowner. In this case the mortgage continues to exist and now secures the reimbursement claim of the debtor. The other scenario is that the hull insurer, who makes payment to the mortgagor according to §§ 34, 36 SchRG (cf.

paragraph 88). Despite the fact that the effect of such payment is that the main claim is extinguished, § 37 SchRG stipulates that the mortgage is transferred to insurer. It now secures the insurer's claim against the shipowner for unjust enrichment.

II. Waiver by the Creditor

95. The creditor, usually the bank which has financed the ship, can also waiver the main claim. If this happens the mortgage is extinguished as well, § 57 (2) SchrRG. A waiver of the main claim requires notification to the Ship Register or the shipowner and must be entered in the Register.

III. Forced Public Sale

96. The forced public sale is the way a mortgagor can obtain satisfaction of the main claim, which is secured by the mortgage. If such enforced sale takes place (for details *see* paragraph 89), according to § 57 (2) 2 SchRG the mortgage is extinguished.

IV. Voluntary Sale of the Encumbered Vessel

97. The mortgagor and the shipowner can agree that the ship is sold voluntarily, i.e., not through an enforced sale. This will often happen if there is a willing buyer, as enforced sales tend to lead to lower proceeds than voluntary, private sales. If the proceeds cover the main claim, the mortgage will be extinguished by satisfaction of the main claim (paragraph 94). If the main claim is not satisfied, the mortgage will continue to exist and now secures the remainder of the main claim. Buyers, however, will be prepared to buy the ship usually only if it is ensured that the mortgage is deleted from the register. Such a voluntary sale, the proceeds of which do not lead to full satisfaction of the claim, will, therefore, only be possible if the mortgagor is prepared to give up the mortgage. If he does, the mortgage will be deleted from the Register upon notification to the Register of a respective agreement between the mortgagor and the shipowner (§ 55 (1) SchRG).

V. Bankruptcy

98. Bankruptcy as such has no effect on the existence of the mortgage. According to § 33 *Insolvenzordnung* (InsO; Insolvency Code) the opening of insolvency proceedings in respect of the shipowner has to be entered into the Ship Register. The mortgage then can be the basis for separate satisfaction according to § 49 InsO.

VI. Modification of the Vessel's Nationality

99. Article 91 of the United Nations Convention on the Law of the Sea stipulates that every state shall fix the conditions for the grant of its nationality to ships, for the registration of ships in its territory, and for the right to fly its flag, and that ships have the nationality of the state whose flag they are entitled to fly. On this basis, a ship has German nationality if it is entitled to fly the German flag. As set out under paragraph 51, commercial ships owned by German nationals must fly the German flag. The same applies to unlimited or limited partnerships or juridical persons with seats in Germany, if there is a majority of German nationals as personally liable partners and as partners generally, or as board members. If nothing changes in this respect, a German ship cannot change its nationality. If, however, ownership of the ship is transferred to an entity which does not qualify for flying the German flag, the ship must be deleted from the German Register, §§ 20 (1), 17 (4) *Schiffsregisterordnung* (SchRegO, Ship Register Ordinance). But if a mortgage is entered in the Register, according to § 20 (3) SchRegO the ship will only be deleted if the mortgagor agrees to the deletion. A change in nationality, thus, cannot lead to the existence of the mortgage being affected.

Chapter 3. Master and Crew

100. The law of master and crew is primarily subject to the *Seearbeitsgesetz* (SeeArbG; Maritime Labor Act), which was enacted 2013 after the Maritime Labor Convention went into force.

§1. Master

101. The master is appointed by the shipowner to command the ship; he must hold a state qualification certificate which entitles him/her to command the ship. If no master is available, or if the master is unable to attend, the First Officer of the deck department or the sole helmsman shall perform the duties and powers of the master (§ 5 SeeArbG). In order to act as a master of vessel under German flag, the master must either be a German national or a national of an EU/EEA Member State, § 4 *Schiffsbesetzungsverordnung* (SchBesV; Ship Manning Ordinance). Such foreign master has to prove knowledge of the German maritime law by passing a respective test (§ 20 (3) *Seeleute-Befähigungsverordnung* (See-BV; Crew Qualification Ordinance)).

I. Public Functions of the Master

102. The master is the highest authority on board. According to § 121 SeeArbG he is in charge of maintaining public safety and order on board of the ship. The shipowner must not prevent the master from taking all decisions which, at his expert discretion, are required for the safety of the ship and her safe voyage, her safe operation or the safety of the crew members and any other person on board. In case of imminent danger to the ship or any person on board, where necessary, the master may take appropriate action, which includes temporarily arresting people. The law expressly states that insofar the human rights as per Article 2 of the German Constitution are restricted. Action taken by the master must not be more severe than necessary, i.e., he has to select the least restrictive measure. In particular, physical force or temporary arrest are only allowed if other means either from the outset appear to be inadequate or have already proven to be inadequate. Physical force or temporary arrest may be applied no longer than required for the master's performance of his task to maintain public order on board of the ship. Any exercise of his powers must be recorded in the deck log book. The master may transfer his mentioned powers to the First Officer and the First Engineer, both for their respective departments, if he cannot exercise his powers himself. Crew members must be informed of any such transfer. Officers so empowered have to report to the master with twenty-four hours what they have done in exercising these powers.

The master has to treat all persons fairly and has to prevent any violations of laws and morals. Despite his powers to maintain public order, he is not allowed punish crew members physically, treat them in an undignified manner, or coerce or mistreat them, but has to protect them from all these. Young crew members of less than 18 years of age must be protected even during their free time against health and moral risks wherever possible.

II. Private Functions of the Master

103. The old Commercial Code (HGB) contained an own charter, Charter 3, which dealt with the private functions, rights and liabilities of the master. This was abolished in the course of the Maritime Law Reform of 2013. The new law of the HGB deals with the master only in one provision. § 479 HGB authorizes the master to conduct all such business and legal transactions on behalf of the Shipowner which ae usual for the operation of the ship. This extends to issuing bills of lading (*see also* § 513 HGB) and, perhaps less obvious, concluding contracts of carriages. Restrictions on this statutory authority, which are possible for the shipowner to make, will be effective in respect of third parties only if they were aware of such restrictions. The public, thus, may generally rely on the statutory authority.

104. But the law contains numerous provisions which deal with activities and provide rights and duties for masters in respect of private functions of the master. He is the one to whom the dangerous nature of goods shall be declared. In salvage cases the master has the power not only to bind the shipowner in salvage contracts, but also the cargo owners (§ 584 HGB). He has the right to reject salvage services at all (§ 579 HGB) or to demand assistance from further salvors if the circumstances require this, but on the other hand he is obliged to cooperate with the salvor (§ 574 HGB). Court actions to exercise a maritime lien of the salvor in respect of cargo not yet delivered must be commenced against the master (§ 586 HGB). If the master delivers cargo prior to salvage security having provided for such cargo, he incurs a personal liability towards the salvor (§ 587 HBB). In case he provides salvage services with his ship, he is entitled to one-sixth of the salvage remuneration.

In case of common danger for ship and cargo (general average), it is the master who may sacrifice cargo or part of the ship or incur expenses in general average to protect ship and cargo. Similar to the situation under salvage law, the master incurs an own liability towards the parties entitled to contribution if he delivers cargo prior to general average securities having provided for such cargo (§ 594 HGB).

If the shipowner gives his ship on time charter, it will be the time charterer under whose instructions the master is regarding employment.

105. In marine cargo insurance law it is settled that action of the master does not affect insurance cover of the cargo owner. The situation is more difficult in hull and machinery insurance. There the courts have held that unseaworthiness caused by the negligence of the master affects cover for the assured. The market has not accepted these decisions and introduced a special clause according to which 'where unseaworthiness is attributable to acts or omissions of the Master, the assured shall not be answerable for such acts or omissions provided the Assured can prove to have exercised all requisite care towards sending the vessel to sea in seaworthy condition and to have ensured by internal organizational procedures that the vessel's command is able to observe and comply with all applicable provisions and rules of good seamanship' (*Seekasko-Druckstück 12/2003*; Marine Print 12/2003).

III. Liability of the Master

106. Though the master has power to bind the shipowner in contract, he incurs no own contractual liability. Other than his personal liability for delivery of cargo despite existing liens on cargo for general average contributions or salvage remuneration (§§ 587, 594 HGB), there exists no special maritime law provisions under which the master would be liable, but if he causes damage to third party he will be liable to the general civil law of delicts (§ 823 Civil Code). However, the Commercial Code avails the master, and all other crew members, the protection of exclusions from and limitations of liability of the Commercial Code (§§ 508, 547 HGB).

§2. Crew

107. Under commercial law, the crew consists of the master, the officers and the ratings (§ 478 HGB). In respect of labour law, rights and liabilities of crew members are dealt with by the *Seearbeitsgesetz* (SeeArbG; Maritime Labor Act). This defines the term 'Crew members' as all persons working on board the ship, regardless of whether they are employed by the shipowner or by another person or are self-employed, including those employed for the purpose of their vocational training (§ 3). The wide definition requires a number of exceptions. The following persons, though fulfilling the definition, are, *inter alia*, not considered to be crew members for the application of the act:

> Pilots; helmsmen on the Kiel Canal; security staff of private security companies licensed in accordance with the 'Gewerbeordnung' (GewO; Trade Regulation Code); shipyard or systems manufacturer personnel working as a rule for no longer than ninety-six hours in order to implement warrantee, guarantee or maintenance or other work necessary on board shipowners; cargo inspectors working on board up to seventy-two hours; artistes working on board for the entertainment of the passengers for up to seventy-two hours; scientists working on board ships temporarily; pupils at technical schools or students at universities or universities of applied sciences undergoing training at training facilities and undergoing practical training and sea-service experience on a ship for this purpose.

Like in many other areas of commerce, also in the marine field trade unions play an important role. The right to form a trade union is protected by the German Constitution (Article 9). The largest German trade union in the maritime field is *Vereinte Dienstleistungsgewerkschaft*, which is better known by its abbreviation *ver.di.* Trade unions negotiate collective bargaining agreements with shipowners' associations, in Germany the *Verein Deutscher Reeder* (German Shipowners Association).

I. Contract of Employment for Crew Members

108. The employment contracts for ships under German flag are subject to the *Seearbeitsgesetz* (SeeArbG; Maritime Labor Act). Traditionally, the crew was employed by the shipowner, in case of a bareboat charter by the bareboat charterer (§ 553 HGB). Modern times have changed this drastically. Nowadays also many German ships are managed by ship managers, who either enter into employment contracts with the crew or contract this out to special crewing managers. Recognizing the aforementioned developments, the Maritime Labor Act treats such service provider, for the purpose of the Act, as shipowners, so that all obligations which a shipowner is subject to in respect of the crew, are also obligations of such service providers (§ 4 SeeArbG).

109. An owner may employ a crew member only if there is an employment contract in place when the service commences. The contract must be in writing and signed by both parties. Electronic format is expressly excluded. Apart from elements, which are more a matter of course, like names of the parties and alike, the contract must address, *inter alia*, the designation or description of the services to be provided by the seafarer; restrictions to specific ships or trading areas, if agreed; the time of commencement of the engagement, the place and date of taking up service, with designation of the ship; the composition and the amount of the wages, including the supplementary allowances, extra payments, bonuses and special payments or the formula to be used for calculating the wages, as well as the due date of the wages; the agreed hours of work and hours of rest; the amount of paid annual leave; the right for repatriation; a reference to collective bargaining agreements, works agreements or shipboard agreements which are applicable to the engagement; the health care services and social security protection benefits provided to the crew member by the owner.

110. The Act puts much weight on the possibility of the crew member to obtain information on his rights and duties. There must be a copy of the employment contract on board, as well as English and German versions of the Maritime Labor Act and any collective bargaining agreements, work agreements or shipboard agreements which are applicable to a crew member.

II. Recruiting

111. For ships under German flag the SeeArbG contains provisions regulating recruiting through recruiting agencies. §§ 24 et seq. SeeArbG give effect to Regulation 1.4 of the Maritime Labor Convention. If a shipowner engages the services of a recruiting agent with seat in Germany, he has to provide the recruitment agent with written confirmation that the employment contract will meet the statutory requirements of the SeeArbG (*see* above at paragraphs 108 et seq.), that he undertakes to fulfil his obligations with regard to repatriation and that he has taken out insurance to indemnify the crew members for financial losses suffered by them due to breaches of the shipowners' obligations under the employment contract. A shipowner may engage the services of a German recruitment agent only if such agent has been certified by the *Berufsgenossenschaft für Transport und Verkehrswirtschaft* (BG Verkehr; Employers Mutual Insurance Association for the Transport and Traffic Industry). Such certificates have a validity of three years. German recruitment agents, which intend serving shipowners with ships under foreign flag, must obtain from such owners a prior written confirmation that the employment agreement that is to be concluded corresponds to the requirements stipulated in the Maritime Labor Convention.

III. Duties of the Employer and Employee

112. The duties of employers and crew members are specified in the SeeArbG. Obviously, one of the employer's main duties is to pay the agreed wages (§ 37 SeeArbG) plus necessary travel expenses to and from the ship (§ 31 SeeArbG). Wages are calculated in months of thirty days each and payable in arrears. Absent any other agreement in the employment contract, they are payable in Euros. If a foreign currency has been agreed it must be converted on the exchange rate fixed by the European Central Bank. Payment must be made, in the choice of the crew member, partly or totally in cash or in a cashless way. The calculation and composition of each payment must be laid down in a payslip.

The shipowner must observe the statutory rules on maximum work and minimum rest hours. These rules are based on the STCW Convention. Regular working hours must not exceed eight hours per day. Maximum hours of work shall not exceed fourteen hours in any twenty-four hour period and seventy-two hours in any seven-day period. Minimum hours of rest shall not be less than ten hours in any twenty-four hour period, and seventy-seven hours in any seven-day period.

The shipowner has to grant paid leave. The minimum leave is thirty calendar days per year of employment. Times of sickness do not count as leave. Leave shall usually be granted after six months of consecutive service on board. Travel expenses to the place of leave are borne by the shipowner.

The shipowner must repatriate a crew member at his own costs in the event of illness or injury; in the event of termination; in the event of a ship being bound for a zone in which particular dangers are immanent because of armed conflict, and to which the crew member does not consent to go, or if the ship fails to leave such a zone without delay; and in the event of the shipowner no longer fulfilling its legal or contractual obligations as an employer by reason of insolvency, sale of ship, change of ship's registration or any other similar reason. It may sound questionable to stipulate a payment obligation in case of a shipowner in case of insolvency. The background is, however, that the *BG Verkehr* is obliged to arrange, and pay for, the repatriation if the shipowner does not fulfil his duties (§ 77 SeeArbG).

113. The crew member's primary duty is to perform, under the orders of the responsible superior officer, the duties to which he is obliged under the employment contract (§ 32 SeeArbG). As a matter of principle, the crew member must be on board also during his off-duty time unless the master has permitted to leave the ship (§ 334 SeeArbG). But the master has to permit shore leave in off-duty times in port or the roads if the ship's operations, in particular including a fair spread of watch-keeping on all qualified crew members, allow this. To the extent reasonable, the master must ensure a connection to land. The crew member is particularly under the master's order in case of peril to the ship. In such situation he has to obey any orders from the master.

If the ship is at risk of foundering, all crew members must not leave the ship without the master's permission as long as he stays on board himself (§ 36 SeeArbG).

IV. Termination

114. Both sides have the right to terminate the employment contract. The notice period within the first three months of employment is one week. Later it is four weeks to the fifteenth or the last day of a month. Notice periods for the shipowner, not the crew member, are longer in case of longer engagement times with the company or enterprise: three months to the end of a calendar month, if the engagement had been at least eight years; four months in case of ten years, five months in case of twelve years, to the end of a calendar month, six months in case of fifteen years and seven months in case of twenty or more years.

Extraordinary termination is possible both for the shipowner and the crew member, but it requires a compelling reason. In the SeeArbG, some reasons are defined as compelling reasons per se. For the shipowner: the crew member is unsuited to perform the service assigned for reasons which existed prior to the establishment of the engagement (unless the shipowner was aware of these reasons at that time or should have been aware of them under the circumstances); infectious disease; persist or particularly grossly breaches of duties under the engagement; commitment of a criminal offence making it unacceptable to keep him on board.

For the crew member: serious breach of duty by the shipowner or the master; serious violation of the crew member's honour by the master; mistreatment by the master or mistreatment by others tolerated by the master; change of the ship's flag; denial to grant leave as obliged; calling of or failure to leave a contaminated port which causes a serious health risk; sailing into or failure to leave an area exposed to particular dangers from armed conflicts; unseaworthiness of the ship; harmful crew compartments; inadequate or spoiled food supplies or drinking water; insufficient manning of the ship.

Chapter 4. Rights and Obligations of the Carrier, the Contractual Shipper, the Documentary Shipper and the Consignee under a Contract for the Carriage of General Cargo by Sea

§1. General

115. Traditionally, the German law on carriage of goods by sea was significantly different from the contract of carriage by other transport means. Both the maritime transportation law and the general transportation law were dealt with in the *Handelsgesetzbuch* (HGB; Commercial Code) but in different books. Sea transportation was dealt in the Fifth Book and general transport in the Fourth Book. The differences between both areas of law even increased, when the general transport law was revised in 1986. This revision brought the German general transport law much in line with the provisions of CMR and introduced numerous new provisions and concepts which previously had not been part of the German national transport law (*see also* paragraph 406). When the German maritime law was revised in 2013, one of the aims was to bring maritime transportation, again, closer to general transportation. Much of what is explained below, thus, can be found partly identical, partly to a certain extent differently also in general transport.

116. Also under German carriage by sea law the contract for carriage of goods by sea is a contract entered into between two parties, the carrier and the consignor, for the benefit of the third party, the consignee. But the law uses partly different terminology when addressing the parties, and it introduces a person who does not exist in general transport law. The difference in terminology on carrier's side is visible only in the German language: the carrier in general transport is called *Frachtführer*, the carrier sea transport is called *Verfrachter.* Similar differences exist when it comes to the contractual partner of the carrier. In general transport law he is called *Absender* and in sea transport law *Befrachter*. Here the translation differs. The *Absender* is usually translated as consigner, while the *Befrachter* is addressed as *contractual shipper.* The reason for adding the word *contractual* to the word *shipper* is that maritime law adds another person: the *documentary shipper.* This person is alien to general transportation law. Why it was introduced and what its characteristics are will be explained below (paragraph 141). Only the receiver of the goods, in English translation usually described as the *consignee*, has the same name in general transport and sea transport: *Empfänger.*

117. German law acknowledges only contracts for the benefit of a third party, but not to its detriment. This is not different in carriage by seas. The contractual parties, thus, cannot burden the consignor with any obligation. What the law accepts, however, is that obligations for the consignee arise if he elects to make use of the benefits availed to him under the contract. One of the major examples is that the consignee becomes liable for the payment of the freight as soon as he makes use of his right to claim delivery of the goods to him.

§2. The Sea Waybill

118. As regards transport documents, the English translations of the words used in the German text make the distinction not easier. In general transport law the main transport document is the *Frachtbrief.* It is usually translated as *consignment bill.* The second, by far less relevant transport document, is the *Ladeschein*, usually translated as *consignment note.* While the consignment bill is a negotiable instrument, the consignment note is not (*see* paragraph 415). Also carriage by sea has two different transport documents, one being a negotiable instrument, the other one not. Here the most relevant document, and the only document addressed in the old German maritime law, had been the *Konnossement* or *bill of lading.* But as in younger times another document has become more and more important, German law now also addresses a document, which is not a negotiable instrument: the *Seefrachtbrief.* Using the internationally accepted term, this document is widely translated as *sea waybill.* The use of the word *bill* in *waybill* indicates that this document may be somewhat similar to the consignment *bill* in general transport law, but it is not. The relationship actually is:

Seefrachtbrief/Sea Waybill–Frachtbrief/ Consignment Note

Konnossement/Consignment Bill–Ladeschein/Consignment Bill

There is one further major difference between the consignment notes in general transport and the sea waybill in sea transport: The consignment note is issued, upon request of the carrier, by the consignor, while the sea waybill is issued by the carrier.

119. The Fifth Book of the Commercial Code deals with the sea waybill in § 526 HGB. Subsection (1) makes it clear that German law still considers the bill of lading (*see* paragraphs 197 et seq.) as the more relevant document: the carrier may issue a sea waybill '*unless he has issued a bill of lading*'. As to the necessary content of a sea waybill, § 526 (1) HGB refers to § 515 HGB, which stipulates the necessary content of a bill of lading. In maritime transport, thus, the situation is exactly opposite to the situation in general transport law, where the necessary content of a consignment note is defined in § 408 HGB; to which § 443 (1) HGB refers as regards the content of the consignment bill. The content of the sea waybill (and the bill of lading) is comparable to the content of a consignment note (and a consignment bill):

- place and date of issue;
- name and address of the contractual shipper;
- name of the ship;
- name and address of the carrier;
- port of loading and destination;

- name and address of the consignee and notify address, if any;
- nature of the goods and their apparent order and condition;
- quantity, number or weight of the goods and their permanent, legible leading marks;
- freight owed on delivery, costs to be incurred up to the time of delivery as well as a statement concerning payment of the freight;
- number of originals.

According to § 408 (1) No. 6 HGB the consignment note in general transports shall in case of dangerous goods contain their description as required by dangerous goods regulations, or, if there are no such regulations, their generally recognized description. This requirement is missing for sea waybills. The reason is that while the consignment note is issued by the consigner, the sea waybill is issued by the carrier. Without any information from the contractual shipper, the carrier would not be in a position to enter any references regarding the dangerous nature of goods into the sea waybill.

120. Just as in general transport law, there is no need for issuing a sea waybill in order for the contract of carriage by sea to be a binding contract. The relevance of the sea waybill, like that of the consignment note, rests with the evidentiary value it is given by the law. According to § 526 (2) HGB there is a, rebuttable, assumption of the conclusion and content of the contract for the carriage. By reference in § 526 (2) HGB, a sea waybill also creates the presumptions referred to in § 517 HGB for bills of lading. First, it establishes the presumption that the carrier has received the goods in the state described in the sea waybill; but if the description given therein refers to the contents of a closed load device, then the sea waybill of lading establishes the mentioned presumption only if the carrier has inspected the contents and the results of said inspection have been recorded in the sea waybill. If the sea waybill does not provide any information regarding the apparent order and condition of the goods, then it establishes the presumption that the apparent order and condition of the goods were satisfactory at the time the carrier received them. The latter presumption is not given if the carrier has made a reservation in the sea waybill. Such reservation must be detailed enough to show the order and condition of the goods when received by the carrier; which information furnished in the sea waybill is incorrect, and what the correct information is; the carrier's reason for assuming that the information is incorrect; or why the carrier had insufficient opportunity to verify the information furnished. All this is the same as for a bill of lading. The major difference for a sea waybill is that it does not limit the objections of the carrier against a claim as the law does for bills of lading in § 522 HGB (*see* paragraph 199).

121. Differences to the general transport law also exist as to the number of originals and the required signatures. In line with the fact that it is not the shipper contractual shipper who issued the sea waybill, but the carrier, it is the carrier has to sign the sea waybill (§ 526 (3) HGB). While the general transport law stipulates that the consignor can request the carrier to sign the consignment note as well (§ 408 (2) 2 HGB), maritime law does not say that, upon request of the carrier, the contractual shipper would have to sign the sea waybill as well. There is a difference also in respect of the number of originals: While the consignment note must be issued on three originals (§ 408 (2) 1 HGB), there is no such requirement for a sea waybill.

§3. The Carrier

I. The Obligations of the Carrier

122. The carrier's obligation under a contract of carriage by sea is to carry the goods by sea by ship to their destination and there to deliver them to the consignee (§ 481 (1) HGB). He has to do this with a seaworthy and cargoworthy ship. According to § 485 HGB the term 'seaworthiness' includes that the ship is properly furnished, equipped, manned, and sufficiently supplied. Cargoworthiness requires that the holds, including the refrigerating and cooling chambers, as well as all other parts of the ship in or on which cargo is stowed, are fit for the reception, carriage, and preservation of the goods.

The carrier's most important obligation is to carry and deliver the goods in their entirety, without damage, and also without delay with such a seaworthy and cargoworthy ship. As will be seen later (paragraph 228), however, contrary to general transport law maritime transport law does not contain a particular (minimum) liability for delay in delivery. The consequence is that the general rules of the Civil Code apply in respect of late performance of an obligation. But there are further obligations of the carrier, which in first instance have nothing to do with liability for damages. The obligations start with the loading process. While in general transport law the obligations are shared by the consignor and the carrier, unless otherwise agreed in maritime transport it is the carrier alone, who is in charge of loading, stowing, securing and discharging the goods (§ 486 (2) HGB). Without the consent of the contractual shipper carrier may not load the goods on deck, unless they are stowed in a container and loaded on deck of a ship which is properly fitted to carry a container on deck (§ 486 (3) HGB). As regards carriage, if the goods are stored in a container, the carrier is entitled to tranship the container (§ 486 (3) HGB). This implies that in any other kind of carriage the carrier is not entitled to transship, unless he agrees this with the contractual shipper in the contract of carriage.

123. The law addresses a certain loading time only for voyage charters (*see* paragraph 189). For transport of general goods the law leaves this to the agreement between the parties alone (§ 490 (12) HGB). If a loading time has been agreed but the cargo has not been handed over for carriage by the expiry of the agreed time, the carrier can set a reasonable time within which the missing cargo has to be handed over (§ 589 (1) HGB). If this additional time has expired, or if it is obvious that the cargo will not be made available within such time, then the carrier may terminate the contract and claim either the agreed freight, as well as – after setting off any costs or expenses he saved as a result of the termination of the contract, or anything he acquired or failed, in bad faith, to acquire – any costs or expenses incurred; or payment of one third of the freight agreed, the so-called dead freight (§§ 490 (2), 489 (2) HGB). If only a part of the cargo has been made available in time, the carrier may carry that part of the cargo which has already been loaded and stowed but still demand the full freight as well as reimbursement of any costs or expenses incurred as a result of the incompleteness of the cargo. This can, for example, be costs to restow the cargo. What would have to be deducted from the full claim, however, is any freight for goods which the carrier transports on the same ship instead of the goods which had not been loaded

If the cargo was not handed over for carriage for reasons within the sphere of risk of the carrier himself, he is not entitled to any of the mentioned rights.

124. Transports cannot always be carried out as the parties had intended. Obstacles may arise which may be required extraordinary measures in order either to deliver the goods at the intended place of delivery or to bring the contract to an end in another orderly way. Such measures usually result in additional costs, which were not calculated as part of the agreed freight. The law must, therefore, provide for mechanisms for such unforeseen developments and their financial consequences. German maritime transport law does so in § 492 HGB. This provision is almost identical with § 419 HGB, after which it was modelled in the course of the Maritime Law Reform of 2013. The carrier must ask for instructions if it becomes evident, after the goods have been taken over, that the transport of the goods or their delivery cannot be performed in accordance with the contract. The carrier must seek such instructions from the proper party. Seeking from and following instructions of the wrong party qualifies as a breach of contract and can make the carrier liable towards those entitled. Prior to arrival at the place of delivery proper party for instructions generally is the contractual shipper (§ 492 (1) 2 HGB), unless a bill of lading has been issued. If this has been the case, the only party entitled to give instructions is the legitimate bill of lading holder.

125. If the contractual shipper interferes with cargo in the course of transit, this may create problems under the underlying contract of sale, under which the buyer/consignee may want to be protected against any alteration of the intended transport by the contractual shipper. One way to do so would be to let the carrier issue a bill of lading, because, as just explained, where such a bill of lading has been issued, the only person entitled to give instructions to the carrier is the rightful holder of the bill of lading. A buyer/consignee, who is in possession of the bill of lading, thus, is protected from interventions of the contractual shipper. Another, less stringent, way is to enter a remark into a sea waybill that instructions may be given by the contractual shipper only upon presentation of the original sea waybill. This protects the buyer/consignee, if he has obtained possession of a sea waybill so specially claused. But it makes handling of such unexpected situations more difficult, because the consignee would have to send the sea waybill to the contractual shipper, so that he could present it to the carrier when giving instructions. Sea waybills claused this way, therefore, are rare in practice.

126. The right of the contractual shipper to give instructions is lost once the goods reach the place of discharge. At this moment it is the consignee who is entitled to give instructions (§ 492 (1), 492 (2) HGB); but again if a bill of lading has been issued, the consignee must be in possession of the bill in order to give instructions himself. If it is not possible to locate the consignee or if the consignee refuses to accept delivery, in the absence of a bill of lading the right to give instructions falls back to the contractual shipper. Should a sea waybill have been claused to request production of the sea waybill, in this particular situation the contractual shipper may give instructions even without being in possession of the sea waybill. If a bill of lading has been issued but is not presented to the carrier, he must not follow instructions of the contractual shipper or the consignee, but has to take such appropriate steps as he has to take if he does not get instructions at all (*see* below).

127. If an obstacle prevents the carrier from continuation or completion of the transport or from delivery to the consignee, the situation for maritime transports is identical to that for all other transports. He has to describe such obstacle in his request for instruction in a way allowing the party entitled to give instructions to form a view of the situation. Insofar the information given must be sufficiently accurate. The carrier then has to wait a reasonable time for instructions. What is reasonable depends on the situation. If the instructing party has additional questions, the carrier must answer such questions to the best of his ability. If finally instructions are given, the carrier has to follow and execute them. It depends on sphere in which the obstacle arose, whether the carrier is entitled to claim indemnification for costs incurred and additional remuneration. If the obstacle arose in his own sphere, e.g., if the ship used for transport suffers a main engine damage, then the carrier is not entitled to expenses and additional remuneration. In all other situations, i.e., in situations where the obstacle arose in the sphere of the contractual shipper (e.g., insufficient packing of the cargo), but also in cases where the obstacle was neither in the consignor's nor the carrier's sphere – the so-called *neutral zone* –, the carrier is entitled to reimbursements of costs incurred and to additional remuneration, which reflects additional time needed for fulfilment of the contract.

128. If the carrier is unable to obtain instructions within reasonable time he is entitled, and obliged, to take such measures as seem to be in the best interest of the party having the right to give instructions (§ 492 (3) HGB). The law sets out possible activity, but the alternatives mentioned in § 492 (3) HGB are not conclusive and final, but just examples. For instance, the carrier may discharge the goods and store them, in latter case he may entrust them to a third party for storage. If he does so, his only liability in respect of such storage is for exercising due diligence in choosing a third party. The carrier also may return the goods to the place of loading. He may sell them if they are perishable or if the condition warrants such a measure, or if the costs to be incurred otherwise would be out of proportion to the good's value. Finally, he is also entitled to destroy goods which cannot be sold. It is settled that out of all these alternatives the carrier has to choose the one which places the least burden on the party entitled to give instructions. If, for example, the goods still have a value and can be returned to the place of shipment, the carrier is obliged to do so and not entitled either to sell them, even less to destroy them.

129. Special rights are availed to the carrier in case of carriage of dangerous goods. The dangerous nature of the goods may be an obstacle for the further transport of the goods. Had the Carrier been properly advised of the danger, such situations fall under § 492 HGB, so that the carrier has to seek instructions from the party entitled to give such instructions (paragraph 124). But if the carrier, the master or the ship's agent had not been advised of the danger, the carrier does not have to seek instructions. Rather he may, according to § 483 (2) HGB to the extent necessary unload, store, or return dangerous goods or, destroy them or render them harmless. Such action does not require that the danger resulting from the goods either already has materialized or is about to materialize, but the carrier may act upon detection of the dangerous characteristics of the goods. The carrier can act without thereby becoming liable in damages to the contractual shipper, and he may claim reimbursement from the contractual shipper of any costs or expenses necessitated by the measures taken. The carrier can pursue such claims also against such third party, which had been designated by the contractual shipper to delivers the goods to the carrier for carriage, if such third have provided incorrect or incomplete information.

Maritime transport law contains a further provision which was also existing prior to the Maritime Law Reform, but which is not part of the general transport law. If the carrier, the master or the ship's agent knew of the nature of the danger, or had at least been informed of the danger, when the goods were received for carriage, the carrier may only, but may, take the measures just described without becoming liable to the contractual shipper if the dangerous goods were likely to become a danger to the ship or its cargo, and such danger was not due to the Contractual Carrier's fault or neglect (§ 493 (2) 2 HGB). What the carrier may do, thus, is the same as if he did not know of the dangerous nature of the goods. The difference is that if he had this knowledge, he may not act at any time, but only if the goods are likely to become a danger.

130. Freight is payable only upon delivery of the goods (§ 493 (1) HGB). The carrier, thus, has to fulfil his contractual duties before he receives his remuneration. Therefore, the carrier needs to be protected against non-payment of the freight. The law does so by availing the carrier a lien on the cargo carried (§ 495 HGB). This lien does not only cover freight, but also any other monetary claim of the carrier under the contract, e.g., claims for reimbursements of costs and additional remuneration which he is entitled to after following instructions (§§ 492, 491 HGB). Such lien is not limited to goods owned by the contractual shipper. If this were the case, in many situations the carrier would not be properly protected. Instead the law provides that also goods owned by the documentary shipper, i.e., the person who hands over the goods to the carrier for carriage and which is shown in a bill of lading or a sea waybill as the shipper (§ 513 (2) HGB), are subject to the lien. The lien even extends to goods owned by third parties, if they had consented to the carriage of their goods. This does not require consent to a particular contract of carriage, but merely to the carriage as such. But the law goes beyond that. It avails the carrier a lien on goods owned by the contractual shipper for all other undisputed claims which the carrier has under other contracts he has concluded with a contractual shipper for the carriage of goods, for the carriage of goods by sea, for freight forwarding or warehousing.

Generally the lien is a possessory lien, i.e., it exists as long as the carrier has possession of the goods, which includes possession by right of disposal by means of the bill of lading, a consignment bill or a warehouse warrant. But there is an extension of the existence of the lien, which goes beyond a strictly possessory lien, because according to § 495 (3) HGB the lien continues to exist for further ten days (in general transport law: three days, cf. paragraph 429) after delivery if during these ten days the carrier asserts the lien by way of a court action. But there is one limit provided by the law. At the time of submitting the application to the court within the mentioned ten days the goods still must be in possession of the consignee. If the consignee has transferred possession of the goods to a third party at the time of submitting the application to court, there is no further protection of the carrier by a lien.

II. The Liability of the Carrier and Its Limitation

131. The liability of the carrier under a contract of carriage by sea is generally the same as his liability under a bill of lading. Details of this liability, and its limitations and exclusions, thus, are dealt with in detail in paragraphs 212 et seq.

§4. The Contractual Shipper

132. The main obligation of the contractual shipper is to pay freight (§ 493 HGB). Freight is only payable upon delivery of the goods, which means that the carrier has to fulfil his obligations before the contractual shipper has to fulfil. The obligation to pay freight falls away if the carriage is impossible. It is only impossible if the goods cannot be brought to the place of delivery. If there are merely obstacles, which can be overcome by adapting the transport upon instructions sought by the carrier given from the party entitled (cf. paragraph 124), the transport is not impossible and the obligation to pay freight does not fall away. Rather, additional obligations in respect of disbursements of the carrier or additional remuneration may arise. The obligation to pay freight also continues to exist if the transport becomes impossible for reasons within the sphere of risk of the contractual shipper or at a time when the consignor is in default of his obligation to accept performance by the carrier.

133. But the contractual shipper is also under various other obligations. One obligation has already been discussed above (paragraph 119): If the goods to be shipped are of dangerous nature, § 483 (1) HGB requires the contractual shipper to inform the carrier in a timely manner of the precise nature of the danger and, to the extent necessary, of any precautionary measures to be taken to count as such dangers. This extra information must be given in text form which, according to § 126b of the *Bürgerliches Gesetzbuch* (BGB German Civil Code), means that the declaration must be made in a document or another manner suitable for its permanent reproduction in writing. The last alternative applies to the most relevant form of communication nowadays, e-mails.

Not only for dangerous cargo, but for any kind of cargo, the contractual shipper is under an obligation to package cargo, which in view of its nature and the carriage agreed requires packaging, to package them in such a way that it is protected against loss and damage and in such a way that the carrier suffers no loss or damage. These two obligations are of different quality. The first obligation is one which is meant to protect the contractual shipper himself from loss or damage. If he does not fulfil it, the consequences resulting therefrom have to be borne by himself. If goods are lost or damaged due to insufficient packaging, the carrier is released from liability according to § 499 (1) No. 5 HGB. A carrier who realizes that packaging may not be insufficient in view of the nature of the goods and the carriage agreed, may be under an obligation to inform the contractual shipper of this fact, but he is not entitled to refrain from carrying such goods, because the consequences of such insufficient packaging would only be borne by the contractual shipper. The situation is different with the second alternative, where the insufficiency of packaging could lead to loss or damage of the carrier. If this actually happens, the contractual shipper is liable according to the general provision for breach of contractual obligations under § 280 BGB. Such liability may be reduced under the principle of contributory negligence as laid down in § 254 BGB, if the carrier realized the insufficiency of packaging but nevertheless performed the transport. If the carrier realizes the insufficiency of the packaging, he is entitled to withhold his own obligation (§ 320 BGB), i.e., he can refrain from commencing the transport until the packaging is sufficient.

Just as the contractual shipper has to care for proper packaging of the goods, he is obliged to label or mark the goods insofar as their contractually agreed handling so requires. The main purpose of this rule is to avoid that goods of similar outer appearance are mixed up and wrongly delivered. Here, usually no damage to the carrier occurs so that the consequences of inferior labelling or marking hit the consignor only: According to § 499 (1) No. 5 HGB the carrier is released from liability for loss of or damage to the goods or for delay in delivery, if same was caused by insufficient labelling or marking.

134. One major difference between sea transport and all other kinds of transport is in the area of loading, stowing and discharge. In general transport, absent contrary agreement between the parties or other customary practice, the consignor is obliged to load, stow and secure and discharge the goods. In sea transport of general goods loading, stowage and discharge of the goods is not the obligation of the contractual shipper but of the carrier (§ 486 (2) HGB). This is again different in case of voyage charters: here the loading obligation rests with the charterer (§ 531 (1) HGB; *see also* paragraph 188).

135. The scenarios, in which difficulties arise for the carrier in respect of performing the agreed transport, have already been discussed above. In these scenarios, the carrier is obliged to seek instructions from the party entitled to give such instructions (for details *see* above paragraph 124). Such scenarios may arise, however, also before the carrier realizes them, or situations may arise which do not affect the transport as such, but which make the transport as agreed less useful or even useless for the contractual shipper. A typical case would be that the contract of sale and purchase, which is underlying the transport of the goods, is cancelled so that it does not make sense anymore for the contractual shipper (as buyer) to continue transporting the goods to the buyer. For all such situations, the law gives the contractual shipper the right to change what had originally been contractually agreed. This effect, the change of the content of the contract, is not really apparent from the words chosen by the lawmakers. § 491 HGB is headed *Nachträgliche Weisungen* (subsequent instructions). The first sentence of subsection 1 does say no more than that the right of disposal in relation to the goods is with the contractual shipper. Then follow certain examples of this right under which the contractual shipper may give certain instructions to the carrier who has to follow them according to the third sentence. What is not directly visible from the wording of the law, but what is settled in German law, is that such instructions actually do change the content of the contract. As long as such 'instructions' remain within the limits provided for by the law, the contract is changed merely by the contractual shipper making such instructions.

136. The right to give instructions is a right in relation to the goods. It follows that the right is limited to the goods as agreed in the contract of carriage. Neither can the contractual shipper replace the contractually agreed goods with other goods nor can he change the quantity of goods to be carried. But in relation to the goods to be carried the law allows him to instruct the carrier to stop the goods in transit, to deliver them to another destination, to deliver them to another place of discharge at the destination or to deliver them to another consignee. To the extent that the law then states that the carrier is obliged to comply with such instructions, this actually means that the carrier is obliged to fulfil the contract in its amended or altered content. But also these rights are not unlimited. The law states that the carrier is not obliged to comply with instructions insofar as this cannot be done without the risk of prejudice to his business or damage to the contractual shippers or consignees of other shipments. If this is the case, not only is the carrier not obliged to follow the instructions, but it is settled that in such scenarios the contractual shipper's instructions do not effectively change the content of the contract.

137. The right of the contractual shipper to change the contract does not come for free. Rather the carrier may claim from the contractual shipper reimbursement of the costs and expenses incurred as a result of having carried out the contractual shipper's instructions. If the transport means is used for a longer time than it would have been used on basis of the original contract of carriage, the consignor is also obliged to pay the carrier a reasonable remuneration.

The wording of § 491 HGB is almost identical with that of § 418 HGB, which relates to general transport. But for practical reasons a sea carrier will be much more often in a situation where he is not bound to follow instructions, because this would mean risking prejudice of the carrier's business. The official reasons stated by the Government in the draft reform bill expressly address insofar the scenario that goods are carried in a containership together with goods of many other shippers, or on basis of a slot charter, which usually is characterized by a multiplicity of carriers.

138. In § 488 HGB the Commercial Code provides for a liability of the contractual shipper to the carrier. He has to compensate the carrier for any damage, costs or expenses caused by the inaccuracy or incompleteness of the required information regarding the goods; by the failure to disclose the goods' dangerous nature; by the insufficient packing or labelling or marking of the goods; or by the lack, incompleteness or inaccuracy of documents or information referred to in § 487 (1) HGB. Comparing this provision with § 414 HGB, which addresses similar scenarios for general transport, despite different structure the provisions are materially identical. But their effect is drastically different due to one major difference: while the consignor's liability in general transport law is a no-fault liability (*see* paragraph 436), in sea carriage the contractual shipper is released from liability if he proves that the breach of duties is not due to his fault or neglect (§ 488 (2) HGB). He can, thus, exonerate himself. This is insofar remarkable as the maritime law prior to the reform in 2013 indeed also provided for a no-fault liability. The lawmaker, thus, has lessened the liability requirements for the contractual carrier and made it more difficult for the carrier to obtain indemnification for loss or damage. The reason stated by the Government in the draft reform bill is that it would be unbalanced if the carrier is liable only fault based (cf. § 498 (2) HGB), while the contractual shipper would be liable without relevance of fault.

But matters get more complex in view of how the lawmaker has dealt with the same scenario in case a bill of lading has been issued. If this is the case the contractual shipper is liable to the carrier, even if he is not at fault, for any damage, costs or expenses caused by the inaccuracy or incompleteness of any information in the bill of lading regarding quantity, number or weight of the goods and their permanent, legible leading marks, or the failure to disclose the dangerous nature of the goods. The explanation given by the lawmakers is that in these cases also the Hague-Visby Rules provide for a no-fault liability of the shipper. This may be true, but it leads to a somewhat strange differentiation. A contractual shipper, who agrees with the carrier on the issue of a sea waybill is better off as regards liability to the carrier than a contractual shipper who agrees on the issue of a bill of lading. What transport document is issued, however, is largely a matter which is determined by the sales contract, which is underlying the contract of carriage. One may well question whether provisions are wise which lead to different legal regimes for situations, which are actually predominantly structured by needs entirely outside the transport arrangements.

139. § 488 (5) HGB allows deviation from the liability provisions only by individually negotiated agreements, but such agreements may be concluded also for agreed several similar contracts between the same parties. Derogation by standard business terms is only possible in respect of the introduction of a limitation of the contractual shipper's liability. On first glance this seems to be a difference from what § 414 HGB provides in general transport, as no such provision is found in § 414 HGB. But the difference is only in structure, not in substance. For sea carriage § 488 HGB had to deal with the mandatory application itself, because the general rules on mandatory application in § 512 HGB only relates to the provisions of Subtitle 2, while § 488 HGB is part of Subtitle 1. Such structure was not necessary for general transport law, because there the rule on mandatory application contained in § 449 HGB also addresses § 414 HGB.

140. Finally, in case of loss of or damage to the goods or delay in delivery the contractual shipper is entitled to claim damages from the carrier (§ 494 (1) HGB).

§5. The Documentary Shipper

141. The documentary shipper is a person peculiar to sea carriage. It does not exist as such in general transport law. It is legally defined in § 513 (2) HGB as the person who delivers the goods to the carrier for carriage and who has been designated by the contractual shipper as such for the purpose of being recorded in the bill of lading. It follows, thus, that the documentary shipper does not exist if a sea waybill is issued instead of a bill of lading. In line with this, when § 526 (1) HGB, dealing with sea waybills, refers to provision applicable to bills of lading, it states that the contractual shipper takes the place of the documentary shipper.

The documentary shipper has widespread rights and responsibilities. Once having been designated by the contractual shipper, he is the one who has to right to request from the carrier the issue of an order bill of lading (§ 513 (1) HGB), which has to identify him by name (§ 515 (2) No. 2 HGB). If the carrier has issued a 'received for shipment' bill of lading, he is the one who can request the so-called 'notice of shipment'), i.e., the carrier's statement in the bill of lading when and by which ship the goods were loaded on board (§ 514 (2) HGB). He is the one who has to consent to the loading of cargo on deck (§ 486 (4) HGB).

From him the carrier can request general information on the goods (§ 482 HGB) and particular information on their dangerous nature (§ 483 HGB). His goods are subject to the lien of the carrier (§ 495 (1) HGB). He can be liable to the carrier for wrong information given (§ 488 (2) HGB). His acts or omissions, in particular in respect of insufficiency of packing or improper labelling or marking of the cargo units release the carrier from liability (§ 499 (1) No. 5 HGB; *see also* paragraph 133). Next to the contractual carrier he is under a no-fault liability to the carrier for damage, costs or expenses caused by the inaccuracy or incompleteness of any information in the bill of lading regarding quantity, number or weight of the goods and their permanent, legible leading marks, or the failure to disclose the dangerous nature of the goods (§ 488 (3) HGB).

§6. The Consignee

142. The main right of the consignee is to demand from the carrier delivery of the goods once the goods have arrived at the place designated for delivery (§ 494 (1) HGB). This right is not unconditional. Rather the consignee, who demands delivery, has to perform certain obligations under the contract. One of these obligations is especially dealt with in § 494 (2) HGB: a consignee who executes his rights must pay any freight still due. The law limits this liability to pay freight up to the amount specified in the transport document (bill of lading according to § 515 (1) No. 9 HGB or sea waybill, § 526 HGB).

143. But the consignee has certain rights even before he has demanded delivery of the goods and by that created own obligations for him. By virtue of § 491 (2) HGB the right to dispose of the goods, which is originally vested in the contractual shipper, expires at the moment the goods arrive at the place of discharge. From this moment on the right of disposal is vested in the consignee. This right is not dependent on the consignee demanding delivery. As a consequence, the consignee is in a position to alter the contract of carriage by giving instructions to the carrier without being subjected to the obligations he is exposed to when demanding delivery. But if the consignee so alters the contract, resulting costs or expenses incurred by the carrier as well as a possible reasonable remuneration will be payable by the consignee (§ 491 (2) 2 HGB). Amongst the rights transferred from the contractual shipper to the consignee upon arrival of the goods at the place of discharge is the right to instruct delivery to another consignee (§ 491 (1) 1 HGB). If the consignee makes use of this right, effectively he puts someone else in the position of the consignee. This new consignee then is the consignee with all the statutory rights vested in a consignee by the law. In general transport law for such a 'subsequent' consignee it is not possible anymore to give instructions to deliver the goods to another, now third, consignee (§ 418 (3) HGB). This limitation has not been taken over into maritime transport law. As a consequence, any consignee can give instructions for the delivery to another consignee, so that the actual and final consignee can be replaced more than one time.

Finally the consignee who has demanded delivery of the goods to him is entitled to claim damages from the carrier in case the goods have been delivered damaged or late or have been lost (§ 494 (1) 2 HGB).

Chapter 5. Liability and Limitation of Liability in Maritime Law

§1. General Principles

144. German law distinguishes between statutory liability and contractual liability. In respect of contractual liability it distinguishes further between liabilities imposed simply as a consequence of the fact that the parties have entered into a respective contract, and liabilities imposed by one party on the other by special contractual provisions. Both latter forms are forms of contractual liability. The general concept of civil law liability in Germany is that of fault and causation. Non-contractual liability, as a matter of principle, requires fault of the wrong-doer in order for him to become liable. No-fault or strict liability requires a special statutory basis. Prominent examples are the strict liabilities of vehicle owners, producers for defective products and owners of nuclear installations. Under the freedom of contract principle parties are free to agree on contractual strict liability, but there are limits for doing so in standard contract terms, which may be held invalid by courts on the ground that they deviate from basic principles of the law. The fault principle has been held repeatedly to be one of those basic principles, so that strict liability cannot be imposed by way of standard contract terms.

If a debtor is a company, for example a company with limited liability (*Gesellschaft mit beschränkter Haftung*/GmbH), then such company is responsible for any act of its directors. § 31 *Bürgerliches Gesetzbuch* (BGB; Civil Code) provides this for associations, but it is settled that it applies to any kind of company or corporation.

145. Liability is not only imposed on the acting party as such but can also be imposed on third parties not acting directly themselves. Such kind of vicarious liability exists both in contractual and non-contractual form. If a party to a contract makes use of someone else for the performance of his obligations, such party is responsible for this person's fault to the same extent as for fault on his own part (§ 278 BGB). Insofar it is possible that a party acting itself without fault becomes contractually liable on basis of someone else's fault. There is no way to avoid such vicarious liability by proving the absence of own fault. This is different for vicarious liability on non-contractual basis. In this case someone using another person to perform a task is liable for unlawful damage inflicted on a third party. In this case exoneration is possible, however, by proof that reasonable care was adopted in the selection and supervision of the acting person (§ 831 Civil Code).

§2. Liability of a Shipowner and the Crew

146. Shipowners and crew members may become liable under statute or contract just as any other person can. Prior to the Maritime Maw Reform in Germany in 2013, the old version of the *Handeslgesetzbuch* (HGB; Commercial Code) contained special provisions imposing certain liability on the master of a ship. No special liability provisions existed for other crew members. But even those existing for masters were abolished by the reform. Nowadays, thus, crew members are liable only as per the general civil law.

147. This is different for shipowners. First, there exists a special provision in § 480 HGB. This provides that if, in the course of performing his duties, a crew member or a pilot on board the ship becomes liable to a third party, the shipowner is also liable for the damages. But it is also provided that in case liability towards a person having an interest in cargo carried on board the owner's ship, the shipowner is only liable as if he were the contractual carrier.

This raises a number of questions, namely:

- For which persons is the shipowner responsible? – *see* paragraph 148.
- What qualifies as something done in the course of performing a duty? – *see* paragraph 149.
- Who are persons interested in cargo? – *see* paragraph 150.
- What is the liability of the contractual carrier, to whose liability the liability of the shipowner is reduced? – *see* paragraph 151.

148. To the first question. The question who is a crew member is answered by the HGB. We have seen above that the Maritime Labor Act (SeeArbG) contains own definitions of a crew member, and that those definitions are fairly wide. But those definitions are relevant only for the purposes of the SeeArbG. For the purpose of determining who is a crew member under § 480 HGB, the definition of the HGB itself is decisive. § 478 HGB describes them as the master, the officers and the crew. Insofar the new law is identical with the old law prior to the Maritime Law Reform of 2013. But the old law then only extended this to other persons employed on the ship. The new law is wider, extending not only to all other persons involved in the operation of the ship who have been employed by the shipowner or by the operator, but also to all persons who have been put at the disposal of the shipowner or operator by a third party for the purpose of performing work relating to the ship's operation, and who are subject to the orders of the master. The requirement of employment nowadays is not absolute anymore, as also such persons are embraced who are not employed by either the shipowner or the operator, but who nevertheless are on board for the purpose of performing work in respect of the ship's operation. The purpose of the new law was to provide answers to questions raised under the old law whether self-employed or independent merchants and their servants, like crew members of tugs, stevedores, longshoremen, could qualify as crew members. The decisive element now is no more employment, but subordination under the master and performance of service for the operation of the ship. As a consequence, crew members of tug boats, which used to be treated under the old law as if they were crew members, do not qualify any more.

Apart from crew members as defined in § 478 HGB, § 480 HGB only refers to pilots onboard of the ship. This was necessary, as according to § 1 *Seelotsgesetz* (SeeLG, Marine Pilotage Act), the marine pilot is not a crew member. For pilots onboard, the law does not distinguish between voluntary and compulsory pilotage.

Neither does it require that the pilot is under the orders of the master. Under German law, there does exist compulsory pilotage, but the master always remains responsible for the navigation of the ship. In other jurisdictions there exists pilotage in which the navigation of the ship is exclusively in the hands of the pilot. But if damage is caused in such jurisdictions, the liability usually will be determined under local law and not under § 480 HGB.

The so-called radar pilots, who perform assistance from radar stations, thus, are not embraced. The shipowner, thus, is not vicariously liable for unlawful damage caused by such radar pilots.

149. To the second question. The shipowner is only responsible for those persons, which have become liable to a third party in the course of the performance of their duties. This narrows the shipowner's responsibility. He is not liable to the third party for damage caused by crew members or pilots on board if they became liable to the third party for acts or omissions done outside the performance of their duties. The German courts have given this a wide meaning. They have accepted that the reason for such liability of the shipowner is that the operation of a ship raises certain dangers, and that the protection of third parties from such dangers requires that the limits of duties in respect of the operation of the ship must be wide. For this reason, not only such activity qualifies, which is carried upon order of the master or which is simply required for the use of the vessel, but also such activity which has a connection to duties which are carried out onboard.

150. To the third question. The Commercial Code does not define who is a person interested in the cargo, neither did the old Commercial Code. It is settled, however, that this refers to the charterer (in the sense of the contractual partner of the owner, either under a contract of carriage on the goods to be carried, or under a charter party; *Befrachter*), the shipper (in the sense of the party delivering the cargo to the ship; *Ablader*) and the consignee (in the sense of the person to whom the good must be delivered under the contract of carriage).

151. To the fourth question. The shipowner's liability under § 480 HGB for damage suffered by an party interested in the cargo due an act or omission of a crew member or a pilot onboard depends on what the Commercial Code itself provides for the carrier's liability and on what has actually been contractually agreed in respect of the cargo in the contract of carriage. Statutory provisions on the liability of the carrier will be dealt with in detail below. Here it should suffice that the shipowner could rely on such limitations as the exclusion of liability for destruction of dangerous cargo in case the master had not been informed of the dangerous nature of the cargo (§ 483 HGB); on the exemption from liability for perils of the sea, war, etc. seizure, etc. strikes and lockouts, etc. acts and omissions of the shipper, inherent vice, etc. carriage of livestock and rescue of life or salvage of property on sea (§ 499 HGB); on the limitation of liability to the value of the damaged goods (§ 502 HGB); on the per package or weight limitation (§ 505 HGB), on the prescription period of one year (§ 605 HGB). Apart from such statutory exclusions, the shipowner may also rely on any particular exclusion agreed by the cargo interests with the carrier, as long as they do not go below the statutory minimum liability.

152. Under German law, the shipowner is exposed to various liabilities outside the Civil Code and the Commercial Code. § 89 *Wasserhaushaltsgesetz* (WHG; Federal

Water Act), applying *inter alia* to inland rivers and lakes as well as to the coastal sea (but not to the EEZ), there is a strict no-fault liability for damage to the water quality caused by any kind of substance. This is the main German provision for water pollution also from ships. Apart from that, there are a number of provisions in international conventions, ratified by Germany, which provide for liability of the shipowner. In the area of oil pollution, the provisions of the *Ölschadengesetz* (ÖlSG; Oil Damage Act) declare the International Convention on Civil Liability for Oil Pollution Damage (CLC 1992) and the International Convention on Civil Liability for Bunker Oil Pollution Damage (Bunkers Convention) applicable. According to Article 2 CLC the owner of a ship at the time of an incident shall be liable for any pollution damage caused by the ship as a result of the incident. The only exceptions is provided for damage resulted from acts of war, hostilities, civil war, insurrection or a natural phenomenon of an exceptional, inevitable and irresistible character, or was wholly caused by an act or omission done with intent to cause damage by a third party, or was wholly caused by the negligence or other wrongful act of any Government or other authority responsible for the maintenance of lights or other navigational aids in the exercise of that function. Rather similar, and modelled after CLC 1992, Article 3 of the Bunkers Convention provides that the shipowner at the time of an incident shall be liable for pollution damage caused by any bunker oil on board or originating from the ship. The exclusions from liability are the same as under CLC 1992.

153. The latest of the international conventions, in force since 14 April 2015, is the Nairobi International Convention on the Removal of Wrecks (Wreck Removal Convention, or Nairobi Convention). Geographically it applies to the EEZ of Member States, but Member States may extend their application also to their national waters and coastal sea (Article 3 (2)), so-called opt-in. Germany has not made use of the opt-in, the reason being that under the national wreck removal laws the state can also go after a party responsible for ship having become a wreck. This is not necessarily the owner of the wreck. As the wreck Removal Convention concentrates, and limits, liability to the owner of the wreck, opting-in would have meant narrowing the rights currently existing under the national law. According to Article 10 the registered owner of a ship shall be liable for the costs of locating, marking and removing the wreck. The exceptions from liability are, again, the same as under CLC.

Finally, there is a strict no-fault based liability also of the owner of a nuclear-powered ship under § 25a *Atomgesetz* (AtomG; Nuclear Act). The Act currently has no relevance, as it applies only to nuclear-powered ships which are entitled to fly the German flag (*see* above at paragraph 51). The only German nuclear-powered ship had been the m/v 'OTTO HAHN', which commenced trading in 1968 and was decommissioned in 1979.

154. For certain damage caused by crew members the law contains exclusions of liability. According to Article 3 (4) CLC 1992, which is applicable under German law not only because Germany has ratified CLC 1992, but because § 611 HGB declares is applicable, no claim for compensation for pollution damage under CLC 1992 or otherwise may be made against, *inter alia*, the servants or agents of the owner or the members of the crew, unless the damage resulted from their personal act or omission, committed with the intent to cause such damage, or recklessly and with knowledge that such damage would probably result.

§3. Limitation of Liability

155. Shipowners have a long-established right to limit their liability. In the past different legal regimes existed, starting with a liability of the owner only with the value of the ship in its current state. In 1972 German adopted the International Convention relating to the Limitation of the Liability of Owners of Sea-Going Ships (1957 Brussels Convention), which introduced a limitation of liability linked to the tonnage measurement of the ship. This was followed by the Convention on Limitation of Liability for Maritime Claims (1976 London Convention or LLMC) with the Protocol of 1996 (1996 Protocol), which lead to a significant increase of the limits. In 2012 the limits were raised further by roughly 51%, the new limits being effective also for Germany since June 2015.

§ 611 *Handelsgesetzbuch* (HGB; Commercial Code) declares CLC 1992 and LLMC 1996 applicable. In respect of the latter, it is expressly provided that also claims for bunker oil damage are subject to LLMC 1996. In respect of pollution claims, which are addressed in CLC 1992 but to which the convention does not apply (most relevant case: the pollution occurs outside the territorial scope of the convention), § 611 (3) HGB provides that the persons listed in Article 1 LLMC 1996 may limit their liability for such claims by applying the provisions of LLMC 1996 mutatis mutandis.

Germany has made use of the right to introduce special provisions in respect of limitation for wreck removal. Wreck removal is not excluded from limitation, which is allowed under the 1976 London Convention, but it is stipulated that a separate limitation in relation to such claims (§ 512 HGB). The national rules on wreck removal and limitation must not be mixed with the Wreck Removal Convention, which entered into force on 14 February 2015. The scope of application of this convention is limited to the EEZ.

§4. Ships for Which the Limitation of Liability Can Be Invoked

156. To the extent that § 611 HGB refers to international conventions on limitation of liability, it will be the requirements of those conventions which determine whether there is a right to limit. CLC 1992 links the liability as well as the right to limitation of this liability to pollution damage caused by a 'ship'. For the purposes of this Convention, Article 1 (1) defines this as 'any sea-going vessel and seaborne craft of any type whatsoever constructed or adapted for the carriage of oil in bulk as cargo, provided that a ship capable of carrying oil and other cargoes shall be regarded as a ship only when it is actually carrying oil in bulk as cargo and during any voyage following such carriage unless it is proved that it has no residues of such carriage of oil in bulk aboard'.

Also the Bunkers Convention uses the term 'ship', but here Article 1 (1) defines it much wider as 'any seagoing vessel and seaborne craft, of any type whatsoever'. Compare also the Wreck Removal Convention, in which according to Article 1 (2) as ship means 'a seagoing vessel of any type whatsoever and includes hydrofoil boats, air-cushion vehicles, submersibles, floating craft and floating platforms, except when such platforms are on location engaged in the exploration, exploitation or production of seabed mineral resources'.

Against that, LLMC 1996 uses the term 'ship' without any further definition other than that it must be a seagoing ship (Article 1 (2) LLMC) in contrast to ships intended for navigation on inland waterways (Article 15 (2) (a) LLMC).

Article 15 (2) (b) LLMC allows state parties to LLMC to regulate by national legislation the system of liability for ships less than 300 tons. Germany has made use of this option. § 613 HGB stipulates that the limitation of ships up to 250 tons is half of the limitation applicable under LLMC for ships up to 2,000 tons.

§5. Claims Subject to Limitation

157. As the Commercial Code refers to various limitation conventions, those conventions determine which claims are subject to limitation. Under Article 2 LLMC 1996 there are six different types of claims which are subject to limitation.

158. The first type (Article 2 (1) (a) LLMC) are claims in respect of loss of life or personal injury or loss of or damage to property, if they occurred on board of the ship or in direct connection with the operation of the ship or with salvage operations, including any consequential loss resulting therefrom. Personal injury claims include those of passengers, but also any other persons who are with or without consent of the shipowner on boards of the ship, i.e., pilots, stevedores, guests, but also stowaways. Generally, personal injury claims by crew members also would be embraced, but they are specially dealt with in the convention (*see* below at paragraph 165). Damage to property includes damage to harbour works, basins and waterways and aids to navigation. In respect of those claims there exists a special, additional provision in § 614 HGB which gives such claims priority over all other property claims. Personal injury and property claims are addressed together here but are treated with different limitation amounts later.

159. The second type (Article 2 (1) (b) LLMC) consists of claims in respect of loss resulting from delay in the carriage by sea of cargo, passengers or their baggage. Liability for delay in delivery of cargo has not played an important role in German law, as neither under the old nor under the reformed maritime law there exists a mandatory liability for delay in delivery. There does exist mandatory liability for delay in delivery of passenger baggage, but it must be extremely rare cases that such claims occur in such magnitude that the limitation amount is reached.

160. The third type (Article 2 (1) (c) LLMC) consists of claims in respect of non-physical loss, i.e., pure financial loss, resulting from non-contractual infringement of rights, occurring in direct connection with the operation of the ship or salvage operations. This does not include consequential financial loss resulting from personal injury or property damage, as those are already included in Article 2 (1) (a) LLMC. The relevance for German law is limited, as under German law non-contractual liability for pure financial loss is rare. One class of cases is that a ship cannot leave a port or berth for a significant period of time due to obstruction caused by the liable party, e.g., a sunken ship. Accepted cases are rare, as in most cases ships are not totally deprived from movement, and as usually obstructions are removed before the period of idleness required by the courts has expired.

161. As fourth and fifth types Article 2 (1) (d) and (e) LLMC address claims in respect of the raising, removal, destruction or rendering harmless of a ship which is sunk, wrecked, stranded or abandoned, including anything that is or has been on board such ship and its cargo. Article 18 LLMC gives State Parties the right to exclude the application of LLMC for these types of claims. Germany has made use of this right in the way that § 612 HGB allows limitation of liability for this type of claims, but that such claims are subject to a separate limit. If only such claims arise, which rarely will be the case, then only one limitation fund for such claims has to be provided. More regular will be cases, in which wreck removal claims will come together with claims for other damage. In those cases the shipowner will be forced to put up two funds.

162. Finally, Article 2 (1) (f) LLMC allows limitation of claims of a person other than the person liable in respect of measures taken in order to avert or minimize loss for which the person liable may limit his liability in accordance with this Convention, and further loss caused by such measures. The idea behind this is that while it is always better to avoid damage than to rectify damage, the liable party shall not be treated worse than if the damage had not been avoided but was incurred. As in such case he would be, on principle, be entitled to limitation, such limitation shall also be available for mitigation costs.

163. Under CLC 1992 limitation is available for the liability imposed by the Convention on the shipowner. This is Liability for pollution damage caused by the ship (Article III (1) CLC 1992), pollution damage being defined by Article I (6) CLC 1992 as '(a) loss or damage caused outside the ship by contamination resulting from the escape or discharge of oil from the ship, wherever such escape or discharge may occur, provided that compensation for impairment of the environment other than loss of profit from such impairment shall be limited to costs of reasonable measures of reinstatement actually undertaken or to be undertaken; (b) the costs of preventive measures and further loss or damage caused by preventive measures'. As mentioned above (paragraph 155), § 611 (3) HGB stipulates that in case CLC 1992 does not apply, persons entitled to limit liability under LLMC 1996 may limit their liability for pollution by application of the provisions of LLMC 1996 mutatis mutandis.

164. § 614 HGB contains special rules on limitation of the liability of pilots, both on board and not on board. The purpose of the provisions is to provide lower limitation amounts than otherwise would be applicable under LLMC 1996. The provisions are detailed and complicated. § 615 (1) HGB stipulated that in case of a pilot on board of the ship even if the piloted ship measures more than 2,000 tons, the pilot may limit his liability to the amount derived under an assumed tonnage of 2,000 tons. In respect of passenger claims, § 615 (2) HGB links the limitation of liability to the number of passengers which the ship is certified to carry. If this number exceeds twelve, then the pilot's liability is nevertheless limited to the limitation amount for twelve passengers, even if the actual number of passengers injured on board is higher.

As a consequence, if the ship measures more than 2,000 tons or is licensed to carry more than twelve passengers, limitations funds which are constituted by a pilot will be of a lower amount than limitation funds constituted by other persons entitled to limitation. Under Article 14 (3) LLMC 1996, a fund constituted by any person entitled to liability is deemed by all persons entitled. As German law does not aim to give other persons the benefit of lower limitations amounts available to a pilot, § 615 (3) HGB stipulates that Article 14 (3) LLMC 1996 in this situation does not apply. A fund constituted by a pilot, thus, only protects the pilot. According to § 1 (2) *Schifffahrtsrechtliche Verteilungsordnung* (SVertO; Shipping Limitation Procedure Ordinance) only claims against the pilot can be pursued against such fund . Such fund can only be constituted by a pilot, if no other person as already constituted a limitation und, which then protects also the pilot as per Article 14 (3) LLMC 1996.

Finally, § 615 (4) HGB deals with limitation of liability available to pilots not on board and provides a regime similar to the one for pilots on board.

§6. Claims Excluded from Limitation

165. First, such claims are excluded from limitation, which are so excluded under the applicable conventions. In this context there are certain provisions which deal with the delineation between the various limitation conventions and, thus, do not really exclude liability, but merely allocate it to a certain convention. Leaving those apart, under LLMC 1996 excludes from this is the case for (a) claims for salvage, including, special compensation (Article 14 Salvage Convention 1989), (b) contributions in general average; (c) claims by servants of the shipowner; and salvors whose duties are connected with the ship or the salvage operations. This latter exclusion applies under LLMC 1996 only if under the law governing the contract of service between the shipowner or salvor and such servants the shipowner or salvor is not entitled to limit his liability in respect of such claims, or if he is by such law only permitted to limit his liability to an amount greater than that provided for in Article 6. In this respect § 611 (3) HGB provides that for contracts subject to German law there is no limitation of liability.

§7. Counter Claims

166. It may be that a person who is entitled to limit liability has a counter-claim against the claimant. A typical scenario is the collision of two ships. In this situation the question arises how the law deals with such counter-claims. The question has two elements. One element is whether the claims are set off against each other so that only one claim remains existing under the law – so-called single liability concept –, or whether both claims exist separately under the law. The other element is how limitation is applied in these scenarios. Under German law generally claims and counter-claims are independent. There is no automatic consolidation. Rather in such situation either party may declare set-off (§ 387 BGB). The result of such set-off then is that only one claim survives, namely that claim which exceeds the other claim. But if no set-off is declared by either party, then both claims remain separately alive under the law and can have different fates.

167. Matters are different, when it comes to limitation of liability. Sedes materiae is not a German provision of law, but Article 5 LLMC 1996, which is applicable by virtue of § 611 (1) HGB. Article 5 LLMC 1996 provides that where a person entitled to limitation of liability has a claim against the claimant arising out of the same occurrence, their respective claims shall be set off against each other and the provisions of this Convention shall only apply to the balance, if any.

§8. Conduct Barring Limitation

168. As § 611 HGB provides that liability for maritime claims may be limited in accordance with LLMC 1996, conduct barring limitation is conduct referred to in Article 4 LLMC. A person's liability is, therefore, barred from limitation if it is proved that the loss resulted from that person's personal act or omission, committed with the intent to cause such loss, or recklessly and with knowledge that such loss would probably result. It must be noted that in maritime law only the fault of the acting person is of relevance. Not the fault of persons a person makes use of for fulfilling certain tasks or obligations. Insofar maritime law differs from general transport law, where limitation is also lost if such other persons fulfils the requirements for barring limitation (§ 435 HGB).

German courts have held that recklessness is a category of fault which is more severe than gross negligence. The test for recklessness is an objective one and requires that the acting party has disregarded the interests of the party damaged in a very substantial way. Against that, knowledge that such loss would probably result is a subjective element. Nevertheless the courts allow to conclude from the objective facts of the case that the party acting must have had such knowledge.

Article 4 LLMC does not deal with the question whose behaviour is to look at in case of the liable person being either a legal entity or commercial partnership. This question is answered by § 616 HGB: such legal entity or commercial partnership is barred from limitation if the requirements of Article 4 LLMC 1996 are fulfilled by a member of the body authorized to represent the legal entity or partnership, or by a shareholder/partner who authorized to represent it.

§9. Persons Entitled to Limit

169. This is dealt with by Article 1 LLMC 1996 and § 1 *Schifffahrtsrechtliche Verteilungsordnung* (SVertO Shipping Limitation Procedure Order). Persons thereby entitled to limitation are shipowners, which include the owner, charterer (including bareboat charterer), manager and operator of the ship; salvors, which includes persons engaged in raising, removal, destruction or the rendering harmless of a wrecked or sunken ship or her cargo, and persons engaged in measures taken in order to avert or minimize loss in respect of further loss caused by such measures. Apart from these persons, all persons are entitled to limit, for whose act, neglect or default the shipowner or salvor is responsible. Furthermore pilots are entitled to limit, as well as insurers of liability subject to limitation, for whom Article 1 (7) LLMC 1996 provides that they are entitled to the benefits of the Convention to the same extent as their assureds themselves.

§10. General Limits of Liability

170. The limits of liability under German law are the limits provided for in LLMC 1996. The Convention distinguishes between passenger liability for loss of life or personal injury and any other liability for which limitation is available under the Convention, and in respect of the latter between claims for loss of life or personal injury and any other claim.

As to claims other than passenger claims, the limits for claims for loss of life or personal injury and for other damage depend on the measurement of the ship:

	Loss of Life/Personal Injury	*Other Claims*
Up to 2,000 tons	2,000,000 SDR	1,000,000 SDR
for each ton from 2,001 to 30,000 tons	800 SDR	400 SDR
for each ton from 30,001 to 70,000 tons	600 SDR	300 SDR
for each ton in excess of 70,000 tons	400 SDR	200 SDR

Where the amount calculated in respect of loss of life or personal injury is not sufficient to settle the full claims, the limitation amount for other claims shall not only be available for such other claims, but also for the unpaid balance of the claims for loss of life or personal injury. In such case, the remaining claims for loss of life or personal injury have no priority but the same ranking as the other claims.

171. As to passenger claims, liability is limited to an amount of 175,000 SDR multiplied by the number of passengers which the ship is authorized to carry according to the ship's certificate.

172. Finally there is a special limit for the liability of salvors either not operating from any ship at all, or operating solely on the ship in respect of which he is rendering salvage services: This limit is to be calculated on basis of a ship of 1,500 tons. As the minimum tonnage for calculating limitation under LLMC 1996 is 2,000 tons, under the Convention such salvors have a liability limitation of 2,000,000 SDR for loss of life or personal injury or 1,000,000 for any other claim respectively.

§11. Limitation Fund, Limitation Without a Fund and Procedure

173. Although in practice the principal way of obtaining limitation of liability under LLMC 1996 seems to be the constitution of a limitation fund. In so far Article

11 LLMC 1996 provides that any person entitled to limit liability may constitute a fund with a Court or other competent authority in any State Party in which legal proceedings are instituted in respect of claims subject to limitation. But LLMC 1996 also allows relying on limitation without constitution of a fund, unless the law of a Member States excludes this and allows limitation only on basis of a fund constituted. If limitation without a fund is permissible, questions of procedure are to be decided in accordance with the national law of the State Party in which action is brought (Article 10 (3) LLMC 1996).

German law does not prohibit limitation without a fund. Rather, the Civil Procedure Code contains in § 305a a provision dealing with this.

174. The procedure for constitution and distribution is laid down in the *Schifffahrtsrechtliche Verteilungsordnung* (SVertO; Shipping Limitation Procedure Order), which does not only apply to maritime limitation, but also inland navigation limitation.

Jurisdiction with limitation proceedings rests with the Local Courts. While the SVertO contains detailed provisions which of the German Local Courts have jurisdiction, there is an agreement between the German states (*Länder)* that all limitation proceedings in maritime matters shall be handled by the Local Court of Hamburg. An application for limitation may be filed by any person entitled to limitation under substantive law, but not before proceedings have been commenced against such person in a German court (§ 1 (3) SVertO). The application must identify the occurrence which has given rise to claims against the applicant, the persons for which limitation shall be limited, the class of claims for which limitation is sought, names and addresses of known claimants, details of the ship involved (name, flag, port of registry), tonnage of the ship, claims and claim amounts raised against the applicant. The application must include a certified copy of the entries on the incident in the deck logbook as well as a certified copy of the Register of Ships.

175. On basis of such an application the court fixes the limitation amount by way of an order. This amount will consist of the limitation amounts as calculated according to LLMC 1996, plus interest of 4% p.a. from the time of the incident until the constitution of the fund. Generally this amount has to be paid in cash to the court cashier, but the court has discretion to allow substitution of cash by other means of security. Courts generally accept guarantees of banks; under EU law they should also be obliged to accept guarantees from banks of other EU states. There is no reported case where a P&I Club Letter of Undertaking or a guarantee of an insurer has been accepted, but practitioners report that at least guarantees by insurers from the EU should be accepted.

176. Once the applicant has either paid the limitation amount to the court or has deposited a security with the court, the court will issue a further order, by which the limitation proceedings are opened. The effects of the opening of the limitation proceedings are that (a) the liability of the applicant is limited to the fund; (b) claims against the liable person can only be pursued by notification of such claims with the fund according to the provisions of SVertO; (c) any proceedings pending at the time of opening of the limitation proceedings are automatically stayed; (d) no separate enforcement into assets of the applicant is allowed any more.

177. Together with the order opening the limitation proceedings the court appoints a liquidator (*Sachwalter*), who is in charge of administering the fund, considering all claims pursued against the fund and either accepting them as valid or rejecting them as unfounded. Not only the liquidator but also the applicant as well as any other claimant have the right to contest claims pursued against the fund. The court will call for a hearing in which all claims should be discussed. In practice, however, objections against claims are usually submitted in writing to the liquidator and the court before the hearing takes place. Claims which have neither been contested by the applicant, nor by the liquidator nor by any other claimant will be entered in the distribution schedule (*Verteilungstabelle*). If objections have been raised against a claim, the respective claimant has the possibility to commence proceedings against any objecting party. Such proceedings must be commenced within one month after publication of the distribution schedule: If not done so, the right to participation in the fund is lost. Once all claims are entered into the distribution schedule, the liquidator prepares a distribution plan showing the participation of each claim in the fund. If claims are contested, respective parts will be withheld by the liquidator from distribution. Should respective claimants be successful with their action against contesting parties, the liquidator will pay them, there reserved shares. Should he be unsuccessful, the reserved shares will be re-distributed pro rata to all accepted claimants.

Chapter 6. Charter Parties

§1. Definition and Varieties of Charter Parties

178. There does not exist a general definition of a charter party in German law. From a broad perspective, charter parties are contracts for the use of ships. As to terminology, the party making the ship available is usually described as the Owner, to the other party the charterer. This does not necessarily mean that such 'owner' is actually owning the vessel in the sense that he has title to the vessel. An 'owner' in this sense can be a charterer himself. The contract entered into by a charterer as 'owner' would be called a sub-charterer. The 'owner' may be described as 'disponent owner', by that indicating that such 'owner' has no own title in the ship.

Depending on the type, a charter party may be linked to the carriage of more or less precisely described cargo between more or less precisely described places. Such charter parties are generally described as voyage charter parties. Or they may not be linked to a certain kind of cargo but rather permit, for an agreed time, the carriage of any kind of cargo, unless specifically excluded, between any places in the world, again unless specifically excluded. Such charter parties would be called time charter parties. Time charter parties may be concluded for the whole ship, or only for parts of the ship, in case of containerships in particular also just for a certain but nor further defied a number of stowage places for containers. Such charters are usually described slot charters. And slot charters may even be concluded in a way that owners so charter out slots on their ships to other owners and also charter in slots form ships from other owners. This is a feature common in joint container services, in which the partners of the service all make ships available for the service and grant each other the rights to book containers for all the vessels for their own account. Such charters are called cross charters.

179. Charter parties may be concluded in a way that all costs and disbursements involved with the operation of the ship are for the owner, which is the usual model for voyage charter parties. Or they may allocate certain costs, like bunkers, port charges, agency fees, with the charterer, which is usually the case for time charter parties.

Charter parties may provide that the ship shall remain fully manned, equipped and maintained by the owner, as is the case both for voyage and time charter parties, or they may provide that the owner simply provides the ship as such, i.e., with crew, and that the charterer shall be responsible for maintenance of the ship. Such charter parties are referred to as bareboat charter parties, as the owner provides nothing but the 'bare boat'.

Charter parties may differ in respect of the remuneration paid by the charterer. Such remuneration may either be a lump sum amount payable for the service provided with the vessel – this is the typical remuneration in case of a so-called voyage charter. Such remuneration is usually called freight. Or it may be a remuneration which is not linked to a particular voyage, but to the time during which the charterer has the ship available. This is the usual remuneration under a time charter. But there also exist hybrid types like trip-time charters, in which a ship is chartered for a particular trip between defined ports, but the charterer does not pay a lump sum, but rather a daily amount for the time the vessel needs for the performance of the voyage.

§2. Statutory Provisions

I. General

180. German law distinguishes between voyage charters, time charters and bareboat charters. The law on voyage charters is basically the same as on contracts for the carriage of general cargo, but subject to a number of special provisions, which have preference over the general rules. The rules on time charters and bareboat charters are independent and do not refer to the provisions on contracts for the carriage of general cargo.

181. None of the provisions on any of the mentioned charterparties is binding, but all can be deviate from by contractual agreement. This is also the case for voyage charters, for which the law makes a general reference to the law governing contracts for the carriage of general cargo., Those provisions are to a vast extent mandatory by virtue of § 512 HGB, but this very provision is excluded from the reference in § 527 (2) *Handelsgesetzbuch* (HGB; Commercial Code).

II. Voyage Charters

182. Traditionally, German law only had very few statutory provisions on charter parties. Rather the law concentrated on statutory provisions for a contract of affreightment (*Frachtvertrag*), which applied to voyage carter parties. A charter party in the sense of a contract relating to the transport of goods with reference either to the whole ship or designated holds of a ship was referred to in § 556 HGB in its version valid until 26 April 2013. § 557 HGB old version then went on to deal with the document issued for such contract, which the law defined as *Chartepartie.*

183. After the reform of the German maritime law in 2013 the basic provisions of German shipping law are those on contracts for the carriage of goods by sea (*Seefrachtverträge*). This includes contracts for the carriage of general cargo (*Stückgutfrachtverträge*) and voyage charters (*Reisefrachtverträge*). While in practice the carrier under a voyage charter is usually referred to as the 'owner', German law uses the term 'contractual carrier' (*Verfrachter)*, as it is also used in the context of carriage of general goods. By a reference contained in § 527 (2) HGB, most of the statutory provisions on contracts for the carriage of general cargo are applicable also on voyage charters, subject to the one exception referred to in paragraph 181 already: parties to a voyage charter have freedom of contract.

184. The statutory law on voyage charters in contained in §§ 527–535 HGB. They address the following aspects:

- The carrier's principal obligation (§ 527 HGB).
- Determination of the load port/load place (§ 528 HGB).
- Loading discharging (§§ 529–531, 535 HGB).
- Termination by the carrier and the charterer (§§ 532, 534 HGB).
- Partial shipments (§ 533 HGB).

III. Time Charters

185. Time charters are dealt with in German statutory law for the first time since the Maritime Law Reform of 2013. The law is not mandatory, but the parties to the contract can deviate from the statutory rules. Different from voyage charters, which only deal with the transport of cargo, time charters may be concluded also for the transport of passengers or other services by the ship, e.g., dredging, cable laying, etc. The statutory law on time charters in contained in §§ 527–535 HGB. They address the following aspects:

- The parties' principal obligations (§ 557 HGB).
- Delivery and redelivery of the ship (§§ 559, 569 HGB).
- Maintenance and operational costs (§ 560, 564 HGB).
- Use of the ship and loading/discharging (§§ 562, 563 HGB).
- Hire, lien for unpaid hire and right of retention (§§ 565, 566, 568 HGB).

IV. Bareboat Charters

186. Bareboat charters are substantially dealt with as a form of rental agreements. Actually, § 553 HGB uses the term 'bareboat charter' only in brackets after the German term *Schiffsmietvertrag,* which literally translated means contract for rent of a ship. The few provisions which the Commercial Code contains in respect of bareboat charters are not mandatory. The statutory law on bareboat charters is contained in §§ 553–556 HGB. They address the following aspects:

- The parties' principal obligations (§§ 553, 555 HGB).
- Delivery, maintenance and redelivery of the ship (§ 554 HGB).
- Termination (§ 556 HGB).

§3. Duties of the Shipowner

I. Voyage Charters

187. As mentioned above, the law on voyage charters declares almost all provisions on contracts for the carriage of general goods applicable. Most of the carrier's obligations under a voyage charter, thus, are identical to the carrier's obligations under contracts for the carriage of general goods. Only in certain areas special provisions on voyage charter take precedence over general provisions. One of those special provision addresses the principal obligation of the carrier under a voyage charter: to carry the cargo to an agreed destination, in one or more specified voyages by sea, using either the entirety of a specified ship, a proportion of a specified ship, or a specifically designated space within such ship, and there to deliver the cargo to the consignee (§ 527 HGB). This is much more specific than the general contained in § 481 HGB, which merely stipulates as the carrier's obligation to carry the goods by sea by ship to their destination and there to deliver them to the consignee. The carriage must be performed in a seaworthy and cargoworthy condition, which means that the carrier must ensure that the ship is seaworthy and properly furnished, equipped, manned and sufficiently supplied (seaworthiness) and that the holds, including the refrigerating and cooling chambers, as well as all other parts of the ship in or on which cargo is stowed, are fit for the reception, carriage and preservation of the goods (cargoworthiness), § 485 HGB.

188. Under a contract for the carriage of general cargo loading and stowage of the cargo is, in the absence of other agreements, an obligation of the carrier. This is different for voyage charters, where, just the other way round, in the absence of other agreements this is the duty of the charterer (§ 531 (1) HGB). But the carrier always remains responsible for the seaworthiness of the ship. Containers may be stowed on deck also under voyage charters without the charterer's consent but different from the general rules, which allow transshipment of cargo at least if it is stowed in container (§ 486 (3) HGB), no transshipment at all is permissible under a voyage charter (§ 531 (2) HGB). There is no special provision on voyage charters for discharge, so that it remains the statutory duty of the carrier to discharge the cargo (§ 486 (2) HGB). But as under a voyage charter all statutory provisions are subject to agreements to the parties, they can agree on duty of the charterer to care of discharge at the destination.

189. According to § 528 HGB, for the purpose of loading and stowage the cargo, the carrier must berth the ship at the loading place designated in the voyage charter contract, or to be designated by the charterer. As soon as the ship is at the loading port ready for loading the cargo, the carrier has to give a notice of readiness (§ 529 HGB). Time for loading (laytime) as agreed between the parties starts on the following day (§ 530 HGB). The carrier is not entitled to remuneration during laytime, but if it is exceeded due a circumstance outside of his own sphere of risk, he is entitled to demurrage (§ 530 (3) HGB). Usually the party agree on the amount of demurrage per day pro rata in the charter party. In the absence of such agreement, the carrier is entitled by law to a reasonable amount, which would be determined by the courts, if not agreed between the parties. If the charterer does not load cargo within the agreed time, the carrier has the right to terminate the charter (§ 534 HGB). In this case the carrier is entitled either (a) to the agreed freight less costs or expenses he saved as a result of the termination, or anything he acquired or failed, in bad faith, to acquire; or (b) to payment of dead freight, which is one third of the freight agreed. In the latter case, no costs saved or other income obtained is deducted from the dead freight.

II. Time Charters

190. Under a time charter the owner (who does not need to be the civil law owner of the ship, but can himself be a time charterer) must make the agreed ship with her crew available for the agreed time to carry goods or passengers or to render other agreed services with the ship (§ 557 HGB). The owner must deliver the ship to the charterer at the agreed time and location and in a condition appropriate for the use contractually agreed (§ 559 HGB). This condition must be maintained throughout the time of the charter. In particular, the owner must keep the ship in a seaworthy, in case of a time charter for the intended carriage of cargo also in a cargoworthy, condition (§ 560 HGB). The fixed operating costs of the ship are for the owner's account (§ 564 (1) HGB). He remains responsible for the navigation and operation of the (§ 561 (2) HGB).

III. Bareboat Charters

191. Before the background that German law treats a bareboat charter as a form of a rental agreement, § 553 HGB addresses the owner as lessor (*Vermieter*). His obligation is to let the agreed ship, without crew, to the charterer. As regards termination, the lessor, as the charterer, may terminate the contract, if concluded for an indeterminate period (which in practice never applies), with effect from midnight of any given Saturday by giving one week's notice by the first workday of the preceding week. More practical is the provision that if the hire is payable monthly or in longer intervals, termination is possible with three-month notice to the end of a calendar quarter (§ 556 HGB).

§4. Duties of the Charterer

I. Voyage Charters

192. The charterer's principal obligation is the payment of the agreed freight (§ 481 (2) HGB). He has to provide the carrier with such information relating to the goods as is required for their carriage, which includes information on the quantity, number, or weight of the goods, as well as the leading marks and the nature of the goods (§ 482 HGB). If the goods are of dangerous nature, the charterer has to inform the carrier of the precise nature of the danger and, to the extent necessary, of any precautionary measures to be taken (§ 483 HGB). If the goods require packing, the charterer has the obligation to package them in such a way that the carrier suffers no loss or damage. Furthermore, that charterer has to provide the carrier with such documentation which is necessary for official processing prior to delivery of the goods, in particular for customs clearance (§ 487 HGB).

193. If the charter does not provide for a load port or loading place, the charterer must exercise due diligence in choosing a safe load port or loading place (§ 528 (2)

HGB). As mentioned above, loading of the cargo onto the ship is the duty of the charterer, the carrier always remaining responsible for the seaworthiness of the ship (§ 531 HGB).

194. The charterer may terminate the charter at any time without reason, but in such case the carrier is entitled to freight or dead freight as described above under paragraph 123 (§ 532 HGB). He can also demand that the carrier perform the voyage with only part of the cargo. If he so demands, the carrier is entitled to the full freight. But if the charter party allows the carrier to carry also other cargo, freight earned by the carrier from the carriage of such other cargo is deducted. Different from the termination cases, here only freight actually earned is deducted, but not also freight which could have been earned but was failed to be earned.

II. Time Charters

195. The charterer's principal obligation is the payment of the agreed hire (§ 557 (2) HGB), which is payable fifteen days in advance (§ 565 (1) HGB). The obligation to pay hire ceases, either fully or partially, for periods in which the ship is not fully available for the charterer's use due to deficiencies or other circumstances resulting from the owner's sphere (§ 565 (2) HGB). When ordering the ship to a certain port or berth he has to exercise due care to choose a safe port or berth (§ 561 (1) HGB). Loading, stowage and discharge of cargo is his duty, but as mentioned the owner remains responsible for the seaworthiness of the ship (§ 563 HGB). While the owner has to bear all fixed operational costs, the charterer has to bear all variable costs, such as port charges, pilotage, tug assistance, additional premiums for insurance of the ship resulting from the particular service the charterer engages the ship in. The charterer also has to provide the ship with the required fuel, the law expressly providing that such fuel must be of normal commercial quality (§ 654 (2) HGB). At the end of the charter period the charterer has to redeliver the ship to the owner at the agreed place (§ 569 HGB).

III. Bareboat Charters

196. The charterer's principal obligation is also here the payment of the agreed hire (§ 553 (2) HGB), which is also payable fifteen days in advance. During the charter period, the charterer has to maintain the ship. The standard of maintenance is that the ship must be maintained to remain suitable for the use contractually agreed in the charter party. At the end of the period the charterer must redeliver the ship to the owner in the same condition as he took delivery of her, wear and tear caused by contractual use of the ship excluded (§ 554 (2) HGB). As regards third parties, the charterer is obliged to protect the owner's interests (§ 555 HGB). The most relevant aspect will be claims for damages which the owner may have against third parties, but which he does not become aware of himself, as the ship is under the sole control of the charterer's crew.

Chapter 7. Transport under Bill of Lading

197. Under German law the issuing of a bill of lading is not mandatory. Contracts of carriage by sea are valid without a bill of lading having been issued. But if a contract of carriage by sea has been concluded, the carrier is under an obligation to issue a bill of lading if so requested (§ 513 HGB). Here a short introduction to the German concept and terminology of persons on the side of the cargo is useful. The law distinguishes between the *Ablader*, usually translated as documentary shipper, who may be but not necessarily is the contractual partner of the carrier, and the *Befrachter*, usually translated as the contractual shipper, who is party to the contract of carriage. The person entitled to the bill of lading is the so-called *Ablader*. The documentary shipper is defined by § 513 (2) HGB as the person who delivers the goods to the carrier for carriage and who has been designated by the contractual chipper as such for the purpose of being recorded in the bill of lading. If the contract does not identify a documentary shipper, or if some else delivers the cargo to the carrier, then the contractual shipper is treated as a documentary shipper.

§1. Definitions and Functions of the Bill of Lading

198. The Commercial Code (HGB) does not itself define what a bill of lading is as such. Basic provision is § 363 HGB, which stipulates that rights under bills of lading can be transferred by endorsement if they are issued to order. The generally accepted definition of a bill of lading is that it is a document, issued under a contract of carriage, which confirms receipt of the cargo and contains the obligation of delivery of such cargo to the person entitled to such delivery under the bill of lading itself. As per § 519 HGB, the bill of lading embodies the contract for the carriage of goods by sea. This mentioned definition embraces most of the functions of a bill of lading. The first function is that of a receipt, that means providing evidence that and when the cargo as such has been received by the carrier. The evidence so provided depends on the content of the bill of lading and may extend to the kind, quantity, weight and outer appearance of the cargo (§ 517 HGB). Beyond this more factual aspect goes a further function, namely that the bill of lading determines the legal relationship between the carrier and the consignee. One aspect of this relationship is that the owner of the ship is considered to be the carrier under a bill of lading, if the bill of lading does not identify the carrier (§ 518 HGB). Another function is that it serves as a document of title: the transfer of the bill of lading to a third party has the same effect, in terms of the acquisition of rights to the goods, as a physical handing over of the goods (§ 524 HGB). A further function is that presentation of the bill of lading is required for obtaining delivery of the goods (§ 521 HGB). Whoever gives credit in respect of cargo, thus, can rely on being properly secured if he holds (all) bill(s) of lading. Another function, closely related to the one before, is that rights under a bill of lading can be easily transferred by simple endorsement of the bill of lading.

199. Finally, the bill of lading cuts of many defences against a claim under it. Only such defences are permissible, (a) which concern the validity of the bill of lading, or (b) which arise from the contents of the bill of lading, or (c) which the carrier has directed against the claimant (§ 522 (1) HGB). As to the content of the bill of lading, § 522 (1) 2 HGB provides that an agreement to which the bill of lading merely makes reference is not incorporated into the bill of lading. This means that under German well-known incorporation clauses like clause 1 (Clause Paramount) of the CONGEN Bill of Lading, do not have the effect of incorporating charter party terms into a bill of lading. The very intentions of a combination of a GENCON voyage charter and a CONGEN Bill of Lading issued under it, thus, cannot be achieved under German law anymore. But the effect is less drastic than it may on first glance. § 522 HGB itself is a provision of substantive German law. It only applies if, under conflict of laws rules, German law is the proper law for the bill of lading. If the charter party, which bill of lading refers to, is subject to foreign law, under conflict of laws rules the court would have to test the validity of the incorporation clause on basis of the law which would be applicable if the incorporation is valid. If such law accepts a valid incorporation, like the widespread English law does, thus, also a German court could not deny incorporation of charter party terms into the bill of lading, because § 52 HGB as a statutory provision of German substantive law would not be applicable. § 533 HGB, thus, has an effect only if the charter party is subject to German law or, for these purposes, to any other law not permitting incorporation of charter party terms into the bill of lading.

200. § 515 HGB describes the content of a bill of lading: place and date of issue; name and address of the Contractual Carrier, the Documentary Shipper and the consignee and notify address, if any; name of the ship; port of loading and destination; nature of the goods and their apparent order and condition; quantity, number or weight of the goods and their permanent, legible leading marks; freight owed on delivery, costs to be incurred up to the time of delivery as well as a statement concerning payment of the freight; and the number of originals issued. The carrier has to sign the bill of lading, but the law allows a reproduction of the personal signature by means of printing or stamp.

201. Bills of lading may be issued also electronically. But the law requires that the authenticity and integrity of the record of such electronic bill of lading is secured. As modern as this legislation sounds, so far it is still an empty shell, because § 516 (3) HGB stipulates that details concerning the issue, presentation, surrender and transfer of an electronic bill of lading, as well as the particulars of the process of making entries to an electronic bill of lading after it has been issued shall be subject to a regulation issued by the German Ministry of Justice. So far, no such regulation has been passed, and it is not expected in the near future.

202. As mentioned above, the carrier is only obliged, and only entitled, to deliver the cargo against presentation of an original bill of lading. If more than one original has been issued, delivery may and must take place against presentation of one original. If more than one bill of lading is presented by different parties, the carrier may not choose one party and deliver to it. Rather he has to store the goods in a public warehouse or in some other form of safe storage and must inform the bill of lading holders accordingly (§ 521 (3) HGB).

203. If the bill of lading has been issued by the master or any other person authorized by the shipowner but does not state the name of the carrier, by virtue of §

518 HGB the shipowner is deemed to be the contractual carrier under the bill of lading. The same applies, if the bill of lading identifies a party as the contractual carrier, who is in fact not the carrier. The well-known so-called Identity-of-Carrier Clauses, which intend to have the effect of having the contract concluded not between the contractual carrier but the shipowner and the cargo interests, are not valid under German law. If the bill of lading does not identify any carrier at all, this is the consequence of § 5187 HGB, just discussed. If the name of carrier is mentioned, e.g., the name of a time charterer, the German courts have deemed such identification an individual agreement, which supersedes a printed identity-of-Carrier Clause.

§2. Various Types of Bills of Lading and Similar Documents of Title

I. Bill of Lading 'Received for Shipment'

204. The 'received for shipment' bill of lading is one of the two standard bills of lading dealt with by the German Commercial Code (HGB). The carrier has to issue it (upon request of the shipper, § 513 HGB) as soon as he has received the cargo. It does not bring proof that the cargo has actually been put on board, but merely that the carrier has received it. The difference has lost part of its relevance. Under the old law, which was built after the Hague Rules, the carrier had a mandatory liability for loss of or damage to cargo only between loading and discharge. Liability for the time between receipt of the cargo and its loading on board and between discharge and the cargo and its delivery, thus, could be excluded by agreement. A clean mere 'receive for shipment' bill of lading, thus, did not bring proof of the condition of the cargo upon loading. After the law reform, the liability now is mandatory between receipt and delivery. A clean 'received for shipment' bill of lading brings the proof which is required for a claim against the carrier.

II. 'On Board' Bill of Lading

205. By issuing this type of bill of lading, the carrier confirms that he has actually loaded the cargo on board of the ship (named in the bill of lading). Once a 'received for shipment' bill of lading has been issued, the shipper cannot request the carrier to issue a further 'on board' bill of lading for the same cargo. But he can request that the carrier enters a 'notice of shipment' into the bill of lading. This is a remark stating when and on which ship the cargo was loaded.

206. German law is serious on incorrect bills of lading. Incorrectness in respect of the cargo as such will be dealt with below (paragraph 237). In context with the issuing of an 'on board' bill of lading before actual loading of the cargo on board of the ship, the stipulates a strict liability, i.e., a no-fault liability for resulting damage suffered by the person entitled to claim under the bill of lading (§ 523 (2) HGB).

III. Through Bill of Lading, Combined Transport Bill of Lading and Multimodal Bill of Lading

207. Such bills of lading are transport documents issued for a transport which is not only performed by a ship, but which combines carriage by sea with carriage by other modes of transport. German law contains certain provisions on multimodal transport (§ 452–452d HGB), but those provisions do not deal with transport documents. § 452 BGB declares the national general transport law as contained in §§ 407 et seq. HGB applicable to such multimodal transport. Transport documents issued for a multimodal transport, thus are subject the provisions on transport documents for general transport. They are either a consignment note (§ 408 HGB), or, in its legal effects similar to bill of lading, a consignment bill (§ 443 HGB).

IV. Sea Waybill

208. Sea waybills are dealt with by statutory law only since the Maritime Law Reform of 2013 (§ 526), but were obviously in use long before. The concept of the law is that a sea waybill may be issued by the carrier, if he had not been required to issue a bill of lading. By reference to § 515 HGB, a sea waybill must have the same contents as a bill of lading (*see* above paragraph 118). Like a bill of lading, a sea waybill must be signed by the carrier, but also here a reproduction of the signature is sufficient. A sea waybill so issued brings the same kind of proof as a bill of lading; in particular it serves as prima facie evidence of the existence and content of the contract for carriage and that the carrier has taken over the cargo. But sea waybills are not documents of title. Neither requires the law their presentation upon delivery.

§3. Charter Party and Bill of Lading

209. The issuing of bill of lading under charter parties is common practice. The old law provided in § 656 HGB that in such a case the bill of lading is decisive for the legal relationship between the carrier and the consignee, while the charter party is decisive for the legal relationship between the owner and the charterer. This provision is no more part of the new version of the Commercial Code (HGB), but the principal obviously apples nevertheless. Rather § 519 HGB now stipulates that any claim under a contract for the carriage of goods by sea embodied in a bill of lading may be brought only by the person entitled to claim under the bill of lading. There is no guiding decision on the consequences of this new statutory provision. There are views in the legal literature that the bill of lading sets aside any kind of contractual claim, even if it avails a party of broader rights than laid down in the bill of lading. What has survived in any event is that in the hands of the charter a bill of lading has no other quality than a receipt for the cargo. It does not avail the charterer any rights which would go beyond his right under the charter party. This is important, because the carrier's obligations under a bill of lading may be deviated from generally only by individual agreement (§ 512 HGB), while under a charter party the parties have freedom of contract. It is common for bills of lading issued under charter parties to refer to and incorporate the terms, conditions and even jurisdiction clauses of the charter party in the bill of lading. As already explained above, this is no more possible under German law. For details *see* above paragraph 199.

§4. Hague Rules, Hague-Visby Rules, Hamburg Rules and Rotterdam Rules

I. National Incorporation of the Hague-Visby Rules, the Hamburg and the Rotterdam Rules

210. Germany is a Member State of the Hague Rules, which were ratified on 1 July 1939 and incorporated into the German Commercial Code. Germany never ratified the Visby Protocol, mainly for political reasons, as Germany hosted the diplomatic conference I leading to the Hamburg Rules. Germany had no intention to ratify the Hamburg Rules but felt it inappropriate to ratify the older Visby Protocol instead. But this did not prevent Germany from incorporating the material provisions of the Visby Protocol into the Commercial Code. For all practical purposes, though under the law of nations, German was a Hague-Visby state. In the course of the Maritime Law Reform, which was underway for many years, the group of experts, appointed by the German Ministry of Justice, had recommended to terminate the Hague Rules Membership, mainly for the reason that the statutory fire and error in navigation defences were deemed by this group inappropriate in modern times. This proposal was heavily debated in the public. In the end the government decided not to terminate the Hague Rules membership. Nevertheless German national law now does not contain the defences of fire and error in navigation anymore (but allows agreeing on such defences by way contract). A breach of Germany's obligations towards other Hague Rules states under the las nations is avoided by a provision contained in the *Einführungsgesetz zum Handelsgesetzbuch* (EGHGB; Introductory Code to the Commercial Code), which stipulates that these defences are available in relation to Hague Rules states.

211. In the course of the discussions on the new maritime law, there was also an intensive debate on the Rotterdam Rules. A number of industry associations, including the German Shipowners Association, the German Maritime Law Association, and the German Lawyers Association, recommended ratification of the Rotterdam Rules, despite concerns in respect of certain features and provisions of this convention. The reason for the support was mainly that the Rotterdam Rules were widely seen as the realistically last opportunity for unification in this sector of law. But the government decided not to ratify at this time. The general expectation is that his position may be revisited once the US and China have ratified.

II. Mandatory Law, Freedom of Contract, Choice of Law and Jurisdiction

212. Under German law, generally the parties enjoy freedom of contract. But this freedom may be limited or even partly excluded by statute. This is what the German lawmaker has done in respect of liability for loss of or damage to the goods under contracts for the carriage of general goods by sea. Freedom of contract is preserved fully inasmuch the parties may deviate from all of the respective statutory provisions by individually negotiated agreements. Were parties sit down and individually agree on something different than the law provides, this is always possible. This extends to individually negotiated agreements which were not made for one contract only, but also for several similar contracts (§ 512 (1) HGB). The limitation of freedom of contract to individual agreements brings along a very effective limitation of the freedom of contract. Generally, parties are free to agree on the terms of their contracts not only be individual agreements, but also by standard terms. In carriage by sea this is one of the main means of contractual agreements, as can be seen by the widespread use of standard bill of lading or booking note conditions. Such standard terms, however, under German law do not have any effect to the extent they deviate from German law. German law is thus subject to individually negotiated agreements but mandatory towards standard contract conditions.

213. There are only two areas left where there is freedom of contract also for standard contract conditions. One is that, as mentioned before, the parties can agree by standard contract terms, in particular by bill of lading conditions, that the carrier shall not be liable for the fault or neglect of his crew or other if the loss or damage results from an act in the navigation or in other management of the ship, save for measures taken predominantly for the benefit of the cargo, or if the loss or damage results from fire or explosion on board the ship. The other is that the carrier's liability for loss or damage may be limited to amounts higher than those set out in section 504, i.e., they may be agreed to be higher than 2 SDR per kilogram or 666,67 SDR per package or unit for loss or damage.

214. But German law does not only limit freedom of contract in respect of the carrier's liability; it does so also in respect of the shipper's liability as dealt with in § 488 HGB. Subsection (3) of the provisions stipulates that an agreement excluding the shipper's liability shall be effective only if individually negotiated (which also here includes individually negotiated agreements for more than one but for several similar contracts). The only area where changes can be made also by way of standard contract conditions is the amount of compensation payable by the shipper. Under the law the liability is unlimited. But the parties may agree on a limitation by standard contract clauses.

III. Liability Period

215. Prior to the Maritime Law Reform of 2013, § 606 HGB in the old version provided for a liability of the carrier between acceptance and delivery of the goods. But in line with the Hague Rules § 662 (2) No. 2 HGB old version allowed exclusion of liability before loading and after discharging. German courts held that the relevant points in time were commencement of loading and completion of discharge, always in relation to the particular piece of cargo. This lead to the widespread use of so-called *tackle-to-tackle* clauses like clause 3 CONLINEBILL, reading: *The Carrier shall in no case be responsible for loss of or damage to cargo arising prior to loading, after discharging.*

216. After the law reform, the principle of § 606 HGB old version is carried forward to the new § 498 HGB. But the law now does no more contain the option for the carrier to exclude liability prior to loading and after discharge. Consequently, the liability period now starts with the acceptance of the goods by the carrier and their delivery by the carrier to the consignee. Also under the new law terminals are considered to be the *allonge* of the vessel, so that the carrier, who accepts cargo at a terminal, is deemed to have received it once the terminal has received it, and he is deemed to have delivered it not but before the terminal has delivered it. This liability regime is subject to the general rules on mandatory application, i.e., the parties can deviate from it only by individually negotiated agreement, which may be concluded also for several similar contracts between the same parties, but no more by standard contract conditions like bill of lading terms (§ 512 HGB).

217. The question arising from this liability regime is whether it is still possible under German law to use the widespread *fio* (free in and out), *fios* (free in and out stowed) or *fiost* (free in and out stowed trimmed) clauses. The question arises only if those clauses are not designed just to deal with the costs of the respective measure, but also to stipulate whose obligation it is. The statutory law itself does not give a clear answer. While for voyage charters §§ 531, 535 HGB stipulate that loading and discharging are the obligations of the charterer, for contracts of carriage of general goods § 486 (2) HGB provides that it is the carrier who has to load, stow, secure and discharge the goods. But, different from § 498 HGB, the obligations under § 486 HGB are subject not only to individually negotiated agreements, but by any kind of agreement, which includes standard contract clauses like the *fio* clause. If by such a clause loading and discharge have been transferred to the shipper, and if the goods are damaged during loading or discharge, then the carrier is exempted from liability by § 499 (1) No. 5 HGB (acts or omissions by the Contractual Shipper or the Documentary Shipper).

IV. Cargo, Dangerous Cargo and Excepted Cargo

218. The carrier's obligations generally apply to any kind of cargo, but the law contains special provisions on the carriage of dangerous cargo and live animals. Regardless of its kind, the law also contains special rules on the carriage of cargo on deck, which will be dealt with in paragraph 223. As regards dangerous cargo, the shipper is under the obligation to inform the carrier of the precise nature of the danger and, if necessary, of any precautionary measures to be taken to counter the dangers resulting from the cargo (§ 483 (1) HGB). What the carrier may do with dangerous cargo depends on whether he, his agent or the master were informed latest at acceptance of the dangerous nature of the cargo. If such information had not been provided, and the carrier later learns of the dangerous nature, he has the right to unload, store, or return the goods or, to destroy them or render them harmless. He is not free in choice, but has to take such action which on the one hand is sufficient to counter the danger, but on the other hand is the least burdensome for cargo interests. He may get active not only upon the dangerous nature of the cargo being about to cause damage, but he may do so at any time. If his acts cause damage to the cargo, he will not be liable for (§ 483 (2) 1 HGB). If the carrier, agent or master has been advised of the dangerous nature, this does not mean that they are not allowed to do anything. But in such case he is permitted to take any of the aforementioned actions only, if the goods will likely become a danger to the ship or its cargo, and if the danger is not the consequence of the carrier's fault (§ 483 (2) 2 HGB). If this is the case, again the carrier will not incur any liability for damage to the goods resulting from his acts.

219. While the carrier, thus, is under no liability for damage caused to dangerous goods, if the above requirements are met, the law provides for a liability of the shipper for loss or damage caused by the dangerous goods, but such liability is only towards the carrier, not towards other cargo interests. But the carrier incur liability towards such other cargo interests for damage caused to their cargo by the dangerous cargo, such liability qualifies as the carrier's own damage, so that he can recover from the shipper of the dangerous cargo. Indirectly, thus, the shipper of dangerous cargo may be liable also for damage caused to other cargo interests, but only if they have claims for damages against the carrier.

220. As regards the requirement of fault, the law makes a rather peculiar distinction between cases where a bill of lading has been issued and cases were not. In the latter category, the shipper's liability requires his fault In respect of his failure to disclose the goods' dangerous nature of the goods (§ 488 (1) 2 HGB), the burden of proof that there was no such fault resting with the shipper. If a bill of lading has been issued, the law is tougher for the shipper. In this case he is liable even without fault (§ 488 (3) HGB). A shipper is better off, thus, if he, where possible, does not make use of his right to request a bill of lading, but rather agrees with the carrier on the issue of a seaway bill, which does not create no-fault liability. Under all circumstances the shipper's liability is unlimited.

221. The shipper's liability for dangerous cargo can be excluded only by an individually negotiated agreement, which may also be entered into for several similar contracts between the same parties. The law is more flexible in respect of limitation of the liability. This can be agreed also by standard contract conditions (§ 488 (5) HGB).

222. After the law reform, live animals are treated by the HGB generally like any other kind of cargo. Different from the old law, which gave complete freedom of contract for the carriage of live animals (§ 663 (2) No. 1 HGB old version), the liability for damage to life animals is identical to that in respect of other cargo. But the carrier is relieved from liability if damage to live animals is the consequence of the very nature of this cargo (§ 499 (1) No. 7 HGB). German law follows in this the Hamburg Rules, thus, while the Rotterdam continue to allow complete exclusion of liability, as the Hague Rules did.

V. Deck Cargo

223. Before the Maritime Law Reform, the carrier was not allowed to stow cargo on deck without the consent of the shipper. Beyond the wording of the law, however, courts allowed carriage of containers on deck, if the ship was proper designed and equipped for such deck carriage. If this exception did not apply and the carrier stowed cargo on deck without the shipper's consent, the carrier was liable for resulting damage and could not rely on the perils of the sea defence. Limitation of liability per package or unit, however, was available. As per § 663 (2) No. 1 HGB old version the carrier could put a deck cargo remark into the bill of lading and was entitled to exclude his liability for cargo so carried on deck. It was settled by court decisions that such exclusion was not complete but only related to the particular risks resulting from deck carriage. For all other risks, e.g., improper stowage, the carrier remained responsible.

224. This situation has changed after the law reform. What is the same, though, is that the carrier generally needs the shipper's consent for stowage of cargo on deck (§ 486 (4) HGB). The jurisprudence of the courts on containers has now been made part of the statutory law, and it has been widened. Rather than referring to containers, § 486 (4) s HGB now refers to loading devices, and allows carriage of goods on deck without the shipper's consent, if they are loaded in in loading devices, which are suitable for on-deck carriage, provided that the deck of the ship has been properly fitted out to carry such a load device. In all other situations, the shipper's consent is required. What has changed are the possibilities to exclude liability for deck cargo, and what also has changed are the consequences for carriage on deck without the shipper's consent. Under the new law the carrier cannot anymore exclude his liability for deck cargo, even if the shipper has consented to such deck carriage. This change is in so far remarkable, as the Maritime Law Reform intended to bring maritime transport law more in line with the general transport law. There the carrier still has the option to exclude his liability for deck cargo (§ 417 (1) No. 1 HGB). Despite this fact the lawmaker decided against this concept. What always remains available, however, is an individually negotiated agreement with the shipper that there shall be no liability of the carrier for deck cargo (§ 512 (1) HGB). But exclusion of liability by bill of lading conditions or remarks entered into the bill of lading by the carrier is no more possible (§ 512 (2) HGB).

225. The consequences for on-deck stowage without the consent of the shipper are severe: Even if there is no fault on the part of the carrier for the unauthorized on-deck stowage, the carrier is liable for any loss of or damage to deck cargo, which was caused by the stowage on deck (§ 500 HGB). Contrary to the general rules of liability, which allows the carrier to exonerate himself, such exoneration is not possible in case of unauthorized deck stowage. But this applies only for the special risks involved in on-deck carriage. In case of damage to unauthorized deck cargo there is a legal presumption that the damage resulted from the fact that they were stowed on deck. If a container stow collapses because cargo was not properly secured in a shipper-packed container, thereby causing damage to other cargo, the carrier can also in case of deck carriage seek to exonerate himself in respect of this cause. He cannot, if damage is caused by a strong wave damaging the container wall or washing a container over board. At least, however, such liability is subject to the limitation per package or unit.

226. The carrier's situation is even worse, if he had agreed with the shipper on under-deck carriage but actually carries on deck. The liability, of course, also here is a no-fault liability (§ 507 No. 2 HGB). But different from the situation, where merely the shipper's consent is missing, in case of agreed under-deck stowage the carrier is liable for the full damage without any limitation of liability. This does not only cut away the package limitation, but any limitation provided for in the liability provisions of the Second Subtitle (§§ 498–512 HGB) or in the contract of carriage. There is no restriction of liability, thus, to the value of the goods at the port of discharge (§ 502 HGB).

VI. Liability for Cargo Damage and Delay

227. Prior to the Maritime Law Reform the law contained two provisions on the carrier's liability for loss of or damage to the goods. As per § 559 HGB old version the carrier was liable to indemnify the claimant for any damage resulting from the unseaworthiness or uncargoworthiness of the ship, though the carrier could exonerate himself by proving that the unseaworthiness or uncargoworthiness could not have been discovered prior to commencement of the voyage by a prudent sea carrier exercising due care. The second provision was § 606 HGB old version, which provided that the carrier is liable for any damage resulting from the loss of or damage to the goods occurring between the time the goods are taken over for carriage and their delivery. The carrier could exonerate himself by proving the loss of, or damage to, the goods was due to circumstances which could not have been avoided by a prudent sea carrier exercising due care. The current law after the Maritime Law Reform now contains in § 498 HGB only one provision dealing with the carrier's liability. § 498 HGB repeats basically § 606 HGB old version but contains a rather special provision on seaworthiness (cf. paragraph 233).

228. Neither the previous not the new law contains any provision on liability for delay in delivery. This liability is governed, thus, by the general civil law as contained in the Civil Code. Under § 286 Civil Code there is a liability for default in the performance of the obligation. This rule is not really suitable, as it not only requires that the claimant proves fault of the carrier, but it also generally requires that the claimant had given a warning notice (*Mahnung*). Even more relevant, as this liability is not dealt with in the second Subtitle of the HGB, it is not protected from the limitations on deviations. Generally, thus, the parties can agree on an exclusion of liability for delay, if such exclusion meets the requirements for a valid exclusion of § 286 Civil Code.

VII. Exemptions and Burden of Proof

229. The carrier's liability under German law is a liability for custodial care (*Obhutshaftung*), but allows the carrier to exonerate himself. There is also a catalogue of circumstances, for which the carrier shall not be liable. It is the general view, however, that for most of the circumstances the carrier could exonerate himself anyway, so that the main purpose of the catalogue exclusions is one of the burden of proof. This, and the complicated rules on burden of proof, will be set out below.

230. The principal way for the carrier to avoid liability under § 498 (1) HGB is to establish that the loss of or damage to the goods was due to circumstances which could not have been avoided by a prudent sea carrier exercising due care (§ 498 (2) 1 HGB). The burden of proof rests with the carrier, the cargo interest merely have to prove that loss of or damage occurred during the liability period of the carrier. The burden of proof is aggravated, if the ship was unseaworthy or uncargoworthy. If this is established – the burden of proof of such unseaworthiness or uncargoworthiness resting with the claimant – and if it is likely that the goods were lost or damaged due to the ship's lack of seaworthiness or cargoworthiness, then the carrier has the additional burden to prove that the lack of seaworthiness or cargoworthiness could not have been discovered prior to commencement of the voyage by a prudent sea carrier exercising due care (§ 498 (2) 2 HGB).

231. As an alternative to exonerating himself, the carrier also has the option to prove that fault on the part of the cargo claimant, who has suffered loss or damage, contributed to the occurrence of that loss or damage, § 498 (3) HGB. The difference to the first exemption is that there the carrier exonerates himself, while here he proves contribution by the shipper.

232. Finally, § 499 HGB contains a catalogue of causes for which the carrier's liability is excluded:

- perils or accidents of the sea or other navigable waters;
- war or hostilities, social unrest, acts by public enemies, or measures taken by sovereigns, and quarantine restrictions;
- seizure under legal process;
- strikes, lockouts, or other restraints of labour;
- acts or omissions of the shipper, in particular insufficiency of packing or improper labelling or marking of the cargo by shipper;
- inherent vice or characteristics of the goods making them especially susceptible to damage, particularly through breakage, rust, internal spoiling, drying out, leakage, or normal wastage in bulk or weight;
- carriage of live animals;
- measures serving to save human life at sea.

This catalogue of exemptions is principally known from the Hague Rules. What is missing, when comparing the catalogue with the Hague Rules, are the exemptions for error in navigation and fire. Liability for these two causes was one of the main concerns in the Maritime Law Reform. It was felt that both causes nowadays should no more give rise to an exemption. But the lawmaker did not go so far to prevent contractual agreements in respect of these two causes. Realizing that the Hague-Visby Rules are still the most widespread legal regime internationally, the lawmaker felt it appropriate to allow also under German law a legal situation which is comparable to the situation under the Hague-Visby Rules. Consequently, § 512 (2) No. 1 HGB no allows a contractual agreement that the carrier is not liable for the fault or neglect of his servants or the crew if the loss or damage results from an act in the navigation or in other management of the ship, save for measures taken predominantly for the benefit of the cargo, or if the loss or damage results from fire or explosion on board the ship. Different from other deviations from the statutory law, this derogation is possible also by way of standard contract terms, e.g., bill of lading conditions. What this all comes down to, thus, is a situation which is similar to that of the Hague-Visby Rules, but only if the carrier was successful in including such a clause into his contracts. The concern of the law reform that the carrier generally should be liable for these causes, thus, will be reached only if something went wrong, either because the clause used by the carrier does not stand the validity test as a standard contract clause under German laws, or that the standard contract clauses were not validly included into the contract. It is fair to say that the concept of the new law is no invention of the German lawmaker, but has a predecessor in international inland navigation law, which applies a similar regime in Article 25 (2) CMNI. But critics have wondered whether a law reform, which is effective only in such defective situations, is meaningful, bearing in mind that the continuing Hague Rules membership of Germany now forces Germany to apply the mentioned exemptions by force of law in relation to other (pure) Hague Rules Member States.

233. In many of the situation addressed above the carrier might also be able to exonerate himself under § 498 (2) HGB. But there he has to bring proof himself. The real benefit for the carrier results from the burden of proof provision contained in § 499 (2) HGB. If, given the circumstances of the case, it is likely that the loss or damage has occurred due to one of the causes set out above, then there is a statutory presumption that it was so caused. Rather than having to exonerate himself, thus, the carrier only has to prove the likeliness of the cause. There is one limitation to that presumption, however, and that is that it does not apply if the ship had been unseaworthy or uncargoworthy. Following the general rules in German law that the burden of proof rest with that persons, which would take the advantage of a proven fact, the burden of proof for unseaworthiness or uncargoworthiness insofar rest with the claimant. But this is not the only way for the claimant to avoid the statutory presumption. He always has the possibility to prove that despite one of the exempted causes being given, loss or damage could have been avoided by a prudent carrier exercising due care. If this proof is brought, the exemptions as such are not available to the carrier (§ 499 (1) 2 HGB), so that subsection 2 is not available to the carrier anymore.

VIII. Extent of Liability

234. Under the general German civil law, a party being liable for loss of or damage to property has to make good the full damage caused, regardless of whether it is property damage, whether it is pure financial damage or whether it is consequential financial damage resulting from property damage. In transport law the extent of such liability is significantly reduced in different ways. First, the liability is reduced to the market value of the goods. For cases of total or partial loss § 502 (1) HGB provides that the carrier shall be liable for the value that the goods would have had if they had been delivered in due time at the contractually agreed destination. This rule is final. Neither can the carrier prove that the loss actually suffered by the claimant is less (e.g., the only buyer of the claimant went bankrupt, so that the goods are of no use for the claimant anymore), nor can the claimant prove that his loss greater (e.g., the claimant's buyer would have paid a price in excess of the market value). Even more important, any consequential damage resulting from the property damage is excluded from liability. If a factory cannot produce because the raw material delivered by the carrier is polluted during carriage, the loss resulting from the business interruption is not covered. Similarly, the costs for disposal of the polluted raw material cannot be recovered from the carrier.

235. Despite the general intention of the lawmaker to bring the law of maritime transport closer to that of general transport, there remains a significant difference here to general transport law. While maritime transport law looks at the value at the place of destination, general transport looks at the value at the place of shipment (§ 429 HGB). As regards damage, the carrier is liable for the difference between the value of the damaged goods at the place and time of delivery and the value that the goods would have had at the place and time of delivery had they not been damaged. Determining such difference may involve difficult questions of fact. For this reason the law contains a simplifying solution by providing yet another statutory presumption: The costs necessary to mitigate or remedy the damage are presumed to be equal to the mentioned difference in values (§ 502 (2) 2 HGB). But, as always unless provided otherwise by the law itself, such presumption is not final. The carrier may prove that the difference is less, the claimant may prove that it is higher.

For both cases there is a need to determine the value of the cargo in sound condition. Here, again, the law helps with a statutory presumption. If the goods were sold immediately prior to shipped, the purchase price noted in the seller's invoice, including the costs of carriage, is presumed to be their market price.

In particular in case of damage to goods, usually costs are incurred by the claimant to determine the extent of the damage. The question arises whether such costs are recoverable or whether they are also excluded by the above mechanism. Here § 503 HGB stipulates that the carrier is liable for the costs of assessing the damage.

236. Apart from limiting the carrier's liability to the value of the goods, there is another limitation of liability, which applies in parallel, not in the alternative. This is the package or weight limitation. The compensation payable for loss or damage is limited to 666,67 Special Drawing Rights (SDR) per package or unit, or to 2 SDR per kilogram of the gross weight, whichever amount is higher, § 504 (1) 1 HGB. There is a special provision if goods are carried in a container or other consolidated manner. In this case each package or unit stated in the bill of lading or seaway bill as being contained in a container or alike is deemed to be a package or unit within the meaning of the first sentence. If the bill of lading or seaway bill does not contain such statement, the container or alike is deemed to be the package or unit (§ 502 (1) 2 HGB).

IX. The Content of the Bill of Lading and the Seaway Bill

237. The HGB describes what a bill of lading shall contain in § 515. But it only describes what it shall contain, not what it must contain. This means that a document may still be a bill lading, if it does not contain all the required information. But it means that a shipper, who has the right to demand the bill lading (§ 513 (1) HGB), may reject a document which does not contain this information. The information, which shall be contained in the bill of lading is:

- place and date of issue;
- name and address of the shipper;
- name of the ship;
- name and address of the carrier;
- ports of loading and destination;
- name and address of the consignee and notify, if any;
- nature of the goods and their apparent order and condition;
- quantity, number or weight of the goods and their permanent, legible leading marks;
- freight owed on delivery, costs to be incurred up to the time of delivery as well as a statement concerning payment of the freight;
- number of originals.

As regards the nature of the goods and their apparent order and condition and their quantity, number or weight and their permanent, legible leading marks, the carrier has to take over this information as described by the shipper (§ 515 (2) HGB). Obviously, all this information may not reflect the true condition of the cargo taken over for shipment or loaded on board. In order to avoid liability for any discrepancy between the sound description in the bill of lading and the actual condition (§ 517 (1) HGB), the carrier, therefore, is entitled to enter reservations into the bill of lading (§ 517 (2) HGB). The law is rather detailed on what such reservation must include: the actual order and condition of the goods when received; which information furnished in the bill of lading, if any, is incorrect, and what the correct information is; the carrier's reason for assuming that the information is incorrect, if any; or why he had insufficient opportunity to verify the information furnished. If a person entitled to claim under bill of lading suffers damage as a result of the carrier not having properly described the cargo in the bill of lading, such person is entitled to a claim for damages according to § 523 (1) HGB, if the carrier knew or should have known, had he exercised due care of a prudent sea carrier that the information was missing or was inaccurate or incomplete.

For the content of a seaway bill, § 526 HGB refers to the mentioned provisions on bills of lading.

X. Right of Action

238. The contractual partner to the carrier in the contract of carriage has a right of action against the carrier. But he is not the only person. Under German law, a contract of carriage qualifies as a contract for the benefit of a third party, namely the consignee. The benefit which the contract avails to him is that he has the right to claim delivery of the goods from the carrier. This would already follow from the general provision on contracts for the benefit of a third party in §§ 328 et seq. Civil Code (BGB). But there is a respective special stipulation contained in § 494 (1) 1 HGB. Hand in hand with this right to claim delivery goes the right to claim damages, if the goods are totally or partly lost or if they are damaged, § 494 (1) 2 HGB. The original consignee under the contract of carriage is not necessarily the party, which actually takes delivery of the goods and who has the rights under § 494 HGB. In line with many other modern transport laws, German maritime law provides for the possibility to make subsequent changes to the contract of carriage. Under § 491 HGB the shipper does not only have the rights to instruct the carrier to stop the goods in transit or to deliver them to another destination, or to deliver them to a different place of discharge, but he may also demand that they shall be delivered to another consignee. The position of a consignee under a contract of carriage, thus, is not a finally secured position but may be varied by the shipper. But the shipper's right to change the consignee end at the moment the goods arrive at the place of discharge. From that moment on the rights mentioned above shift from the shipper to the consignee (§ 491 (2) HGB). As a consequence, it is now the consignee who may instruct the carrier to deliver the cargo to another consignee. Such new consignee then will be the consignee in the meaning of § 494 HGB, who has the right of action against the carrier.

239. It is noteworthy, however, that in all these cases the contractual shipper, who is party to the contract of carriage, despite losing the right to vary the contract once the goods arrive at their destination, retains a right of action as well. In Germany this is addressed as double legitimation. This results in certain procedural problems. Even if the carrier was successful against, say, the shipper, who had commenced an action against him, he remains exposed to the risk that the consignee commences a fresh action. The denial of the shipper's claim has no procedural effect on the consignee's claim. As there is usually more than one place, where actions can be commenced, the only protection of the carrier results from an action for negative declaration, commenced by the carrier against both the shipper and the consignee.

240. If a bill of lading has been issued, it may be that the lawful holder of the bill of lading is someone different from the shipper and consignee under the bill of lading. If, for example, the shipper has sold the cargo to the consignee, the first lawful holder may be the shipper. If he endorses the bill of lading to the consignee, the consignee will be the lawful holder. The right of action rests solely with the party entitled under the bill of lading, § 519 HGB. Different from a bill of lading, a seaway bill generally is not relevant for determining who has a right of action. A seaway bill is of relevance only in an indirect way. It may be issued in a way that instructions of vary the content of the contract may only be followed by the carrier, if the seaway bill is presented to him (§ 491 (3) HGB). A seaway bill, thus, can be an appropriate way to protect a buyer/consignee from deviation of the cargo to another consignee, as long as such buyer/consignee has possession of such a seaway bill carrying the mentioned remark.

§5. Liability of the Actual Carrier

241. General transport law contained the concept of an actual carrier since the transport law reform in 1998, though it was not addressed as actual carrier but rather as performing carrier. The intention behind this terminology was to distinguish between someone who merely enters into a contract of carriage, but does not perform it, from such a person, which performs the carriage. For maritime law this concept was only introduced by the Maritime Law Reform of 2013. § 509 HGB provides that where the carriage is performed, in whole or in part, by a third party who is not the contractual carrier, then such third party, also here addressed as performing carrier, is in the same way liable, as if he were the contractual carrier, for any damage resulting from loss of or damage to the goods. Such liability is limited, however, to the period during which he performs the carriage. Damage may occur during such time but have its root before such performing carrier took over the cargo. In such scenarios the actual carrier may be able to rely on the defence that he could not avoid the damage with the care of a prudent sea carrier.

Performing carriage is not limited to performance of the carriage by ship. Rather, it does include everything which is part of the carriage. As such, part of such carriage is also the loading or discharging of cargo to and from the ship. Such activities make the performing parties, e.g., terminals, performing carriers under § 509 HGB. As they are the same way liable as the contractual carrier, their liability is mandatory in the same way as it is for the contractual carrier. Terminals, thus, can only limit their liability within the framework of § 512 HGB, i.e., by individual agreement, but generally not by standard contract terms.

Chapter 8. Piloting

§1. Introduction

242. Pilotage has a long tradition in Germany. Already in the fourteenth century experienced fishermen acted on river Elbe as pilots for other ships not familiar with the river. In 1610 in Hamburg the first formal pilot was sworn in by the city council. This was followed by the first German pilotage regulation, the Hamburg Pilotage Rules of 1656. Nowadays there are different kinds of pilots active, sea pilots, river pilots and harbour pilots.

§2. Statutory Provisions

243. Basic law for pilotage is the *Seelotsgesetz* (Marine Pilotage Act, SeeLG), which is complemented by the *Allgemeine Lotsverordnung* (ALV General Pilotage Ordinance). Under those acts, pilotage as such is a task of the Federal Republic of Germany. But pilots are not public employees. Rather they are independent professionals, organized in pilots associations called *Lotsenbrüderschaften*. For each maritime pilotage area there exists one pilot association. Currently there exist seven pilot associations:

(1) Ems.
(2) Weser I (from Geestemünde to Bremen).
(3) Weser II / Jade (Outer Weser and Jade).
(4) Elbe.
(5) Nord-Ostsee-Kanal I.
(6) Nord-Ostsee-Kanal II/Kieler Förde/Trave/Flensburger Förde.
(7) Wismar/Rostock/Stralsund.

§3. Duties of the Pilot

244. Under the law, the pilot does not have the nautical command of the ship, but he only advises the master. § 23 (1) SeeLG states that the pilot advises the master in commanding the ship. In practice, though, pilots often give direct orders relating to the movement of the ship. Insofar § 23 (2) SeeLG stipulates that the master remains responsible for the navigation of the ship, even if he allows independent orders of the pilots in respect of the navigation. The pilot is under various duties, which shall secure that he can render his services properly. No surprise, he is not allowed to provide pilotage services if he is not able doing so because he is intoxicated. Similarly obvious is that it forbidden for him to consume alcohol during his pilotage (§ 23 (4) and (5) SeeLG). As to his time of duty, a pilot has to provide his services until he is replaced by another pilot, until he is released by the master of the ship or until he has reached the border of the pilotage area of his pilot's association (§ 24 (1) SeeLG). In areas where pilotage is compulsory, he has to perform his services even if the master releases him (§ 24 (2) SeeLG). Apart from his duties to advise the master, the pilot has to inform his supervising body and his pilot's association of any accident the ship he advises has. He also has to inform of observation relevant for the safety of shipping traffic, and of any pollution of the water (§ 26 (1) SeeLG).

§4. Liability of the Pilot

245. As pilots are not public servants, they are not protected by the statutory provisions which channel liabilities of public servants to the state. Rather, the pilot can be liable for breach of his obligations under the pilotage contract entered into with him as an independent profession. But the SeeLG contains special provisions. According to § 21 (3) SeeLG the pilot is liable towards the owner of the ship he advises only in cases of intent or gross neglect. Ordinary negligence, thus, does not lead to liability of the pilot. If the pilot has caused damage to third parties in the course of his services, and if apart from the pilot either the owner of the ship or another party is also liable, then the owner of the ship and such other party internally have to hold the pilot free, unless the pilot acted with gross negligence or intent. The remaining liability of the pilot is subject to limitation. As per § 615 HGB the pilot can avail of the limitations of liability under the Convention on Limitation of Liability for Maritime Claims, 1976 or 1996. The maximum liability, regardless of the size of the vessel, is 1,000,000 SDR.

Chapter 9. Towage and Push Contract

§1. Introduction

246. Towing and pushing of vessels occur in maritime practice in very diverse situations. While pushing mostly occurs in inland navigation, where pushboats push barges, this is rather rare in ocean shipping. Ocean-going ships are the objects of pushing generally only during assistance by harbour tugs in the course of approaching or leaving the berth. Towing, in contrast, is a regular feature also for sea transport where ocean-going barges are towed by tugs even over very long distances. Commercial towing must be distinguished from towing in distress and salvage situations. In such context towing services are usually not provided on basis of a towage contract, but either as part of a salvage contract or even without any contract just on basis of the statutory salvage law.

§2. Statutory Provisions

247. Contracts for the towing or pushing of a ship are not the subject of special maritime legislation. The legal qualification of a towage contract depends on whether the tug has custody over the tow or not. If the tug has custody, German courts treat such a contract as a contract of carriage, under which the tow is cargo. In such a scenario, thus, the carrier will incur carrier's liabilities in respect of the cargo in the same way as any carrier incurs in respect of his cargo. The tug is treated as having custody of the tow if the tow is unmanned. If it is manned, usually custody of the tug is denied. In such cases, a towage contract is usually deemed to be a contract for services under § 631 Civil Code. Towage can also be performed under charter contract, be it voyage or time charters. Insofar the statutory provisions on voyage charters or time charters apply (*see* paragraphs 180 et seq.).

§3. Liability and Limitation of Liability

248. If the towage contract qualifies as a contract of carriage and if the towage is done by sea, the usual provisions on liability under a contract of carriage by sea apply. This means that the tug incurs a liability under § 498 HGB from the time of accepting the tow for carriage until delivery to the consignee. The tug can exonerate itself according to § 498 (2) HGB, and is exempted from liability for loss or damage resulting from the perils addressed in § 499 HGB. Most notably, the statutory law does not contain an exemption for erroring navigation, one of the major causes for loss of or damage to the tow. For details please *see* paragraphs 232 et seq. If the tow is lost on account of the weather conditions met during the voyage, this may qualify for the perils of the sea defence (§ 499 (1) No. 1 HGB). But the tug may nevertheless be liable, if it was foreseeable that the tug and tow would meet such weather conditions and that the tow would not be able to withstand them. Often parties agree, not the least as this is required by their insurance covers, that there must be towage approvals both for the tug and the tow. Such approvals are issued by special surveyors experienced in towage arrangements. They address such aspects as the fitness of tug and tow for the intended voyage, including stability and water tightness of the tow; the strength and seaworthiness of the tug; the suitability and condition of the towage equipment; the maximum wind fore and wave height permissible for the voyage; the maximum distance from the shore, etc. A breach of such conditions may qualify as a breach of the contract.

249. If the contract does not qualify as a contract of carriage, but as a contract for services according to § 631 Civil Code, the tug will be liable for any damage caused in breach of any of the carrier's duties. Such breach would have to be proven by the tow. Once it is proven the carrier has the possibility that he was not at fault in respect of such breach (§ 280 Civil Code).

250. Many of the towage services for ocean towage are performed on basis of BIMCO contracts, mainly TOWCON or TOWHIRE. The contracts contain special so-called knock-for-knock liability provisions alien to most other contracts, but found also in the field of supply vessels (e.g., SUPPLYTIME). The knock-for-knock principle means that the parties are responsible for loss and damage caused to them, even if caused by the other party. The principle, thus, is one which excludes liability towards the other party completely. Apart from that, both parties undertake to the respective party free from claims for personal injury from persons put on board either the tug or the tow by the respective party. Under German law the validity of such liability arrangement is in dispute. Once they are treated as standard contract conditions, they are subject to the validity test under the law on standard contract conditions in §§ 305 et seq. *Bürgerliches Gesetzbuch* (BGB; Civil Code). A standard contract clause may be treated as invalid, if it is found by a court that, contrary to the requirement of good faith, it unreasonably disadvantages the other party to the contract. As long as one party can be identified as the 'user' of the conditions, i.e., the party on whose initiative the conditions were included in the contract, it does not help such party to refer to the fact that the liability terms are reciprocal, so that both parties have actually the same position under the contract. There is no court decision yet which has dealt with such clauses. The fate under German law, thus, remains unclear.

251. Regarding claims by third parties for loss caused by either the tug or the tow, German tort law does not contain any special provisions, but the general tort law is applicable. If loss or damage was caused by the tug master, he will incur a personal liability under § 823 (1) BGB. But as tug masters usually will not have sufficient funds to satisfy larger claims, liability of the tug owner is of more relevance. Such liability may be based on § 831 BGB, which provides that a person who uses another person to perform a task is liable to make compensation for the damage that the other unlawfully inflicts on a third party when carrying out the task. This provision, thus, only requires establishing causation between the act of the tug master and the damage caused to the injured party. It is not necessary to show fault of the tug master. But the tug owner has the possibility to exonerate himself by demonstrating that he had exercised reasonable care when selecting the tug master. In most cases this proof can be brought, so that in practice § 831 BGB usually does not provide the basis for compensation. But the tug owner can also be liable under § 480 HGB. This stipulates that where, in the course of performing his duties, a member of the crew incurs liability to a third party for damages the shipowner is also liable for the damages. Different from § 831 BGB, thus, here it is not sufficient to show causation by the master, but to establish liability of the master. Such liability may be based on the mentioned § 823 (1) BGB, but it requires fault on part of the master. Once this is established, the owner is liable and, contrary to § 831 BGB, cannot exonerate himself by establishing that he had exercised reasonable care when selecting the tug master.

Chapter 10. Salvage and Assistance

§1. Definition

252. German law defines what salvage is by defining who is a salvor. § 574 (1) HGB defines the salvor as a person that renders assistance (1) to a seagoing ship or inland navigation vessel or other property that is in danger at sea; (2) to a seagoing ship that is in danger in inland waters; or (3) to an inland navigation vessel or other property that is in danger in inland waters, insofar as the assistance is provided by a seagoing ship. Salvage under maritime law, thus, includes assistance not only to seagoing ships, but also to inland navigation ships, and it does not only apply to assistance at sea, but. If carried out from a seagoing ship, also to assistance in inland waters. The decisive element is that the assistance is provided by a seagoing ship. If assistance is rendered to an inland navigation ship or any other property, but if this assistance is not provided by a salvor not acting from a seagoing ship, the maritime salvage law of §§ 574 et seq. HGB are not directly applicable. But § 93 *Binnenschifffahrtsgesetz* (BSchG; Inland Navigation Code), which deals with assistance to an inland navigation ship or other property on inland waters, refers to the maritime salvage law as contained in the HGB. Under § 93 BSchG it is not required that the salvor acts from an inland navigation ship. On internal waterways, thus, assistance to an inland navigation ship can qualify as salvage, and thus be subject to the substantive law of maritime salvage, if it is carried out even without a ship at all.

§2. Statutory Provisions

253. Germany has adopted the International Convention on Salvage of 1989 and has incorporated it into the Commercial Code. The relevant provisions can be found in §§ 574–587 HGB. Foreign lawyers may find it somewhat difficult in finding their way through those provisions, as the German legislator decided to incorporate the Convention into German law not following the structure of the Convention itself, but following the old traditional structure of German salvage law. The consequence is that German law now reflects the Salvage Convention, albeit in a different order of the individual provisions.

254. As provided for in the definition of a salvor, salvage is not limited to assistance for ships, but it embraces assistance for any other property in danger at sea. Both terms, ship and property, are more closely defined in § 574 (2) HGB. The term 'ship' includes floating equipment and floating structures, and the term 'property' includes freight at risk(§ 574 (2) 1 HGB). Not expressly addressed, but certainly also embraced, are bunkers and equipment of the ship, containers, and cargo, regardless of whether it is still on board of a ship in danger, or whether it is lost from a ship. Even a sunken ship or sunken cargo can be the object of salvage. As regards wreck removal *see* also paragraph 270. Neither ship nor property are objects attached permanently and intentionally to the shoreline or fixed or floating platforms, or mobile offshore drilling rigs, which used for the exploration, exploitation or production of sea-bed mineral resources (§ 574 (2) 2 HGB).

255. The ship or property must have been in danger. The law itself does not describe what this means. In respect of ships the courts have held that this means a situation in which there is a danger, which the crew cannot counter the danger with the means available on board. Dangers may not only exist on the high sea, but also on rivers and even in ports. The decisive aspect is that the ship cannot counter the danger on its own. An objective danger is always sufficient for triggering the reward of a salvor. But even without an objective danger courts have allowed a reward, where the master reasonably assumed that there was a danger.

256. Even in the absence of any contract (for salvage contracts *see* paragraph 269) salvage creates a legal relationship between the salvor and the salved interests. The salvor is obliged to carry out the salvage with due care; to seek assistance from other salvors, if the circumstances reasonably so require, and to accept the intervention of other salvors when reasonably requested to do so by the master or owner of the ship in danger or the owner of property in danger (§ 574 (2) HGB). He is further obliged on the other side, the owner and the master of the ship and the owner of other property in danger owe the salvor the duty to cooperate in every regard with the salvor during the salvage operation. Even more important, once the salvor has brought the ship or other property to a port of refuge or other place of safety, the owners of the ship and the saved property are under the obligation to take redelivery of the ship and property (§ 574 (3) HGB). The owners of ship and other property, thus, cannot just leave ship or property to the salvor, regardless of the state in which both are. This is an important aspect, as damaged cargo nowadays often creates huge disposal costs. Both sides owe each other special duties in respect of environmental damage. When rendering his assistance, the salvor has to exercise due care in order to prevent or minimize damage to the environment, and the owner of the ship and proper owe the salvor the same duty. Any agreement to the contrary is null and void (§ 575 HGB).

257. The saving of human life does not qualify as salvage, as a salvor is only a person who gives assistance to a ship and property, but not to persons. Nevertheless salvage law addresses saving of human life, mainly to clarify that for saving of human life generally no salvage reward is payable (§ 583 (1) HGB). A salvor, who saves the ship or property and at the same time saves human life, thus, is rewarded only for the saving of property, not for the saving of human life. But the amount of his reward is also influenced by his skill and efforts of saving human life (§ 577 (1) No. 5 HGB). Apart from lifesaving by the salvor, the law contains special rules, if during salvage operations human life is saved by someone who is not a salvor. If this is the case, such person may demand a fair share of the salvage reward payable to the salvor (§ 538 (2) HGB). This does not only relate to the reward for saving ship and/or property, but also to the special compensation for prevention or mitigation of damage to the environment (*see* paragraph 261). The law even addresses what shall happen, if the salvor should have lost all or part of its right for reward to his own misbehaviour (*see* paragraph 267). In such situation the law recognizes that a person, who has saved human life, shall not be less rewarded only because the salvor has not fulfilled his duties. But still the persons whose lives have been saved, do not have to pay a reward. Rather, in such situation the owners of the salved ship and other property have to pay to such person that such person otherwise would have received from the salvor.

258. This obviously includes cargo on board of a ship, but also cargo lost over board from a ship. It also includes any other fixed or floating object on the sea, like rigs, platforms, buoys. The only requirements are that they qualify as property and that they are in danger.

§3. Salvage Reward

259. Salvors are entitled to a reward. Since ancient time they provide their assistance under the principles of *no cure – no pay*. This means that no reward is payable, if nothing was salved (§ 576 (1) HGB). A further consequence of the principle is that the reward cannot exceed the salved value (§ 577 (2) HGB).

260. The salvage reward includes all costs and expenses incurred by the salvor in carrying out his assistance with the exception of except costs and fees charged by public authorities, customs and other duties payable and all costs of warehousing, preserving, appraising, and selling the salved property (§ 576 (2) HGB). The amount of a reward depends on a number of criteria, the sequence of which as set out in § 577 HGB being expressly declared as irrelevant:

- the salved value of the ship and of any other salved property;
- the skill and efforts of the salvor in preventing or minimizing damage to the environment;
- the measure of success obtained by the salvor;
- the nature and degree of the danger;
- the skill and efforts of the salvor in salving the ship, other property and human life;
- the time, expenses, and losses incurred by the salvor;
- the potential liability and other risks the salvor or his equipment was exposed to;
- the promptness of the services rendered;
- the availability and deployment of vessels or other equipment intended for the salvage operations;
- the state of readiness and efficiency of the salvor's equipment along with its value.

261. The salvage reward is paid as a consideration for the salvor having salved property. This was the very principle of salvage for centuries. The disastrous consequences of tanker accidents involving tankers then shed light on the fact that protection of the environment is an important aspect as well, and that salvors often prevent severe damage to the environment. If they are successful in their efforts and earn a reward, the amount of this reward is also dependent on their skills and efforts of in preventing or minimizing damage to the environment (§ 577 (1) No. 3 HGB). But as the reward cannot exceed the value of the salved property, in case of little slaved values there might not be a proper remuneration for a very successful mitigation of significant damage to the environment. And they might not get any remuneration for their protection of the environment, if no values at all are salved, so that under the *no cure – no pay* principle no reward is earned at all. As salvors nevertheless should be encouraged to engage in the protection of the environment, that Salvage Convention 1989 has introduced a further remuneration of salvors, which is on principle separate and independent from the salvage reward as such: the so-called special compensation. § 578 HGB stipulates that if the salvor has carried out salvage operations in respect of a ship that threatened, either by herself or by her cargo, environmental damage, then the salvor is entitled to a special compensation, but only to the extent that it exceeds any salvage reward to which the salvor is entitled.

As per § 578 (2) HGB, the special compensation in principle is nothing more than the expenses incurred by him, such expenses being all expenses reasonably incurred in the salvage operation plus a fair rate for any equipment and personnel reasonably deployed in the salvage operation. If the salvor actually has prevented environmental damage, the amount that results from this can be increased by up to 30% or even by up to 100%, if this is fair and equitable.

Given the rather vague parameter of the law, in practice mostly the so-called SCOPIC clause is agreed in salvage contracts (*see* for salvage contracts paragraph 269). This clause basically contains a tariff by which the special compensation is calculated on basis of equipment used and time spent.

262. The salvage reward is owed by the owner of the salved ship and the owners of the other salved property pro rata of the value of the ship in proportion to that of the other property (§ 578 (1) HGB). The obligation is separate, and not joint and several. Against that, special compensation is only owed by the owner of the ship (§ 576 (3) HGB), even if it was not the ship itself, which posed a danger to the environment, but the cargo.

263. Assistance to a ship or other property in danger can be rendered either by one salvor alone or a majority of salvors. In the latter case, under the law there still exists only one salvage situation, and not two or more depending on the number of salvors involved. As a consequence, not each of the more than one salvors is entitled to separate remuneration, but under the law there is one remuneration, which all salvors involved share.

264. A salvor may be totally or partially be deprived of a salvage reward or special compensation, if the salvage operations have become necessary or more difficult due to the salvor's fault or neglect, or if the salvor has engaged in fraud or other dishonest conduct (§ 580 HGB).

265. Salvors have maritime lien on the vessel for their reward payable by the owner of the ship, (§§ 585 (1), 596 (1) No. 4 HGB) and a lien on other salved property (§ 585 (2) HGB). Apart from this, the salvor can demand security from liable parties for his reward (§ 587 HGB). As it is usually difficult for a salvor to exercise his right of security, as in practice he is neither aware of the identity of the cargo owners, nor has he means to contact them, the law burdens the shipowner with the obligation to use his best endeavours to ensure that the cargo owners provide security, before the cargo is released. Without the salvor's express consent neither the ship nor other salved property may leave respectively be removed from the port of refuge or other safe place at which they first arrive after completion of the salvage operations, unless the salvor's claims have been satisfied or properly secured. To encourage the fulfilment of this obligation, the law further provides that the shipowner and the master, who deliver cargo without security, are liable for any damage caused by his fault or neglect to the salvor.

§4. Reward of the Crew

266. Salvage of seagoing ships is usually performed by other seagoing ships. § 581 HGB contains a provision dealing with the question, whether and how the crew of the salving ships, which actually performs the salvage job, participates in the reward and, if payable, the special compensation. The reward and the special compensation then will be apportioned between the shipowner, the master, and the other crew members by way of a certain formula. First, the shipowner is compensated for the damage to the ship and for the expenses incurred. Of what remains the shipowner receives two thirds, the master on sixth and the other crew members jointly the remaining sixth.

§5. Liability and Limitation of Liability of Salvors

267. As mentioned above, salvage creates a legal relationship between the salvor and the owners of ship or other property in danger, under which the salvor has to carry out the salvage operations with due care (§ 574 (3) HGB). If he breaches this obligation, making thereby the more salvage operations necessary or making them more difficult, the salvor can lose his right for a reward (§ 580 HGB). But it is also possible that the salvor causes damage to the ship or the cargo. The law of salvage does not deal with this aspect. But as § 574 (3) HGB created the obligation to carry out salvage operations with due care, a breach of this obligation leading to loss or damage to the shipowner or the cargo owners may lead to a claim for damages under § 280 Civil Code. Such liability is, under civil law, an unlimited liability. It would, thus, not only relate to the value of the damaged or lost property, but it would also extend to consequential losses like loss of profit.

268. But the maritime law of the Commercial Code allows in § 611 HGB the salvor to limit his liability in line with the Convention on Limitation of Liability for Maritime Claims 1976 or 1996 (LLMC 1996). Article 1 (1) LLMC 1996 gives, *inter alia*, the salvor the right to limitation. According to Article 1 (3) LLMC 1996 a 'salvor' means any person rendering services in direct connection with salvage operations. This is wide enough to cover whatever a salvor does under German law (cf. § 574 HGB). For salvors not operating from a ship, Article 6 (4) LLMC 1996 provides that the limits of liability shall be calculated according to a tonnage of 1,500 tons. For salvors operating from a ship, the limits are to be calculated on basis of the tonnage of that ship. The calculation as such follows the formulae of Article 6 (1) LLMC 1996.

§6. Salvage Contracts

269. While salvage may be performed without a contractual basis, in most cases, in particular if professional salvors are involved, it is carried out under a salvage contract. Most widespread is the so-called Lloyd's Open Form (LOF), the current form being that of 2011. German statutory law addresses salvage contracts only in one provision. § 584 (1) HGB authorizes the master of a ship in danger the owner and the master of a ship in danger to conclude salvage contracts on behalf of the owner of the ship; and it authorizes the owner and the master to conclude such contracts on behalf of the owners of property on board the ship. The only other provision is that a court may annul or modify a salvage contract if the contract was entered into as a result of undue influence or under the influence of danger, and the contract's terms are inequitable; or that the payment provided under the contract is in an excessive degree too large or too small in view of the services actually rendered.

§7. Removal of Wrecks

270. Traditionally, German does not contain a definition of a wreck. The only civil law provision addressing wrecks was § 873 HGB in the version prior to the insurance law reform of 2008. The provision was a provision on marine insurance, and all it did was indication that the law distinguished between a ship and a wreck. As the German law on wreck removal is not dependent on classifying an object as a wreck, the question what actually is a wreck is not of relevance, at last as far as wreck removal itself is concerned (it remains relevant for insurance cover).

271. Removal of wrecks is in Germany subject to the provisions of the *Bundeswasserstraßengesetz* (WaStrG; Federal Waterways Act). § 24 WaStrG stipulates that the authority in charge of safety is the federal water and shipping administration. There exist a number of Water and Shipping Offices (*Wasser- und Schifffahrtsamt*; WSA*) as* branches of a number of Water and Shipping Directorates (*Wasser- und Schifffahrtsdirektion;* WSD), which are in charge of different regions of Germany. § 24 WaStrG empowers the WSA to take all necessary measures to keep the German water ways in a state and condition suitable for shipping. The basic provision for WSA activities in connection with wreck removal is § 25 WaStrG. This allows the WSA to issue orders to persons, who have caused a danger to or disturbance of a water way. As regards danger or disturbance, such persons can be the target of orders, who either have caused the danger or disturbance by their own behaviour (acts or omissions), or who are in charge of a thing which creates the danger or disturbance. Turning to wreck removal, obviously the owner of a wreck lying in a German water way, is in this context in charge of the wreck, so that removal orders may be issued against such persons. But if a ship turned into a wreck as the result of a collision, the owner of the other ship involved in the collision could also be the addressee of a removal order, as he has caused the wreck with his ship.

272. Orders so issued by the WSA are administrative orders under German public administration law. They need to be served on the addressee, and they need to contain a reference as to how the addressee can challenge the order. The first step of such challenge is an objection, which is filed with the administration itself. If the administration does not change its order, the addressee has the right to start proceedings in the Administrative Courts with the aim of setting the order aside. Usually court actions against administrative order have suspensive effect, but the administration may issue the order as immediately enforceable if this is required by the situation. In such case the order can be executed immediately despite a pending lawsuit. But the addressee can still apply for a court order staying the enforcement.

273. If there is a wreck lying in a water way, usually time is of essence to remove danger or disturbance. Issuing of orders against responsible persons, and possibly taking enforcement measures against such persons may take more time than available for rectifying the situation. The law, therefore, allows the WSA also to become active on its own. The complex details are dealt with in § 30 WaStrG. In case of necessity the WSA may remove a sunken ship or wreck immediately, if it must be expected that responsible persons will or cannot do this. Once the WSA has commenced its removal activities, no other person may interfere anymore. Once the ship or wreck has been removed, the WSA has to inform the responsible persons, who are liable for the removal costs. Most important, § 30 (12) 2 WaStrG expressly refers to §§ 611–617 HGB, so that the right to limit liability is not affected by public law. The right to limit liability is one of the main reasons, why owners of sunken ships or wrecks usually do not engage in the removal operation. If they did, under the removal contracts they obviously would have to pay the agreed remuneration, even if it exceeds the limitation amount. remaining inactive, letting the WSA remove the wreck and then awaiting a payment request is the usual way to invoke limitation of liability. For this limitation *see* paragraphs 155 et seq.

274. In 2013 Germany ratified the Nairobi International Convention on the Removal of Wrecks. Article 1(4) of the Convention defines a wreck as a sunken or stranded ship or any part thereof; including any object that is or has been on board such a ship; or any object that is lost at sea from a ship and that is stranded, sunken or adrift at sea; or a ship that is about, or may reasonably be expected, to sink or to strand, where effective measures to assist the ship or any property. This definition, thus, goes far beyond what usually might be understood as a wreck. The scope of application is the exclusive economic zone of a State Party (Article 1 (1), Article 3). State Parties may extend the scope of application to their territorial waters (Article 3 (2), but Germany has not done so. Once a wreck has been detected, the state authority must investigate if it causes a danger (Article 6). If this is the case, the registered owner of the ship has to remove the wreck. As mentioned, also cargo lost from a ship qualifies as wreck under the Convention. Nevertheless all liability for wreck removal is channelled to the shipowner. The shipowner is liable for all costs of locating, marking and removing the wreck, unless the owner proves that the casualty, which has caused the wreck, resulted from an act of war, hostilities, civil war, insurrection, or a natural phenomenon of an exceptional, inevitable and irresistible character; or if it was wholly caused by an act or omission done with intent to cause damage by a third party; or if it was wholly caused by the negligence or other wrongful act of any Government or other authority responsible for the maintenance of lights or other navigational aids in the exercise of that function (Article 10). The Convention allows limitation of liability, but does not provide own limits or procedures. Rather, Article 10 (2) allows the shipowner to limit his liability according to LLMC 1996 (*see* paragraph 155). Every shipowner trading in the German EEZ has to prove the existence of mandatory insurance cover for his convention liabilities. Such cover must allow direct actions of injured parties against the insurer (Article 12).

Chapter 11. General Average

§1. The Concept of General Average

275. General average is an ancient concept dating back to the laws of Rhodes (*Lex Rhodia de iactu*) and Rome (Justinian's *Digesta*). The basic idea and principle is that ship, cargo and unpaid fright, payable only upon safe completion of the voyage, are exposed to common perils during the voyage. Different from transport on land, a ship usually is in a secluded position when such peril strikes, so usually it is on its own when countering the peril. Such countering may consist of will harm caused to ship or cargo or expenses incurred to their benefit. Rather than letting the loss lie were it falls, or letting the owner of the sacrificed property pursue his rights against other parties to the adventure, general average provides for a set of rules which evenly distributed the sacrifices made or costs incurred on all parties to the adventure which have benefited from the sacrifice or expenditure. Before this background, sacrifice and expenditure are evenly spread to the extent that they were required for the *common safety*. As a consequence, general average would end once a position of safety has been reached, e.g., a port of refuge. Time went beyond this concept, realizing that the purpose of an ocean carriage is not to reach a port of safety, but to reach the port of destination. Nowadays, therefore, sacrifices made and expenditure incurred in order to complete the voyage are also dealt with under general average. This is the so-called principle of *common benefit*.

276. In essence general average means that all sacrifices and expenditures are spread over al saved property. Sacrifices and expenditures give rise to hat the law of general average describes as an allowance. Saved property must contribute. The total sum of all expenditures and sacrifices is reflected in the total sum of all contributions. Saved property insofar includes the right to contribution for sacrifices suffered or expenditure incurred. This is necessary in order to prevent that those whose property is sacrificed or who incur expenditure are privileged over the other members of the general average community. This can be demonstrated by a simple example. If the general average consists of one cargo thrown overboard, and if all contributing interest were to compensate the owner of such cargo for its sacrifice, in result the owner of such cargo would be fully indemnified, while all other interest would have born the loss. This avoided by the owner of such cargo participating with his right for an allowance.

277. In the nineteenth century early attempts were made to harmonize the law of general average by way of an international, but the attempts failed. Following this, the industry started to develop own rules, which only apply if agreed. After a first set of rules, the Glasgow Rules, the York Rules were passed, later amended in Antwerp to become the York-Antwerp Rules (YAR). Their first version dates to 1877, with revisions in 1890, 1924, 1950, 1974 (with an amendment in 1990), 1995 and 2004. The current version of 2016 was approved by the *guardian* of the YAR, the Comité Maritime International (CMI) on its conference in New York in May 2016.

278. The YAR 2016 consist of a Rule Paramount, seven so-called lettered rules (Rules A–G) and 23 so-called numbered rules (Rules I-XXIII). The first rule is the Rule of Interpretation, stating that except as provided by the Rule Paramount and the numbered Rules, general average shall be adjusted according to the lettered Rules. As mentioned above, for their application they require agreement between the parties. Basically all charter party and bill of lading forms in use do contain references to the York-Antwerp Rules, but all of them to the same version. The 2016 Rules having been adopted recently only, one may expect that for a considerable time also older versions will be agreed, just as until now adjusters were confronted with different versions agreed for one and the same voyage. As all versions differ from each other, in such cases the adjuster has to prepare an adjustment, which gives effect to the rules as agreed between the respective parties. This can complicate and adjustment significantly, and it can make it even more difficult to understand for people rarely studying adjustments.

§2. Statutory Provisions

279. The first rule of the York-Antwerp Rules, the Rule of Interpretation, starts with the statement that in the adjustment of general average the following rules shall apply 'to the exclusion of any Law and Practice inconsistent therewith'. Statutory provisions, thus, would be of relevance only if they are mandatory, or if no agreement on the York-Antwerp Rules was made. German statutory law does contain provisions on general average (§§ 588–599 HGB), but none of them is mandatory. As in most cases one or the other form of the York-Antwerp Rules is agreed, the German statutory law generally plays no significant role, with the exception of those provisions which fill gaps left by the York-Antwerp Rules. This justifies limiting the explanation to the following remarks.

280. § 588 HGB restricts general average to sacrifice and expenditure in order to protect from common peril. Parties to the adventure, and thereby members of the general average community, is the owner of the ship or fuel on board, or who bears the risk of loss with regard to a cargo unit or a claim to freight. There is a change of the law in respect of the relevant time for ownership. Before the Maritime Law Reform the relevant time for ownership was the arrival at the discharge port. Now it is ownership at the time of the general average act. The aim was to make determination of ownership easier. One may question whether this is achieved.

281. Rule D of the York-Antwerp Rules stipulates that general average shall not be affected, through the event which gave rise to the sacrifice or expenditure may have been due to the fault of one of the parties to the adventure, but this shall not prejudice any remedies or defences which may be open against or to that party in respect of such fault. The York-Antwerp Rules, thus, only state that general average is as such not affected by fault of a member of the general average community, but they do not state what consequences this has. This is left to the underlying law applying. German law deals with this aspect in § 589 HGB. It starts with repeating the principle of Rule A: the provisions on general average apply even in a case where the peril is caused by the fault or neglect of a party to the adventure. What the law then avails, can be described as a shield and a sword in the hands of those members of the general average community, who were not at fault. First, § 589 (1) HGB stipulates that the party at fault is not entitled to an allowance in general average. The other members, thus, can defend such a claim. But this is of help only, if it is only the party at fault which has suffered sacrifices or expenditure. If any other, innocent, member of the general average community has suffered sacrifices or expenditure due to the fault of another member, it does not help those, who have to contribute, that allowances for the member at fault are excluded: They still have to contribute in order to make good the sacrifices and expenditure of innocent members. They need means to claim this back from the party fault. One can say: a shield is not enough, it is only good for defence. If they want to attack, they also need a sword. It is here where § 589 (2) HGB steps in and provides that party at fault has to compensate the contributing parties for the damage they have suffered as a result of having to contribute to other members' sacrifices and expenditure.

282. Allowances in general average are to be calculated on basis of the value which sacrificed property would have had at the place and time of the termination of the adventure (§ 590 (1) HGB). In respect of sacrificed cargo, there exists an important legal assumption. If such cargo, immediately prior to the commencement of the voyage, was the subject of a sales contract, it is assumed that the purchase price stated in the sales invoice reflects the market value of such cargo (§ 590 (4) HGB). As to contributions, they are calculated on basis of their values at the termination of the adventure, plus any general average allowance. Based on such values, allowances and contributions are assessed based on the proportion between the allowances on the one hand, and the total contributions on the other (§ 592 HGB). Allowances are secured by a maritime lien on the ship and liens on other saved property (§§ 593, 594 HGB). As a further protection for those entitled to allowances, the master must not deliver cargo without having obtained security in respect of all allowance, failing which he is personally liable for the damage caused to the parties entitled to allowances. This is even the case, if the master delivers upon instructions of the shipowner (§ 594 (2) HGB). This remedy seems, on first glance, of little relief for those entitled to allowances, as the master of a ship usually will not have the financial means to make good such damage. But as per § 480 HGB the shipowner is liable for any damage for which a member of the crew is liable if caused in the course of performing his duties. Ultimately, thus, those entitled to allowances can pursue their claims against the shipowner, if the master delivers cargo without having obtained security for the allowances before.

283. Finally, the law deals with the adjustment. § 595 HGB provides that each party to the adventure may demand an adjustment of general average at the destination or, if it is not reached, at the port where the adventure ends. In practice, however, usually it is the shipowner who instructs an adjuster with the preparation of the adjustment. But there may be cases where the shipowner believes it is beneficial to him not to have an adjustment prepared. This is why the law stipulates that if the fuel or cargo was damaged or sacrificed intentionally, the shipowner is obliged to promptly initiate the adjustment. Any failure to do so makes him liable to the parties which could have claimed an allowance. There no reported cases on this scenario. Presumably, as the claimants would have to show what losses they have suffered from the lack of preparation of an adjustment, a kind of 'as if' adjustment will have to be prepared, showing what allowances the claimant could have obtained. But there will be huge practically obstacles for such a claim, as it will be rather difficult to obtain contributory values, or even information on what property was exposed to the common peril.

§3. Definition and Application of the New York-Antwerp Rules

I. The Principle of Common Safety

284. Rule A of the York-Antwerp Rules provides that there is a general average act, and only when, any extraordinary sacrifice or expenditure is intentionally and reasonably made or incurred for the common safety for the purpose of preserving from peril the property involved in a common maritime adventure. This Rule contains various requirements for a situation to be qualifying as general average. First, there must be a peril, which is endangering the safety for the property at risk. Any real danger is sufficient, but it is common view in Germany that the reasonable assessment of the master in the given situation is decisive. What he considers as a danger, and what he may reasonably consider to be a danger taking all relevant facts into consideration, that is a danger for all purposes of general average, even if with hindsight this assessment proves to be incorrect. If reasonably he should have realized that there was no danger, his assessment to the contrary, however, is not sufficient to create a general average situation.

But not every danger is sufficient. Rather it must have certain significance. A well-known example is that not every grounding leads to a danger significant enough for general average. All depends on the circumstances, whether measures to get the ship afloat again qualify as general average.

Furthermore, the danger must be already present, and not only expected for the future. But this does not mean that the master would have to wait for the peril to do harm to the property at risk. It is accepted that imminent danger is sufficient.

Finally, the danger must be a common danger, which means that one and the same danger must put the property at risk. If only the ship is in danger or only the cargo, measures to counter such danger do not qualify as general average.

Prior to the Maritime Law Reform of 2013, under German law there was only general average, if the ship as well as the cargo were saved from the danger at least partially. If either the ship or the cargo was completely lost, this did not qualify as general average. This has changed with the law reform. Now also cases, in which only some of the property is saved, qualify as general average.

II. The Principle of Common Benefit

285. The common safety principle covers all such sacrifices and expenditures until such time and situation, when and where the danger is successfully countered, so that the property is no more at risk. This must not be applied too narrowly. Arguably, a ship drifting into the direction of a shoreline after engine breakdown is no more in danger of grounding, once a tug could make a towing connection, but the danger of grounding is only countered by the continued assistance of the tug. Safety in such cases is deemed reached only once the tug has brought the ship into a port of refuge. Some port of refuge expenses, thus, will be covered already by the principle of common benefit, e.g., port dues, agency fees, etc. But once the ship is in the port of refuge, usually all dangers are countered, except in such cases were danger continues, e.g., water continues to get into the ship through a leakage so that the ship is at risk of capsizing even in port. Leaving aside such cases, having reached the port and being in safety, expenses incurred in a port of refuge cannot qualify for allowance in general average under the principle of common safety. But as the purpose of the common maritime adventure has never been to reach nothing but a port of refuge, but rather to reach the final destination, the principle of common safety has been amended by the principle of common benefit. It provides for the allowance of mostly expenditure, but potentially also sacrifices made in order to bring ship and cargo to the place of destination. The York-Antwerp Rules deal with this mainly in Rules X, XI and XIV. Expenditure allowed under these Rules includes, *inter alia*, cost of handling on board or discharging cargo, fuel or stores (if the handling or discharge was necessary to enable damage to the ship caused by sacrifice or accident to be repaired); wages and maintenance of the crew as well as fuel and stores consumed during the time the ship is in the port of refuge (under certain conditions); temporary repairs of the ship in order to enable the completion of the adventure; expenses of leaving a port of refuge.

286. The rules insofar are casuistic and rather narrowly define what is and what is not allowable in general average. But the whole system gets much more flexibility, but thereby also to a certain extent, uncertainty by Rule F. This Rule states that any additional expense incurred in place of another expense which would have been allowable as general average, shall be deemed to be general average and so allowed without regard to the saving, if any, to other interests, but only up to the amount of the general average expense avoided.

Another Rule which can be understood only before the background of the principle of common benefit is the so-called non-separation agreement. This previously separate agreement forms now part of the York-Antwerp Rules in Rule G. There may be situations in which the completion of the common adventure may be significantly delayed, e.g., by repairs which are necessary for the ship. Cargo interests may wish to take delivery of their cargo at the port of refuge and forward it to the intended destination. Any costs incurred after such ‘separation’ of the cargo from this ship, would, thus, only be for the benefit for the ship, and no more for the benefit of the cargo. The non-separation agreement now treats the cargo in respect of expenses allowable under Rules X and XI as if it had not been separated from the ship. But Rules G also states that allowances made in general average attaching proportionally to the cargo by this reason shall not exceed the cost which would have been borne by the owners of cargo if the cargo had been forwarded at their expense.

III. New Features under the York-Antwerp Rules 2016

287. The York-Antwerp Rules 2016 were put in force by the Comitè Maritime International on its conference in New York in May 2016. They serve as a compromise between the two major players in this area, the property insurers represented by the International Union of Insurance (IUMI), and the shipowners, represented by the International Chamber of Shipowners (ICS) and the Baltic and International Maritime Conference (BIMCO), after the 2004 rules, which had been largely influenced by the insurers, had not found market acceptance and not been put in the standard contract forms used worldwide. The 2016 rules to a great extent go back to the 1994 principles, with the following alterations.

288. One of the major aspects of dispute had been the treatment of salvage. The 1994 Rules, continuing what had first become part of the Rules in 1974, Rule VI had provided that salvage expenditure incurred shall be allowed. The 2004 Rules reversed that and provided that salvage payments shall lie where they fall and shall not be allowed in General Average, save only cases in which one party to the salvage paid all or any of the proportion of salvage due from another party, when special rules applied. The 2016 Rules are a true compromise. They uphold the 1994 principle that salvage payments are allowable in general average (Rule VI.a), but provide for certain qualifications if the members of the general average community have separate contractual or legal liability to salvors – a situation always existing where the salvage is subject to legislation in line with the International Salvage Convention 1989. This is also the situation under German law. If this is the case, which thus will be the clear majority of cases, salvage payments will only be allowable in five distinct situations: (i) if there is a subsequent accident resulting in loss or damage to property during the voyage resulting in significant differences between salved and contributory values; (ii) if there are significant general average sacrifices, (iii) if salved values are manifestly incorrect and there is a significantly incorrect apportionment of salvage expenses, (iv) if any of the parties have paid a significant proportion of salvage due from another party (this is the exception with was part also of the 2004 Rules), and (v) if a significant proportion of the parties have satisfied the salvage claim on substantially different terms.

289. Another area heavily in dispute between the commercial stakeholders had been port of refuge expenses and temporary repairs. Rule XI (b) (ii) now reinstalls that fuel and stores consumed during the extra time of detention in the port of refuge caused repairs necessary for the safe prosecution of the voyage by shall be allowed as general average, except such fuel and stores as are consumed in effecting repairs not allowable in general average. For repairs which are only temporary, the 2004 Rules had provided in Rule XIV b) that the cost of temporary repairs falling for consideration shall be limited to the extent that the cost of temporary repairs effected at the port of loading, call or refuge, together with either the cost of permanent repairs eventually effected or, if unrepaired at the time of the adjustment, the reasonable depreciation in the value of the vessel at the completion of the voyage, exceeds the cost of permanent repairs had they been effected at the port of loading, call or refuge. The 2016 Rules have abolished this limitation and reinstated the 1994 rule on this.

290. Certain provisions have been made with the aim to simplify and speed up the preparation of the general adjustment and thereby save costs. Commercial invoices may be deemed by the adjuster to reflect the value at the time of discharge, even if the place of final delivery under the contract of carriage is different from the place where the common maritime adventure ends (Rule XVI (a) (i)). Cargo may be excluded from general average should the adjuster consider that the cost of including it in the adjustment would be likely to be disproportionate to its eventual contribution (Rule XVII (a) (ii)). The 2016 Rules have retained the time bar provision of Rule XXIII, which had been introduced by the 2004 Rules. Subject to any mandatory rule on time limitation contained in the applicable law, claims for contributions shall be extinguished unless an action is brought within a period of one year after the adjustment was issued, but in no case after six years from the date of termination of the common maritime adventure. The one-year time limit is in line with the German provision of § 605 No. 3 HGB (Commercial Code). Under German law this time limit starts to run at the end of the year when the claim came into existence, which is the moment when the adjustment is issued. The 2016 Rules, thus, shorten the German statutory time limit by letting the limit tart to run when the adjustment is issued. This is permitted by German law.

291. Finally, there are important changes in respect of commission and interest. Commission at 2% as provided for in Rule XX of the 1994 Rules had been abolished by the 2004 Rules. The 2016 Rules in so far follow the 2004 Rules, so that commission is not payable anymore. As regards interests, the 1994 Rules had provided for a fixed interest rate of 7% p.a. The 2004 Rules replaced this by stipulating that the relevant interest rate is fixed by CMI every year for the following year. The major guideline for this was what would be charged by a first-class commercial bank to a shipowner of good credit rating. The 2016 Rules stick to the concept of a formula, but disconnects this from any activity of CMI. Rather, the relevant interest rate will be that of the twelve months ICE LIBOR as published on the first banking day of every year, plus 4% points.

§4. The General Average Adjustment

292. § 595 HGB provides that each party to the adventure may demand an adjustment of general average at the destination or, it is not reached, at the harbour where the adventure ends. The law is really short when it comes to the content of the adjustment and the duties of the parties involved. Section 595 HGB does no more than provide that each party to the adventure may demand an adjustment of general average at the destination or, if the destination is not reached, at the port where the adventure ends. It goes on to say in subsection 2 that the adjustment is to be made up either way by a licensed adjuster or by a *Dispacheur* (general average adjuster), who is defined as an expert person specially appointed by the court. Nothing is said in the HGB what the adjustment should consist of and state. § 595 (3) HGB merely states that each party to the adventure must provide the average adjuster with all documents in his possession that are necessary to perform the average adjustment. This is enforced by a procedural provision contained in the *Gesetz über das Verfahren in Familiensachen und in den Angelegenheiten der freiwilligen Gerichtsbarkeit* (FamFG; Act on Procedure in Family and Voluntary Matters), where § 404 FamFG gives the average adjuster the right to apply to court for an order that any party, which is legally so obliged, has to hand over to the average adjuster documents in its possession. Somewhat surprisingly, also the York-Antwerp Rules, though repeatedly referring to the general average adjustment, do not specify what such an adjustment has to contain. Only since 2016 there exist guidelines by CMI which, by referring to what is expected from an average adjuster, indirectly sets out what an adjustment should contain. The list starts with particulars, 'in a prominent position in the adjustment', of the clause or clauses contained in the charter party or bills of lading that relate to the adjustment of general average. Next, the adjuster is expected to set out the facts that give rise to the general average. Allowances and contributions referred to in the adjustment should be referred to by identifying lettered and/or numbered rules, if the York-Antwerp Rules apply. This, again, is rather indirect but contains the very heart of an adjustment: the sacrifices and expenditure allowable in general average, the contributing values of salved property and, finally, the resulting calculation of respective contributions. In practice, German adjustments usually also contain an incident report by the master and report prepared by the so-called general average surveyor, who is assessing contributory values in case of part damage to cargo, and who is distinguishing e.g., in fire cases between damages caused by fire and damages caused by extinguishing water.

§5. The Contributing Fund

293. As all sacrifices and expenditures in general average are to be spread evenly on salved values, it is one of the prime tasks of average adjusters to determine those salved values, which commonly are described as the contributing fund. German law deals with this, not much different from the provisions of the York-Antwerp Rules, in § 591 HGB. It states that contributions shall be assessed based on the value of the property subject to common peril. Here one must distinguish between the time and place for which values are determined and the time and place relevant to decide which party personally owes the contributions. As regards assessment of the value, the law provides that such values shall be determined on current market value at the termination of the adventure. This may either be a place of destination or, if their place is not reached but the voyage abandoned earlier, the place where the voyage is abandoned. To these values any general average allowed in respect of damage or sacrifice must be added. The consequence is that totally sacrificed cargo, which has no current market value at the termination of the adventure, contributes with its allowance. Otherwise such cargo would merely benefit from the contributions of others, without having to contribute itself. For identifying which party is liable for the contributions, the law reform of 2013 brought a new concept to the German law. Previously it were the owners of ship and cargo at the time of commencement of discharge at the place of destination. § 588 (2) HGB now provides that the relevant time is not that of commencement of discharge but that of the general average act. In respect of ship and fuel the law now refers to the owner, in respect of cargo it is not the owner but the party bearing the risk of loss. It is not expected that this new regime will have any practical significance, because it is a common practice also in Germany for average adjusters, in so far appointed upon instructions of the shipowners, to collect the standard general average securities. Whoever signs a general average bond takes over the obligation to contribute as stipulated in the average adjustment. Such undertaking is independent from and irrespective of what the law as such provides in respect of liability for contribution. Theoretically, the question could arise whether next to someone having signed a general average bond, the party at risk of the cargo at the time of the general average act is also liable for contributions. In practices this question probably will never be raised, because it will be almost impossible to identify such person at risk and, even if this turn out to be possible later, the claim against such party will be unsecured and therefore, for all practical purposes, mostly without any value.

294. The German provisions on contributory values, however, are in practice overridden by what the York-Antwerp Rules provide in Rule XVII. This is partly in line with German statutory law, but partly much more detailed. Also here it is stated that the relevant place for determining the values is that of the termination of the common maritime adventure. In respect of cargo it is stipulated that its values shall be ascertained from the commercial invoice surrendered to the receiver. Admittedly, such invoice does not necessarily have to reflect the value at the place where the common maritime adventure ended. In particular this will not be the case, if after such termination of the common maritime adventure extended on-travel by other transport means takes place. Freight for this on-transport is already included in the invoice value. This may, indeed, be the case for the clear majority of all container shipments, which usually do not end at the yard in a container hub. Rather most of the containers are forwarded either by other ships or by inland craft or by trucks. The 2016 Rules now have legitimized a practice already exercised by many adjusters around the globe, including Germany, namely to disregard the fact that the invoices in front of them in such cases do not properly reflect the actual value at the place of termination. Costs involved for determining the costs for on carriage would have simply been too high and the time for respective investigation in case of even only mid-sized container vessels would have extremely delayed finalization of the adjustment. What Rule XVII also provides is that the value of the cargo shall include the costs of insurance and freight – an aspect, which usually will already follow from the commercial invoice. The aforementioned is sufficient to determine the contributing value of unaffected cargo. In respect of damaged cargo, Rule XVII provides that loss or damage suffered by the cargo prior or at the time of discharge is to be deducted from its invoice value. As a matter of principle, all salved properties have to contribute in general average. Practice has shown, however, that there may be cargo on board which is of such relatively low value, that the costs for chasing for cargo details allowing the assessment of their values may be out of proportion in comparison with the likely contribution payable by that cargo. As a matter of practice, thus, many adjusters had already shut out such kinds of cargo from contribution in order to speed up the finalization of the adjustment and safe costs. This practice now has also been legitimized by Rule XVII (a) (ii) of the York-Antwerp Rules 2016.

295. As regards the ship, the rules say that the value of the ship shall be assessed without taking into account the beneficial or detrimental effect of any demise or time charter party to which the ship maybe committed. In times of great fluctuations this stipulation may be of great relevance. At times of depressed freight rates a high time charter rate may render the vessel much more valuable for her current owner than for any other owner who would have to seek employment of that vessel in the depressed freight market. Rule XVII (a) (iii) clarifies that this excess value, merely depending on the profitable time charter party, has to be disregarded when assessing the value of the ship.

§6. The Receiving Fund

296. While the contributing fund sets out all served values, the receiving fund consists of what has been allowed in general average in respect of sacrifices and expenses. Whether the contributing fund is exhausted or not even sufficient to satisfy the receiving fund, depends on the extent of sacrifices and expenses made. If the total amount of the receiving fund exceeds the total amount of the contributing fund, then it will not be possible to satisfy all allowances in general average. The York-Antwerp Rules describe in detail how the receiving fund is to be calculated (Rules 13, 15, 16 and 18). Even if the contributing fund is large enough to satisfy the full receiving fund, actual satisfaction will in practice depend on the question whether sufficient security for the contributions has been provided. As mentioned above (paragraph 282) the shipowner must not deliver cargo without prior sufficient security having been provided. If the shipowner delivered without such security, he will be liable towards the receiving parties to make good what covered and respect of non-secured cargo.

§7. Proceedings

297. The York-Antwerp Rules are silent on the question who can declare general average. In practice it is usually the shipowner. Under German Law he is bound to do so, if fuel or cargo was damaged or sacrificed (§ 595 (1) HGB). This creates an obligation of the shipowner, but apart from that each party to the adventure may itself demand that an adjustment of general average is prepared. If an adjuster is appointed, but denies that there was a common danger for ship and cargo, § 403 of the *Gesetz über das Verfahren in Familiensachen in den Angelegenheiten der Freiwilligen Gerichtsbarkeit* (FamFG; Act and Procedure in Family and Voluntary Matters) gives each party to the maritime adventure the right to apply to the court to determine whether the adjuster, contrary to his own views, is obliged to prepare an adjustment. The court in charge is the local court at the place where the adjustment is to be prepared.

298. If parties to the adventure do not voluntarily furnish the adjuster with documents of their possession, the adjuster can apply to the same court for a respective order (§ 404 FamFG). Once the adjustment is issued, each party is entitled to apply to the same court for an oral hearing on the adjustment. The purpose of such hearing is to find clarification on objections against the adjustment. The court will summon to such hearing only those parties, which have been identified by the applicant. Each party so summoned has the possibility to raise objections against the adjustment either in writing prior to or orally during the hearing. If no objections have been raised in this way, the court will confirm the adjustment. In order confirming the adjustment is enforceable between the parties and in so far has the same effect as an enforceable judgment (§ 409 FamFG). If an objection has been raised either prior to or during the hearing, all participating parties have to take a position in this respect. If all parties attending agree to the objection, the adjustment is corrected respectively and then confirmed by the court with the consequences just described (§ 406 FamFG). If objections are not agreed, the objecting party, not all other parties, has the right to follow up its objection by starting an action against all other participating parties. Such an action has to be commenced within one month. The local court has jurisdiction only for claims of a value of up to EUR 10,000,00. Any higher claim has to be pursued in the regional court. If the time for the commencement of the action is expired, the local court will confirm the adjustment. If proceedings have been commenced in time, the court in charge (local court or regional court) will decide on the justification of the objection. If it decides the objection to be justified, the court changes the adjustment by judgment, § 880 *Zivilprozessordnung* (ZPO, Civil Procedure Code). The mentioned procedure is a block to any other ordinary procedures. Ordinary actions commenced in respect of general average matters will be dismissed as impermissible in view of the procedures available under FamFG.

Chapter 12. Particular Average

§1. General Concepts

299. The general maritime Law prior to the law reform in 2013 is used to distinguish between general average and special average *(besondere Haverei).* The latter was defined to be accidental damage or costs airing outside general average, and it was to be borne by the owners of the ship and cargo respectively and separately. The new law since 2013 does not contain such a provision anymore, but the effect is the same. Particular average is borne by the owner of the subject matter affected and not distributed over all owners of property exposed to a marine peril. Particular average and general average may, and often do, arise in the same scenario. If, for example, fire breaks out on a ship and the fire is put out by water, some cargo may be damaged by fire and smoke, some may be damaged by water. Fire and smoke damage are particular average and borne by the respective owners, water damage is generally average, to which all saved property must contribute.

300. The statement that the owner of the damaged thing must bear the damage itself is correct only in comparison to the general average community. Under the law the owner of the damaged thing may very well have a claim for damages, if a third party is liable for such damage. Reverting to the previous example: Owners of cargo damaged by fire and smoke may have claims for damages against other cargo owners, whose dangerous cargos had caused the fire which led to the damage. But such claims in many cases require proof of fault and in all cases require proof of causation. Both may be difficult to establish. And they may be damaged for which the injured party cannot hold anyone responsible, simply because there is no responsible party. If a container goes overboard in a full-fledged storm despite customary and seamen-like securing of the container, the carrier will be able to rely on the perils of the sea defence, so that the owner of the lost cargo will not have a claim against the carrier. But not only cargo owners are exposed to those risks, but shipowners are alike. If their ships are damaged in collision, they may partly have a claim against the other shipowner, but only in proportion of the other ship's fault. If the own ship is at fault as well, then such part of the damage has to be borne by the shipowner. And there can obviously, also be damage to a ship, for which no one can be liable, for example, the sinking of a ship in a severe storm.

301. This is the reason why insurance exists. It takes away the risks for the insured, that he may either not at all or only after a long time and a lot of expenses be able to recover his damage from third parties. Being a mature insurance market, Germany has a long tradition of statutory regulations and insurance. Traditionally German Law distinguishes between marine and non-marine insurance. The non-marine insurance is dealt with in the *Versicherungsvertragsgesetz* (VVG; Insurance Contract Act). § 209 VVG stipulates that its provisions are not applicable to marine insurance and to reinsurance. Marine Insurance traditionally was dealt with in the Commercial Code. But this law was widely considered to be 'dead law' for the reason that in practice it had over the time being completely set aside by contractual agreements between the parties. As a consequence the lawmaker did not update the statutory marine insurance law, which basically came from times when cargo was carried over the oceans still by sailing ships. When the non-marine insurance law was reformed in 2008, there were discussions whether to bring marine insurance law simply under the insurance contract Act and give up the traditional separation between marine and non-marine insurance law. Both reinsurers and shipowners, however, reacted adversely, as they feared that the consumer protection concepts of the non-marine insurance Law, in particular after the law reform in 2008 would penetrate marine insurance. Much to the surprise of many, the lawmaker then decided to abolish the statutory marine insurance law in the Commercial Code. As a consequence, Germany is one of the few mature marine insurance markets with no statutory marine insurance law applying. The reasons given by the lawmaker for the new non-marine insurance law clearly state that the non-marine insurance law is not to be considered a model for marine insurance, but that marine insurance should continue to be self-regulated by contractual agreements.

302. Both hull and cargo insurance traditionally have been dominated by the *Allgemeine Deutsche Seeversicherungsbedingungen* (ADS; German General Rules of Marine Insurance). They are of 1919 and provide in their § 126 that German law applies, but except the statutory law and marine insurance. It was this very provision which made statutory marine and insurance superfluous since 1919. ADS contain all that is needed for general regulation of an insurance contract in their first part (§§ 1–57). This is followed by special provisions on hull insurance and on cargo insurance. Over the years, insurance technique, market practice and technical development rendered certain provisions of ADS outdated. In 1973 all special provisions on cargo insurance in ADS were set aside and replaced by *ADS Güterversicherung 1973* (ADS Cargo 1973), which were amended a couple of times in later years, the most common version in use nowadays being that of 1984. Hull insurance was changed in 1978 by the *DTV Kaskoklauseln 1978* (DTV Hull Clauses 1978), which also were amended in later years, the most common clauses in the market being those of 1992. In 2000 the German Insurers Association put in force the *DTV Güterversicherung 2000* (DTV Cargo 2000) which replaced the old combination of ADS and ADS Cargo. In 2009 new ship insurance conditions DTV-ADS 2009 followed and replaced the previous combination of ADS and DTV Hull Clauses.

§2. Particular Average on the Vessel

I. Definition

303. While in the general context the term 'particular average' is used to distinguish it from general average, in marine insurance particular average splits up in total loss and part damage. A case of total loss is given if the ship is indeed lost, for example, sunken in 5,000 m deep water, or if it is damaged in such a way that it is not a ship anymore, for example, so badly exploded and burned that only metal scrap is left. Such cases have to be distinguished from cases where there is only part damage to the vessel, but where the ship either technically cannot be repaired anymore or it would be uneconomical to repair, because the repair expenses exceed the value. In both cases we are confronted with part damage, but the insurance conditions treat those cases more like total losses. A further category is that of missing ships. These cases are characterized by the fact that there is no information in the respect of the vessel. In particular there is no information that the vessel is actually lost or damaged. As will we see later, the insurance conditions treat such cases as total losses.

II. Insurance

304. Hull and machinery insurance in the German market is an all risk insurance (§ 28 ADS, clause 27 DTV-ADS). This means that all perils are covered by the insurance unless they are expressly excluded. As a matter of fact, the conditions do exclude quite a number of perils (like war risks, nuclear risks, unseaworthiness), so that at the end of the day an all risk cover under German clauses may provide more or less the same extent of coverage as a named peril cover in the English market. The important difference between the two concepts lies in the burden of proof. Under a named peril policy the insured must prove that loss of or damage to his ship was caused by one of the designated perils insured. In contrast, under an all risk cover all the assured has to prove that the loss was caused during the cover period, but he does not identify any particular peril. If the insurer wants to avoid payment, he would have to discharge the burden of proof that the damage was caused by an excluded peril.

305. As regards causation, the two main causation concepts of the German General Civil Law apply also to German Marine Insurance Law. A fact is causative for a consequence if the consequence would not have occurred without this fact (theory of equivalent causation). But there may be equivalent causes for a consequence which are so remote that they should not be taken into account for causation purposes. Insofar only such equivalent causes are relevant causes, which have adequately caused the damage (theory of adequate causation). Marine insurance law adds another tier to this concept by the theory of proximate causation. If damage is the consequence of a combination of insured and uninsured perils, then the judge has to determine which of those perils has approximately caused the damage. Proximity in this respect is not proximity in time, but proximity in effect. This sounds nice in theory but may cause considerable practical difficulties. If, for example, the shell plating of a ship is weakened by rust but could withstand all but the most severe storm, which, on the other hand, would not have damaged a ship without rust-affected shell plating, then it is difficult to determine whether the most effective cause was the storm or the rust-damage.

306. In the German insurance market generally it is not of relevance when the damage occurred, but when it was caused. A well-known text book example is a ship which breaks loose in a port in severe storm on 31 December, 23:50 hour, shifts through the port for twenty minutes and collides with another ship on 1 January, 00:10 hour. Suppose that the policy here expired midnight, then cover will rest with the expired policy, because the risk materialized before expiry, despite the fact that the damage occurred only when the new policy was in force already. There is only one class of cases where the German market deviates from the concept the damage must be caused, but not necessarily incurred during the policy period. Those cases are the cases of error in construction, bad workmanship and faulty material. As regards error in construction, these errors generally occur prior to the building of the ship, which means that they occur prior even to the first hull and machinery policy ever issued for such ship. Damage may result many years later. For machinery damage resulting from errors in construction clause 20 DTV Hull Clauses provides cover under the policy during which damage to machinery occurs. Such cover is limited to consequential damage to machinery and does not extend to consequential damage for the hull itself. DTV-ADS have broadened this concept and now provide cover for consequential damage also to the hull. But damage must be consequential, i.e., the cover generally does not include replacement of the wrongly construed part. What has been set out here applies respectively also to faulty material and to bad workmanship.

307. In case of total loss the assured is entitled to claim the sum insured. Policies in the German market are valued policies, so that generally no discussions come up whether the ship was overinsured or underinsured. The sum insured is payable also if a ship is missed without information. The right to demand the sum insured in this case arises after expiry of one month since the last information received on the vessel. This cover element used to be of considerable relevance at times when information from ship where scarce. It has lost much of its relevance with the technical development which now allows keeping contact with the ship in almost any situation. If the ship cannot be repaired or if it is uneconomical to repair because the repair costs would exceed the value of the ship, different from other markets under the German conditions the assured cannot abandon the ship to the insurer and demand payment of the sum insured. Rather the value of the ship in unrepaired condition is assessed (under ADS by public auction, under DTV-ADS also by agreement between the insurer and assured), and the assured is entitled only to the balance between such residual value and the sum insured.

308. As regards part damage, this must be assessed before any repair steps are taken. ADS provide in § 74 for a special way of assessment of the damage by way of experts appointed by both sides, and a third expert appointed by the two so appointed experts if they cannot agree on the cause and amount of damage. In practice this complicated procedure has no relevance anymore. Rather German insurers appoint their own experts from their expert organization *Verein Hanseatischer Transportversicherer* (VHT), who then jointly with an inspector of the technical department of the assured assesses and quantifies the damage. Repairs may only be carried out after such assessment, and under ADS the insurer has a right to deny payment as long as the damage has not been assessed (§ 74 (9) ADS). Once the damage has been assessed, as a matter of principle the insured is obliged to carry out repairs immediately (§ 75 (1) ADS, clause 62.2 DTV-ADS). Repairs may only be postponed if the classification society of the vessel confirms the seaworthiness of the ship in unrepaired condition. Generally the assured cannot claim payment from the insurer mainly on basis of the damage assessed in a survey report. Rather actual performance of the repairs is the condition for a cover claim. There is only one exception to this rule, namely the sale of the vessel in unrepaired condition. If this happens, the assured can claim payment of the damage assessed.

309. The assured has to present at least two offers for repairs from different yards to the insurer. The insurer then can decide whether to demand further offers from other yards which the assured then must obtain. The decision where the repairs are carried out rests alone with the assured. Even if the insurer expresses a preference for a certain yard and its offer, the assured is free to carry out the repairs elsewhere. But if he does, the liability of the insurer under the insurance policy is limited to what would have to be paid if the assured had repaired at the yard preferred by the insurer. Frequently it happens that the assured carries out uninsured work, particular ordinary maintenance work, at the same time when damage insured is repaired. The conditions are silent on what happens with general expenses incurred, for example the use of a dry-dock to carry out both welding to a damaged rudder (damage insured) and new bottom painting of the vessel (maintenance work). The market practice in these cases is that the assured and the insurer share 50% of dock expenses used for both types of work.

310. The assured and his insurer partly have common but partly also separate interests when it comes to repairs. They both have the common interest that the repairs are leading to a technically sound ship, because neither of them has an interest that the ship has to be repaired a second time simply because the first repairs were not carried out properly. But interests of the assured and his insurer are different when it comes to the cost and time of repairs. Being hull-insured for the costs, the insured is less interested in the repair costs but highly interested in fast repairs, because this enables him to make use of his ship and earn freight. The hull-insurer, in contrast, is interested in low repair costs, even if repairs take longer. It is here that a further insurer and his product have to be taken into account, namely the so-called loss of hire insurer. He pays to the assured an agreed amount per day if the ship cannot be used to earn freight or hire due to insured hull damage. Here the interests of the insurer and the assured are the same. The loss of hire insurer does not mind high repair expenses, as long as the repairs are carried out quickly. The assured, thus, is somewhat between the chairs if he has taken out hull insurance as well as loss of hire insurance, because his insurers' interests are conflicting. In practice the problem is solved by the loss of hire insurance conditions stipulating that the loss of hire insurer accepts repairs at a yard for which the repair costs are fully born by the hull-insurer.

III. Settlement

311. The assured is under an obligation to notify the insurer of any accident of his vessel (§ 40 ADS, clause 43 DTV-ADS). The insurer is entitled to demand from the assured any information and documentation required to determine whether the insurer is liable under the policy at all and if so to what extent. If an accident is investigated by the German Federal Bureau for Maritime Casual Investigation, or a similar authority in another country, the insurer may demand presentation of the report before any payment falls due under the policy. In any other case claims fall due under the policy when all reasonable answers have been provided and documents submitted by the assured and one month has passed since then. Above it has been mentioned that it is a condition for indemnification under the policy that repairs actually been carried out. In case of severe part damage huge amounts may have to be paid to yards, and yards may be careful not to perform their work before payment of their work is secured. The assured, thus, seems to come into a situation where he has to fund repairs in order to carry them out and only be able to claim promise insurer later. A solution to this problem is that the insured is entitled to an advance of 75% of what the insurer under the circumstances likely will have to pay (§ 44 ADS, clause 48.2 DTV-ADS). Special rules apply if the ship is mortgaged. In such situation the insurer must make sure that repairs will be carried out before he pays under the policy.

312. Insurance cover claims are subject to a five year limitation period (§ 48 ADS, clause 89 DTV-ADS). The period starts to run at the end of the year during which the insurance policy expired. The limitation period can be extended by mutual agreement between the parties and protected like any other limitation period under German law, for example by commencing court proceedings. But there exists a further much shorter time limit which the assured has to observe. Within fifteen months after the expiry of the policy period (not the end of the year when the policy expired) the assured must declare to the insurer that he demands settlement of his loss. If this period expires without a respective demand, the cover claim finally extinguishes.

313. The insurer's liability is limited to the sum insured (§ 37 ADS, clause 41 DTV-ADS). But this is true only for repair expenses. Expenses incurred by the insured in order to avoid or mitigate damage are recoverable also beyond the sum insured. Theoretically there is no limit for such cover, as long as the expenses were reasonably incurred. Generally speaking this is the case if the assured reasonably assumes that by making the expenses he saves more money for the insurer than the amount of the expenses. The counter-balance to the far-reaching cover is that the insurer can cut off any further liability for further use and labour expenses by declaring that he will pay a sum insured (§ 38 ADS, clause 42 DTV-ADS). This declaration changes the content of the contract. Once it is given, the claim for the sum insured falls immediately due, and the insurer cannot rely on any breach or of obligation or any exclusion clause, even if he learns of the breach or the exclusion only after he made the declaration.

§3. Particular Average on Cargo

I. Definition

314. Particular average on cargo can arise in the form of total loss, partial loss or damage. While total loss of cargo follows the same concept as that of total loss of a ship, damage to cargo follows somewhat different rules.

II. Insurance

315. Insurance. Cargo insurance is offered in the German market usually on basis of a combination of ADS and ADS Cargo or on basis of DTV Cargo. All sets of conditions are designed to address the insurance of a single cargo. It may nowadays happen that a trader insurers one single cargo with his insurer. In most cases, however, an assured ships more than one cargo per year. Rather than insuring each and every cargo under separate insurance contracts, assureds take out open policies with their insurers. Such open policies are not only frame contracts, which determine the content of individual insurance contracts to be concluded later for the individual cargos. Rather they are insurance contracts themselves. They are concluded on basis of special conditions for open policies, which exist both for covers under ADS/ADS Cargo and for covers under DTV Cargo. Under such covers all cargos shipped by the assured are automatically insured under the open cover. But the assured has to make declarations to the insurer in respect of goods shipped and insured. The conditions provide different mechanics on which the parties can agree. If an assured ships only few cargos in an insurance year, the parties can agree on individual declaration of each cargo shipped. Alternatively the parties can agree that the insurer does not declare individual transports but turnover either monthly, quarterly, semi-annually or annually.

316. While in hull insurance the interest in the subject matter insured – the ship – usually does not change during the policy period, in cargo insurance it is normal that interest in the changes while the goods are in transit. This may be different if the cargo owner ships his own cargo for himself to another destination, for example if a manufacturer assembles his product in different factories. But as a matter of fact, most of transports of cargo are performed in the fulfilment of sales contracts, under which sooner or later risk and/or ownership in the goods will pass from the seller to the buyer. In such cases it depends on the trade terms who is taking out insurance. Sellers may sell their goods *ex works,* so that buyers have to arrange transport for themselves and then will also arrange insurance for themselves. Sellers can also sell on c+f under which they arrange for transport, but arrangement of insurance remains for the buyer. But a frequent trade term is cif (costs, insurance freight), under which the seller does not only arrange for transport but also for insurance of the goods. Under the cif clause risks in respect of the goods passes to the buyer at the moment the goods are loaded on the transport means. Any loss of or damage to the goods from that moment on commercially will have to be borne by the buyer. The insurance cover, which the seller buys, thus, must be construed in a way that the buyer is protected by the insurance policy as soon as risk passes to him. Under a cif-contract the seller, amongst others, has to provide the buyer with a certificate of insurance, which sets out the insurer and the terms of cover. Usually such certificates of insurance will be issued '*to whom it may concern'*. Such insurance certificates are documents of title. Rights under such certificates can be transferred by endorsement and handing over of the document.

317. While open policies are time policies, usually concluded for the period of one year, commencement and expiry of cover for the individual risk are linked to the respective transport. Cover usually is 'from warehouse to warehouse' (clause 5 ADS Cargo, clause 8 DTV Cargo) and commences at the moment the goods are removed for immediate transport from their place of storage. For termination of the cover the conditions provide different alternatives, and the cover actually terminates at the earliest of those events: the moments the goods arrive at the place of final delivery stipulated by the consignee; the moment the goods are forwarded after discharge at the port of destination to a place of delivery not named in the policy, if this changes the risk; after expiry of an agreed number of days after the goods have been discharged from the vessel or, if goods are carried on basis of INCOTERMS fob or cfr when they are stowed on board of the vessel.

318. Cargo insurance, just like hull insurance, in Germany is offered as an all risk insurance (§ 48 ADS, clause 2.1 DTV Cargo). Certain perils are, however, excluded, like war risks, strikes or lockouts, confiscation, delay in transport, inherent vice, customary weight differences, ordinary humidity or inappropriate or inadequate packaging.

319. In case of total loss and of missing goods the assured is entitled to claim the sum insured. In case of missing goods such right arises for inner European transport thirty days after the last information on the goods was received, in case of all other transports after sixty days. If the insured claims the sum insured, the insurer may decide whether or not the rights to the goods shall transfer to him upon payment of the sum insured. In most cases, however, this will require additional steps by the assured. Transfer of title under private international law usually is subject to the law where the goods are resting. Many such laws do not allow transfer of title by simple agreement between the parties but require some additional step like handing over of the goods, assigning storage warrants or alike. In case of damage to the goods the conditions offer to the assured two different ways of calculating his loss. He can either determine the fair market value they would have had in sound condition at the place of discharge and the value in damaged condition and then claim such proportion of the sum insured as the gross damaged value bears to the gross sound value. All he may claim the necessary costs incurred at the time of loss for repairing or replacing damaged goods. There exist special rules in respect of insurance of used machines, devices, equipment, vehicles and their components. In such case the insurer generally reimburses without any deductible 'new for old' the necessary cost of repairs. But if the current market value of such equipment amounts to less than 40% of its new value, the conditions stipulate that the amount payable by the insurer shall not exceed the current value.

III. Settlement

320. The assured has to notify the insurer immediately of any loss or damage. While hull insurance under ADS provides for assessment of the damage by way of a formalized expert procedure, the expert procedure provided for in cargo insurance is an option only and usually is performed only if the parties disagree on cause or quantum of the damage. Once the damage has been assessed in this formal or any other way, the insurer is obliged to indemnify the assured within two weeks of the final assessment. If the amount of the claim cannot be determined within one month after the loss being notified, the insurer is entitled to demand a part-payment of the minimum amount likely payable under the circumstances. While claims under hull insurance policy are subject to a time limitation of five years, the time limitation in cargo insurance under DTV Cargo is three years only (clause 24 DTV Cargo). Like in hull insurance the assured has to demand cover within fifteen months after termination of the risk covered, and all rights under the policy extinguish if the demand is not made within this time limit.

Chapter 13. Collisions

321. The German law of collisions between ships is contained in §§ 570–573 *Handelsgesetzbuch*, (HGB; Commercial Code). The provisions are based on the Convention for the Unification of Certain Rules of Law with respect to Collisions between Vessels of 23 September 1910 (Collision Convention), which applies directly with the force of law in respect of collisions between ships flying the flag of convention countries. The direct application of German statutory law is, thus, limited to collisions in German waters involving ships flying flags of countries which have not ratified the Collision Convention. The Collision Convention is much more detailed than German law, but the main principles are the same.

§1. Definitions

322. In accordance with Article 1 Collision Convention § 570 HGB deals with collision between seagoing ships. The provisions are, thus, not applicable if a ship collides with anything else than a seagoing ship, like a pier, a bridge or a lighthouse. Such cases are governed by the general civil tort law. Obviously inland navigation vessels are not seagoing ships. For collisions involving inland navigation vessels, § 573 HGB stipulates that the collision law of HGB applies. In order to determine the application both of the Convention and of HGB, thus, it has to be determined what a seagoing ship is. There does not exist any statutory definition of either ship or seagoing ship. The German Federal Court of Justice has held that a ship is a buoyant vessel with a hollow space of not only negligible size the purpose of which is to be moved on or in the water and thereby carry persons or goods. Ships do not necessarily need an engine, so that also barges without engines can be ships. The requirement of a hollow space excludes floats and drafts from the definition of a ship. The requirement of a certain size excludes canoes and alike. The requirement of the purpose of the vessel being moved in or on the water excludes storage vessels. Vessels which are not designed to carry persons or things, like remote controlled vehicles for underwater works, are not ships under German law. As the collision law of HGB applies also in case of collisions involving inland vessels, it is not necessary to define the dividing line between seagoing ships and inland vessels. It should suffice here to say that under German law it is not relevant whether a ship is entered into a sea ship register or a register of inland craft. The decisive aspect is whether the ship is usually employed for ocean or inland transport. If the ship is regularly employed in both areas, it is considered to be a seagoing ship.

§2. Statutory Provisions

323. The German collision law in the HGB consists of only of three substantive provisions, all of which have their basis in the Collision Convention. According to § 570 HGB, where a collision occurs between seagoing ships, the shipowner of the ship causing the collision shall be liable for the damage to the other ship and to the persons and properties on board on either or both of the ships. But it is further stipulated that the obligation to pay damages arises only if there is fault or neglect on the part of the shipowner of the ship causing the collision, or on one of his servants, in particular the master or a pilot of the ship. This reflects Article 3 of the Collision Convention. If shipowners of several ships involved in a collision are liable for damages, § 571 HGB stipulates that the amount payable by any of the shipowners shall be determined by reference to the degree of fault or neglect of that shipowner compared with a fault or neglect on the part of the other shipowners. If such degree cannot be determined, the liability of all shipowners concerned shall be apportioned equally between them. This provision reflects Article 4 of the Collision Convention.

324. For death or personal injury to persons on board § 571 (2) HGB contains a special provision. In such case the shipowners of several ships involved in a collision are jointly and severally liable for damages to the injured persons or their heirs. Internally, the amount payable by each shipowner is again depending on the degree of fault. This reflects Article 4 (3) of the Collision Convention. Finally, § 572 HGB deals with damage without collision. If a ship, either by the execution or non-execution of a navigational manoeuvre, or by the non-observance of a navigation rule, causes damage to another to another ship or the persons and property on board of such ship, without a collision taking place, the aforementioned §§ 570 and 571 HGB apply mutatis mutandis. This provision does not find any counterpart in the Collision Convention.

I. Incorporation of Treaty Law

325. As mentioned, Germany has ratified the Collision Convention of 1910. According to Article 12 of the Convention the provisions of the Convention apply when all vessels concerned belong to Convention States, but Article 11 excludes the application in respect of warships and government ships exclusively in public service. The provisions of the Convention are much more detailed than the German statutory collision law, but many of those provisions are embodied in case law in Germany anyhow. Article 2 of the Convention, for example, provides that in case of accidental collision, collision due to force majeure or unknown cause of a collision damages are borne by those who have suffered them. German law does not contain such statutory provision, but reaches the same effect, because it provides for claims only on basis of the statutory law, which states in the second sentence of § 570 HGB that the obligation to pay damages arises only if there is fault or neglect. Article 2 (2) of the Convention states that the Convention is applicable regardless of whether one or more ships are at anchor or otherwise made fast. German law reaches the same conclusion because nothing in the statutory provisions declares them inapplicable in case of vessels being at anchor or otherwise made fast. The same applies to Article 6 of the Convention which provides that the right of action for recovery of damages resulting from a collision is not conditional upon the entering of a protest or the fulfilment of any other special formality. German law does not require such protest or any other special formality, so that provisions like Article 6 are not required under German law. The situation is somewhat different with the abolishment of legal presumptions of fault in regard of liability for collision, as provided for in Article 6 (2) of the Convention. While the German law does not contain any statutory regulation on this, it is set procedural law that there is prima facie evidence of fault, if a ship underway collides with a ship at anchor or otherwise made fast. Article 8 of the Convention contains obligations for the masters of vessels in collision to render assistance to the other vessel, her crew and her passengers. This is not part of German collision law but follows from the *Verordnung über die Sicherung der Seefahrt* (SeeFSichV; Ordinance for the Safety of Ocean-Shipping) of 1993.

II. Damages and Procedure

A. Basic Rules on Liability

326. The starting provision of the German statutory law on collisions seems to stipulate that liability for damage cost and collisions is independent of any fault of the vessels involved. It is true that § 570 first sentence HGB does not at all address fault, but simply states that where a collision occurs the ship *causing* the collision shall be liable for the damage to the other ship and to persons and property on board. But § 570 HGB continues with a second sentence saying that an obligation to pay damages arises only, if there is fault or neglect on the part of the shipowner. There is no strict liability in collision cases under German law, thus, but next to causation also fault must be established. German law, thus, does not contain a provision comparable to Article 2 of the Collision Convention, which provides that in case of force majeure or in cases where the cause of the collision is left in doubt, damages are to be borne by those who have suffered them. But the combined requirements of causation and fault under German law lead to the same result. While Article 3 of the Collision Convention refers to fault of vessels, under the German concept a vessel, being a thing, cannot be at fault. Fault is a subjective category and can only be allocated to persons. Prior to the Maritime Law Reform of 2013, the statutory law only referred to fault of the crew of a vessel (§ 735 HGB old version). This now has been broadened. § 570 second sentence HGB addresses fault either of the shipowner or those persons, for whom he is liable according to § 480 HGB, namely a crew member or a pilot. But § 480 HGB contains a limitation, which will be later dealt with in more detail: Towards cargo interests under § 480 HGB the shipowner is only in the same way liable, as if he were the contractual carrier. This is a legal fiction. A shipowner held liable by his own cargo interests for collision damage, thus, may invoke all the legal defences of a contractual carrier.

Collisions between ships without any fault in respect of the crews on either vessel may happen, but in practice are rare. Usually fault is involved.

327. If fault is established in respect of one ship, the owner of this ship is liable for damages. The liability extends to damage to persons and property, not only on board of the other ship, but also on board of the ship at fault. As shipowners nowadays usually are companies and not individual persons anymore, fault in respect of the shipowner itself must be linked to an individual having acted or omitted to act for the shipowner. Under German law, companies are liable for acts and omissions of their directors. Unless a crew member on board is a director of the shipowning company, thus, no act or omission of those on board can qualify as fault of the shipowner. But a collisions may be caused despite greatest care of those on board, for example if vital equipment on board fails due to lack of maintenance or due to lack of a proper administration. The introduction of the ISM-Code has led to a new safety culture on sea and has drastically increased the requirements for proper management of a shipping company. Deficiencies under the ISM-Code, thus, may qualify as fault of the shipowning company. But in practice in many of the cases fault is resting with the crew members, here usually the officer on watch.

328. It happens that only one ship may be at fault for a collision, for example if one ship is safely moored or properly anchored in an anchorage displaying all the required signals and lights, and is hit by another moving vessel. But where both ships are underway, in many cases both ships are at fault. The International Collisions Regulations, which will be dealt with in more detail later, do provide clear rules on how ships shall act to avoid collisions and allocate clear responsibility of what is to be done in order to avoid that ships even get so close that there is a danger of collision. But once such a situation is reached, obligations to avoid a collision are placed on both ships, and in many cases those obligations are breached on both sides. In such a situation § 571 HGB stipulates that liability shall depend on the degree of fault or neglect of the shipowners (or the persons they are liable for). If the degree of fault cannot be properly determined, the owners of all ships involved in the collision bear liability in equal shares. But this latter rule only applies once fault is established as such. The rule applies only to degree of fault. Therefore, fault must be established before the rule can be applied.

329. German statutory collision law does not limit its application to collisions between two vessels. There can be multi-vessel collisions, which are subject to the application of §§ 570 et seq. HGB. In such cases the degree of fault must be allocated to all the vessels involved, which then will bear the respective share of liability.

B. The Evaluation of Fault

330. § 570 HGB stipulates the requirement of fault (*Verschulden*), without specifying what fault this is. As a consequence, the general provisions of the Civil Code have to be applied. In respect of fault § 276 *Bürgerliches Gesetzbuch* (BGB; Civil Code) refers to intent and negligence. There do exist other grades of fault between (ordinary) negligence and intent, namely gross negligence and recklessness. For the purposes of establishing fault under § 570 HGB these differences are not of relevance, because ordinary negligence is sufficient in order to fulfil the fault requirement. Negligence is the disregard respectively non-application of due diligence. While the determination of fault requires to look at the subjective behaviour of a certain person, it is established that the criteria for fault and the required due diligence are objective ones. If fault of a master is in discussion, thus, the applicable criteria are those of an ordinary master with average capabilities. It is accepted that the general standard of care as provided for in § 276 Civil Code is amended for the special situations on sea by § 3 of the *Seeschifffahrtstraßenordnung* (SeeSchStrO; Traffic Regulations for Navigable Maritime Waterways). It provides that the conduct of every person taking part in shipping traffic shall be such as to ensure the safety and easy flow of shipping traffic and to avoid any other person to be exposed to any damage or detriment, to be put at risk, or to be impeded or molested any more than is inevitable in the circumstances prevailing. Furthermore, it is stipulated that every person taking part in shipping traffic shall in particular take any precaution as may be required by the practice of good seamanship or by the special circumstances of the case. For determining whether a member of the ship's crew or the director of the shipowning company were at fault, the court will take into account all relevant facts of the case. It is settled that customary disregard of good seamanship does not mean that a crew member following such a bad practice would not be at fault. What has to be done in the individual situation also depends on what can be done. If a ship is equipped with technical means which go beyond statutory requirements for such a ship, a crew member may be at fault if it does not use such means, despite the fact that it could not have been blamed if the ship had not been respectively equipped.

331. Of vital importance for determining fault of crew members are the mentioned German Traffic Regulations for Navigable Maritime Waterways and the Collisions Regulations of 1972. The latter were adopted as an international convention by IMO, in Germany they are in force since 1977 on basis of the *Verordnung zu den Internationalen Regeln von 1972 zur Verhütung von Zusammenstößen auf See* (SeeStrOV; Ordinance on the International Rules of 1972 for the Prevention of Collisions at Sea). This Ordinance stipulates that the Collisions Regulations, a German translation of which is an attachment to the Ordinance, are applicable (a) on all German waterways including the coastal sea and (b) on the high seas for all ships entitled to fly the German flag. Some of the major rules of the Collision Regulations are addressed here, because those rules will be the basis of a court for determining whether persons on board of ships have been at fault in respect of the collision. Of great importance are the steering and sailing rules of Part B of the Collision Regulations, which apply in any condition of visibility. Rule 5 requires every vessel at all times to maintain a proper look-out by sight and hearing. Even today too often collisions occur at night time with the officer on watch falling asleep and no look-out being on the bridge. An officer of the watch who does not secure a look-out during his watch clearly is in breach of Rule 5 of the Collision Regulations and thereby at fault for a collision resulting therefrom. Shipowners may be at fault for a lack of look-out on their ships, if they could have identified such a practice on basis of work hour and overtime lists, because they easily identify whether at the required times a look-out was on duty.

332. Rule 6 requires all vessels at all times to proceed in a safe speed so that proper and effective action can be taken to avoid a collision and that the ship may be stopped within a distance appropriate to the prevailing circumstances and conditions. What is a safe speed depends on the circumstances, including the state of visibility, the traffic density and the manoeuvrability of the ship.

333. At the heart of the Collision Regulations are Rules 7 and 8. The purpose of Rule 7 is to avoid that possible risks of collisions remain unidentified. To achieve this every ship must at all times determine the risk of collisions, and if there is any doubt in this respect such a risk must be deemed to exist. If a risk has been identified, Rule 8 stipulates certain steps which then have to be taken. The basic rule is that any action taken to avoid a collision shall be positive and made in ample time. Alterations of courses and speed to avoid collisions shall be large enough to be readily apparent to other vessels observing such manoeuvre, in order to make for such vessels clear what the intentions of the manoeuvring vessel are. A succession of small alterations of course or speed can irritate other vessels and is, therefore, not allowed.

334. Special rules exist for typical situations when ships meet on the ocean, namely overtaking (Rule 13), head-on (Rule 14) and crossing situations (Rule 15). Rule 13 requires the overtaking vessel to keep out of the way of the vessel being overtaken. In head-on situations, both ships shall alter their courses to starboard so that they pass each other on port side. In crossing situations the vessel which has the other on her starboard side shall keep out of the way of the other vessel and shall avoid crossing ahead of the other vessel.

The aforementioned rules clearly describe which of the ships, in some cases both ships, have to take action. For these vessels Rule 16 makes clear that such action shall be taken early and substantial in order to keep well clear from the other vessel. Rule 17 describes what is required from the other vessel, called the stand-on vessel. She is principally required to keep her course and speed and may only change this, if it becomes apparent that the other vessel, which is required to keep out of her way, is not taking appropriate action. If a close-quarters situation arises, i.e., if the collision can no longer be avoided by the action of the give-way vessel alone, the stand-on vessel shall take such action as will best aid to avoid collision.

With these clear rules for both vessels it is obvious that in many cases both ships will be at fault, either because a stand-on vessel, contrary to the rules changes course or speed and thereby creates confusion, or because a give-way vessel does not give way or creates confusion by unclear behaviour.

C. Liability for Damage to Other Vessels

335. § 570 HGB does in no way address to what extent a shipowner liable in a collision has to compensate the owners of other ships. As a consequence, the general principles of the *Bürgerliches Gesetzbuch* (BGB; Civil Code) as contained in §§ 249 et seq. BGB apply. They provide that the liable party has to put the injured party in the same position as it has been before the damage occurred. Under the law the injured party does not have to accept that the liable party carries out repairs itself, but the injured party may claim the necessary amount of money in order to carry out the repairs itself. But there is no condition in the law that a claim for damages depends on repairs actually having been carried out. The injured party can decide to leave the damaged ship unrepaired and just collect the monetary indemnification. The injured party can claim to be put in the same position as before the damage occurred, but it cannot claim to be put in a better position. If, as a consequence of repairs, the ship is after the incident in a better condition than before, for example because new parts have been installed in the vessel and replaced old, used parts then the claim for damages will be reduced by the difference in value under the concept of 'new for old'.

336. The claim for damages is not limited to rectifying physical damages to the ship. § 252 BGB provides that the claim for damages includes damages for loss of profit. For the time during which the owner of the other ship cannot use his ship, thus, he is entitled to compensation. Similarly, if the owner of the damaged ship makes use of the repair time for doing other work which is not related to the collision, by way of adjustment of profit (*Vorteilsausgleichung*) he must give credit to the liable party for the benefits he has drawn from the incident. As far as loss of profit is concerned, if the ship had been employed in a charter, the owner will be entitled to the net charter hire less expenses saved. If the ship was not on charter but trading freely, customarily the net profit from the last three voyages prior to the collision and the first three voyages after the collisions are used to calculate the net loss during the repair time.

Part of the recoverable damage is also what the other shipowner has to spend by following orders of public authorities. If, for example, his ship was sunk and he receives an order for removal of the ship and or pollutants, costs incurred in consequence of following such orders are part of the recoverable damage.

D. Liability for Cargo Claims

337. As mentioned, § 570 HGB is a basis not only for claims of owners of cargo on the other ship involved in the collision, but also basis for claims of the owners of cargo on board of the ship causing the collision. If only one ship is at fault, the cargo owners of both ships can hold the ship at fault liable. But the legal situation of the two different classes of cargo owners is different. Owners of cargo on board of the other ship have a full claim for their damage suffered, which includes loss of physical damage to the cargo and any further consequential damage like loss of profit from the prevented on-sale of the cargo to their customers. As far as cargo on board of the ship at fault is concerned, claims for damages of such cargo are affected by the law on contracts of carriage. If the shipowner is contractual carrier himself, he can rely on all statutory defences available to him as a contractual carrier also in respect of non-contractual claims, because § 506 HGB stipulates that the exemptions from and limitations on liability provided for in the statutory provisions on carriage by sea apply equally to any non-contractual claims.

338. If the shipowner is not contractual carrier, in other jurisdictions it may be necessary for him to rely on a Himalaya Clause for the protection by contractual defences. Under German law this is stipulated in the law itself by § 509 HGB, which provides that where carriage is performed by a third party who is not the contractual carrier then that third party – named by the law as performing carrier – may rely on all objections and defences which the contractual carriers entitled to raise under the contract. But the shipowner cannot become liable only due to his own fault (more precisely: due to the fault of its directors, § 31 Civil Code), but also by fault of one of the crew members or a pilot. But the reference to § 480 HGB, as contained in § 570 HGB, includes the provision of § 480 second sentence HGB, according to which the shipowner's liability to cargo interests is no greater than if he was the carrier. The effect of §§ 480, 506 and 509 HGB, thus, is that the owners of the cargo on board the ship at fault cannot recover from the shipowner more than they can recover from the contractual carrier.

339. Most noteworthy, however, is that since the Maritime Law Reform of 2013 there is no statutory error in navigation defence anymore. Under the law, thus, a carrier now is liable also for negligent navigation by his crew. But contractually a carrier may agree, even by bill of lading conditions, on an error in navigation defence. And if it was so agreed, also the shipowner can rely on such defence. While in theory there was a drastic change by the Maritime Law Reform, in practice all bills of lading contain sufficient wording to exclude liability for error in navigation, because a Paramount Clause, which declares the Hague or Hague-Visby Rules applicable to the contract, is generally accepted as sufficient to exclude liability for error in navigation.

If there is not only one of the two vessels at fault of a collision, but if both vessels are at fault, then the owners of cargo of all ships have claims against both shipowners. According to § 571 HGB the amounts payable by the shipowners then are determined by reference to the degree of fault or neglect of the shipowners. If for example, this leads to a fault ratio of 60% for shipowner A and 40% for shipowner B, then cargo interests can recover 60% of their damage from shipowner A and 40% from shipowner B. The limitations in respect of claims for cargo owners against the shipowner of their carrying vessels are under the same limitations as just described. If their bills of lading contain exclusions for error in navigation, the consequence is that they may recover 40% of their claims from the other shipowner in full, i.e., including consequential damage, for the remaining 60% they would be completely excluded in view of the error in navigation defence.

At all times the liability of the shipowners involved is separate and not joint at several.

E. Liability for Personal Injury

340. While liability for damage to the other ship and property on both ships is only separate, and not joint at several, but also limited to the proportion of the fault falling on each vessel, for personal injury on all vessels involved in a collision the situation is different. Here § 570 (2) HGB provides for a joint and several liability of all vessels involved in the collision, subject only to the requirement that a shipowner only is liable if he, his crew or the pilot on his ship have been at fault in respect of the collision. The owner of a ship involved in a collision which is not in this respect at fault, is not liable for personal injury on board of his ship. As to establishment of fault, the same principles as described above apply also here.

Also in collision cases the general civil law rule of contributory negligence of § 254 BGB applies. This means that a claim for personal injury may be reduced if the injury is caused or aggravated by the injured person itself.

341. The effects of joint and several liability are in German law dealt within §§ 421 et seq. BGB. According to § 421 BGB in case of joint and several liability each of the debtors is obliged to affect the entire performance, but the claimant is only entitled to demand the performance once. As regards the choice of the party, it is the claimant who may demand at its discretion full or part performance for each of the obligors. In the context of collision liability for personal injury this means that the injured person can decide from which shipowner it claims indemnity. It can demand the full indemnity from one shipowner, but it can also be split between the two shipowners. In particular the injured person is not prevented from claiming from a shipowner more than his share of fault in the collision. Under civil law the settlement of a claim by one of the joint debtors has certain effects. First, according to § 426 (1) BGB, internally between joint at several debtors they are obliged in equal proportions in relation to another, unless otherwise determined. § 571(2) second sentence HGB contains such a determination by providing that amongst each other the amount payable by each shipowner shall be determined in accordance with subsection 571 (1) HGB, i.e., on basis of the degree of fault and neglect of the collision. A further civil law consequence of settlement of a claim by one debtor is that the claimant's claim against other debtors passes to the paying debtor. In the collision context this means that the personal injury claim of the injured person against the other shipowner according to § 571 (1) HGB passes to the paying shipowner to the extent that he has settled the claim. But this does not mean that the paying shipowner could pursue the full claim against the other shipowner. Rather § 571 (2) second sentence HGB limits the recourse claim proportionally to the other shipowner's share of fault.

342. In respect of personal injury the injured party can claim costs for medical treatment. If the personal injury affects the livelihood or advancement of the injured person, this is recoverable under § 842 Civil Code. In particular, if the earning capacity of the injured person is affected or if his needs for daily life are increased, then he is entitled to payment of an annuity making good these deficiencies. Over and above such losses which result in financial disadvantages of the injured person, the injured person is also entitled to moral damages (§ 253 BGB). If the collision causes death to a person on board of a ship, the shipowners are jointly and severally liable for the funeral costs (§ 844 (1) BGB. More relevant is that such third parties which were in such a close relationship with the deceased person that the deceased person was obliged by operation of law to provide maintenance for that person, and if such person as a result of the death has been deprived of his right to maintenance, then the shipowners must provide an annuity to such person to the extent that the person killed would have been obliged to provide maintenance for such person for the presumed duration of the person killed (§ 844 (2) BGB).

343. Should the persons on board of the vessel be passengers, §§ 536 et seq. HGB contain special provisions on liability which supersedes those of § 571 HGB.

F. Procedure, Especially the Determination of Damages

344. For a collision claim to be pursued in German courts it is necessary that German courts have international jurisdiction. Germany is a signatory to the 1952 International Convention on certain Rules concerning Civil Jurisdiction in Matters of Collision. Article 1 of this Convention limits jurisdiction to the courts where the defendant has his habitual residence or a place of business, the courts of the place where a ship arrest has been effected of the defendant ship or of security has been furnished in lieu of arrest, or the courts of the place of collision. The 1952 Convention takes precedence over the Brussels 1a Regulation as per the latter's Article 71.

A German court can arrest a vessel for a collision claim, if the vessel within the local jurisdiction of the respective court. Such an arrest is possible, if the main action will be decided by a German court or by any other court in a European Member State. The arrest as such does not found jurisdiction, so that in cases where the defendant is not a German shipowner and the collision did not occur in German waters it is possible to obtain security by way of an arrest in Germany, but it is not possible to found jurisdiction by way of such an arrest.

If German courts have international jurisdiction on basis of the 1952 Convention, the determination of the court which actually will hear the case depends on the provisions of the Civil Procedure Code. Such court will have jurisdiction, in whose local territory the defendant shipowner is domiciled. Alternatively, the claimant can also start an action in the court, in whose territory the collision took place.

345. For smaller claims up to an amount of EUR 10,000 jurisdiction rests with the local courts (*Amtsgerichte*). Which judge at the local court hears which case is governed by the organizational chart of each court. Courts on rivers and coasts sometimes provide in their organizational charts that all collision cases are handled by certain judges in certain departments of the court. Cases with a claim value of more than EUR 10,000 are subject to the jurisdiction of the regional courts (*Landgerichte*). Following the rules of the Courts Constitution Act, regional courts have special chambers for commercial matters (*Kammer für Handelssachen*). § 95 (1) No. 4 f of the *Gerichtsverfassungsgesetz* (GVG; Constitution of Courts Act) expressly provides that actions for compensation for damages in the event of collisions between ships are commercial matters so that they fall under the special jurisdiction of the chambers for commercial matters at the regional courts. Courts with a higher frequency of collision cases, like the Regional Court of Hamburg, may provide by their organizational charts that only a limited number of chambers for commercial matters hear collision cases. In the Regional Court of Hamburg only two of these chambers hear collision cases.

Appeals in collision cases against local court judgments go the regional court and are there dealt with by the chambers for commercial matters. Appeals from regional court decisions go to the respective Court of Appeal. On Court of Appeal level, usually all maritime cases are concentrated on one senate. Appeals against Court of Appeal decisions go to the Federal Court of Justice, where also one senate is in charge of maritime matters.

346. There are no special rules on collision case procedure in the Civil Procedure Code. All general rules and principles apply, but with one specialty. In civil proceedings a claimant pursuing not his own rights but rights of someone else may only do so, if he has a legitimate commercial and legal interest, and if he makes clear in his action that he is pursuing someone else's rights. In collision cases it is accepted that a shipowner may pursue claims for damage to his vessel even after he has been indemnified by his hull insurer with the consequence that the claim for damages against the other shipowner has been transferred to the insurer.

347. As regards evidence, the general rules on taking of evidence under the *Zivilprozessoprdnung* (ZPO; Civil Procedure Code) apply. § 286 ZPO stipulates that the court is to decide, at its discretion and conviction, and taking account of the entire content of the hearings and results obtained by evidence being taken, if any, whether an allegation as to fact is to be deemed true or untrue. The court has to give reasons which specify the conviction of the judges. But the burden of proof is lowered by § 287 ZPO when it comes to determination of damage. Here the court determines to what extent evidence has to be taken for the assessment of damage, and the court is entitled to assess damages by estimation.

III. Limitation of Liability

348. Collision claims are subject to the statutory provisions on limitation of liability. In so far reference is made to paragraph 155.

Chapter 14. Marine Pollution

§1. Introduction

349. While legislative activity for the protection of water can be followed back in time for quite a long time, and while water protection legislation, not only in respect of ground water, dates back in Germany to the 1950s, pollution of water has come into the focus of the legislator with the catastrophic damage caused by tanker accidents like the 'TORREY CANYON' disaster in 1967 where the English and French coasts were for the first time hit by a serious oil pollution caused by about 120,000 tons of crude oil escaped from the vessel when she broke apart. Since then intense international legislative activity in the form of various conventions occurred, for the mentioned historic reasons mainly and originally in the area of oil pollution. Attempts for an international convention on other hazardous substances (HNS Convention) followed later, were not yet successful. Latest development in international legislation is the Bunker Convention.

§2. Statutory Provisions: Sources of Law

350. National German law deals with pollution of water in the *Wasserhaushaltsgesetz* (WHG Water Management Act). This Act applies to the German coastal sea but does not only deal with marine pollution. Rather it deals with any pollution of water including lakes and rivers. It is not limited to pollution from ships, but from any installation, ships being treated as such installations.

There also exists a dense web of legislation for the protection of the environment, which is mainly based on EU law. Of prime importance are the *Bundesnaturschutzgesetz* (BNatSchG; Federal Act on the Protection of Nature) and the *Umweltschadengesetz* (USchadG; Environmental Damage Act). According to § 3 USchadG this Act also applies to the German coastal sea and the German EEZ. § 6 USchadG stipulates a responsibility to mitigate and rectify damage to nature as defined in the BNatSchG. Responsible party is any natural or legal person who engages in or controls the occupational activity, including the holder of a permit or authorization for such an activity or the person registering or notifying such an activity, thereby directly causing environmental damage or the immediate threat of such damage (§ 2 No. 3 USchadG).

351. On international level, Germany has ratified most of the international conventions for prevention of oil pollution and handling of all pollutions occurred. This applies foremost to the MARPOL Convention of 1973 or 1978 with the Annexes I–V and the MARPOL Protocol of 1997 with Annex VI. Germany has also ratified the Intervention Convention 1969 and the 1973 Protocol. In respect of liability from oil pollution Germany has ratified the CLC Convention of 1969 with the Protocols of 1976 and 1992, the Fund Convention of 1976 with the Protocols of 1992 and 2003 and the Bunkers Convention 2001. The HNS Convention of 1996, recently amended by the 2010 Protocol, has not yet entered into force. It is under consideration by the German government, and it is expected that Germany will sooner or later ratify. Finally, Germany has also ratified the Antifouling Convention 2001 and the Ballast Water Convention 2004.

§3. Sources of Pollution

I. Pollution from Ships

352. As mentioned, the national German law deals with pollution of water in the Water Management Act (WHG). According to § 1 WHG the purpose of the Act is sustainable water management as part of the natural resources, as part of the livelihood for human beings and habitat and biotope for animals and plants, as well as a usable resource. As per § 2 WHG, the Act applies to all ground water, surface water and coastal waters. Parts of the Act also apply to the German Exclusive Economic Zone (EEZ), but only to the extent that the Act provides an authority to the Federal Government to make further regulations in respect of water quality and requirements for the use of the EEZ, and to the extent that § 45a–45l WHG rules stipulate for the assessment of water quality and the management of the EEZ. As to liability for water pollution, the WHG contains provisions only for rivers and lakes and the coastal sea, but those provisions do not apply to the EEZ.

The main liability provision is § 89 (1) WHG. It stipulates that anyone who introduces or discharges substances into the water or anyone who affects water in such a way that physical or chemical or biological properties are changed is liable to compensate for damage thereby caused to another. If several parties are responsible for such effects their liability is joined and several (§ 427 Civil Code). Introduction and discharge require an intentional behaviour, intentional not in the sense that the water is polluted, but in the sense that the acting person is aware of what it is doing. Such introduction or discharge leads to the liability of the acting person. The liability extends to any kind of damage, including pure economic loss. This provision is complemented by Article 89 (2) WHG. It stipulates that if there is no case of introduction and discharge according to subsection (1), then the owner of an installation designed to manufacture, process, store, deposit, convey or dispose of substances is liable to compensate damages caused by the release of such substances from such installation. In respect of ships, the acting persons who discharge or introduce substances into the water usually will be crew members. They incur, thus, personal liability under § 89 (1) WHG. This will result in a liability of the shipowner according to § 480 Commercial Code (cf. paragraph 147). If there is no discharge introduction of substances into the water, but a release according to § 89 (2) WHG, then the shipowner (or in case of a bareboat charterer: the bareboat charterer) will be liable under § 89 (2) WHG.

353. Liabilities both under § 89 (1) and § 89 (2) WHG are strict liabilities, so that no fault is required. The WHG itself does not contain any stipulations on limited liability. But it is settled that claims under the WHG are subject to the general limitation of liability provision as per §§ 611 et seq. HGB. The WHG does not stipulate mandatory insurance for water pollution; consequently, it neither introduces direct claims for damages against liable parties. It must be noted that the WHG is applicable only where no international convention applies. If a convention applies, then liability is only subject to such a convention.

354. Turning to international conventions, the most pertinent rules on prevention of oil pollution on the seas are contained in the 1973 International Convention for the Prevention of Marine Pollution from Ships (MARPOL), as amended by the 1978 and 1997 Protocols. The Convention in in its original 1973 version consists of no more than twenty articles. One of the most important provisions is Article 4, stating in subsection (2) that any violation of the requirements of the MARPOL Convention within the jurisdiction of any Convention Party shall be prohibited and sanctions shall be established therefore under the law of the party. Germany has done so by §§ 324 et seq. *Strafgesetzbuch* (StGB; Criminal Code). The articles of the MARPOL Convention themselves fix the administrative framework for dealing with marine pollution, the substantive provisions to avoid such pollution are contained in the annexes, namely Annex I: Regulations for the prevention of pollution by oil; Annex II: Regulations for the control of pollution by noxious liquid substances in bulk; Annex III: Regulations for the prevention of pollution by harmful substances carried by sea in packaged form, or in freight containers, portable tanks or road or rail tank wagons; Annex IV: Regulations for the prevention of pollution by sewage from ships; and Annex V: Regulations for the prevention of pollution by garbage from ships. Annexes I to V are very detailed and fill more than 500 pages of provisions. The MARPOL Convention is not a civil liability convention.

Neither is the International Convention relating to the Intervention on the High Seas in Cases of Oil Pollution Casualties of 1969, which has been ratified by Germany as well. The purpose of this Convention is to allow Convention States to take such measures on the high seas as may be necessary to prevent, mitigate or eliminate grave or imminent danger to the coast line or related interest from pollution or threat of pollution, of the sea by oil.

355. The first civil liability convention in respect of marine pollution was the International Convention of Civil Liability for Oil Pollution Damage of 1969 (CLC), in Germany in force in the version of the 1992 Protocol. In the CLC is supplemented by the International Convention on the Establishment of an International Fund for Compensation for Oil Pollution Damage of 1969, currently in force also in the version of the 1992 Protocol. Finally, Germany is also a Member State of the Convention for the Protection of the Marine Environment of the North-East Atlantic 1992 (OSPAR) and the International Convention on Civil Liability for Bunker Oil Pollution Damage 2001.

356. The conventions on civil liability in respect of oil pollution follow patterns which are also used in case of other international liability conventions: strict liability, combined with mandatory insurance and direct action against the insurer. CLC 1992 deals with pollution damage by escape or discharge of oil carried as cargo. Article III (1) CLC stipulates that the owner a ship at the time of an incident is liable for any pollution damage caused by the ship as a result of the incident. This is a strict liability, so that no fault is required. Exclusions to the liability are very narrow and limited to damage resulting from act of war, hostilities, civil war, insurrection or a natural phenomenon of an exceptional, inevitable and irresistible character; damage wholly caused by a third party by an act or omission done with the intent to cause damage; or only caused by the negligence or other wrongful act of any government or authority responsible for the maintenance of lights or other navigational aids. If the shipowner is able to prove that the pollution damage resulted wholly or partially either from an act or a mission done with the intent to cause damage by the person suffering the damage or from the negligence of such person, the shipowner may be exonerated wholly or partially from his liability.

357. Article 3 (4) CLC clarifies that the shipowner's liability for oil pollution is exclusively determined by the Convention, so that no other national legislation is relevant. The same provision also channels all liability under CLC to the shipowner and expressly excludes claims against crew members or other servants to agents of the owner, pilots or other persons performing services for the ship, charterers, managers or operators of the ship, salvors or any other person taking preventing measures, including servants or agents of the aforementioned. The only exception to this is that such persons may be held responsible if damage resulted from their own personal act or admission, performed with the intent to cause oil pollution damage, or recklessly and with knowledge that such damage would probably result.

358. Liability under CLC is limited. The limitation amount depends on the gross tonnage of the ship calculated in accordance with the International Convention on Tonnage Measurements of Ships 1969. For ships not exceeding 5,000 gross tons the limitation amount is 4,510,000 SDR. For ships in excess of 5,000 GT, the limitation amount is raised by 631 SDR for each GT. The maximum liability amount is 89,770,000 SDR. Similar to most of the other international liability conventions, limitation is not available for an owner who acts intentionally or recklessly and with knowledge that such damage would probably result.

Limitation is effected by the owner constituting a limitation fund for the total sum representing the limit of his liability as calculated aforementioned. Details of the constitution administration of such fund in Germany are subject to the *Schifffahrtsrechtliches Verteilungsverfahren* (cf. paragraph 174).

359. For ships with the oil carrying capacity of more than 2,000 tons Article 7 CLC requires the owner to maintain the insurance or other financial security in the limitation amount applicable to that vessel. In practice such cover as provided by the P&I Clubs. The owner has to obtain a certificate attesting such an insurance, which has to be issued by a contracting state. Contracting states will do so if the owner provides them with evidence of insurance. In case of insurance by P&I Clubs, such evidence is known in the market as *blue card.* P&I insurers providing such cover are in two ways exposed to situations they are otherwise not used to under their rules or insurance condition: should cover with them cease for any reason other than expiry of the period of validity, for example, by termination due to non-payment of premium, then the insurer will remain at risk for convention liability for three months counted from the day when the insurer had informed the authorities of the termination of cover. And the insurance must give third parties, who are entitled to damages under CLC, a direct right of action against the insurer. In particular the last aspect is one usually avoided by P&I insurers, whose rules or conditions of insurance regularly contain *pay first* or *pay to be paid* rules, giving rise to a cover claim from the shipowner only after he has settled his liability towards in the third party himself.

360. Next to CLC Germany has also ratified the International Convention on the Establishment of an International Fund for Compensation for Oil Pollution Damage, currently in force in the version of the 1992 Protocol (Fund Convention). While it is the concept of CLC to provide for liability of the shipowner, limit this liability and stipulate insurance cover with direct action of entitled parties against the insurer, the Fund Convention neither establishes liability nor requires insurance. Rather it is the purpose of the Fund Convention to provide cover if and to the extent parties having suffered damage from oil pollution are not indemnified under CLC. This may be for the reason that no liability for damage arises under CLC (e.g., because one of the exception applies), because the owner and the insurer are financially incapable of meeting their obligations under CLC or because the CLC limits are exhausted. A limitation fund under CLC is an ad-hoc fund, which is usually administered by the court in charge of the limitation proceedings. Against that, the fund under the Fund Convention, the International Oil Pollution Compensation Fund (IOPC-Fund) is a permanent institution administered in London. While by way of the insurance requirement under CLC oil pollution damage recoverable under CLC is effectively financed by shipowners (through their calls or premiums), funding under the Fund Convention is not done by the shipowners, but by annual contributions by any person receiving in one calendar year more than 150,000 tons of oil. One can say, thus, that under CLC the first tier of oil pollution compensation is financed by those who carry the oil, while the following second tier under the Fund Convention is financed by those who consume it. There are only two situations under which the IOPC Fund is not liable to compensate for all pollution damage: act of war, hostilities, civil war or insurrection; or escape of all from a warship or any other ship owned or operated by a state and used only for government non-commercial services; or lack of proof by the claimant that the damage resulted from an incident involving one or more ships. The maximum liability of the fund is 3,740,000 SDR.

361. Liability for oil pollution resulting from bunker oil is subject to the Bunker Convention, which Germany has ratified as well. The features of the Bunker Convention are similar to those of CLC. Limitation is channelled exclusively to the shipowner (Article III (1) Bunker Convention), and claims for bunker oil pollution can only be pursued under the Bunker Convention. The liability is strict liability, so that no fault has to be established. Liability is excluded for the same reasons as there is exclusion under CLC: acts of war, hostilities, civil war, insurrection and exceptional, inevitable and irresistible natural phenomenon; causation exclusively by act or omission done by a third party with the intention to cause damage; causation exclusively by negligence or other wrongful act of any government or authority responsible for the maintenance of lights or other navigational aids in an exercise of that function. Special feature is that in case of two or more ships involved in an incident with resulting bunker oil pollution damage, the owners of all ships involved are jointly and severally liable for such damage which is not reasonably separable (Art. V Bunker Convention).

362. Liability under the Bunker Convention is limited, but the Bunker Convention itself does not provide for limitation amounts or administration of funds. Rather Article VI stipulates that the Bunker Convention does not affect the right of the shipowner to limit his liability in accordance with the London Limitation Convention 1976 (currently in force in the form of the Protocol of 1996), so that the limitation amounts under the London Convention apply to liability under the Bunker Convention (for details to the London Convention *see* paragraph 155). Owners of ships of more than 1,000 GT have to provide evidence of insurance or other financial security covering liability of the owner for bunker oil pollution damage (Article VII Bunker Convention). Comparable to the regime under CLC, contracting states issue certificates confirming that such conventions exist. Also here cover providers usually are P&I clubs and P&I insurers. Also here such insurers remain on risk for three further months after they notify termination (other than regular expiry) of the insurance cover. Also here inter parties have a direct right of action against the insurer.

II. Pollution from Land-Based Sources

363. As mentioned above, the central liability provision under the *Wasserhaushaltsgesetz* (WHG; Federal Management Water Act), § 89 WHG, refers to activities of persons: introduction or discharge of substances into the water. The law is silent in respect of the question wherefrom such introduction or discharge is done. This is the reason why introduction and discharge from ships falls under § 89 (1) WHG. All introduction and discharge from land-based sources are embraced as well. Also here liability is imposed on the acting person by § 89 (1) WHG and on the owner of an installation designed, defector, process, store, deposit, convey or dispose of substances from which such substances are released into the water. The liability is strict, so that no fault is required. It extends to any kind of damage.

III. Pollution from Sea-Bed Activities

364. Apart from one oil platform in the coastal sea off Schleswig-Holstein and one gas platform in the German EEZ there are no sea-bed activities in German waters or the German EEZ. As regards the coastal sea, the provisions of the WHG apply (*see* paragraph 352).

Chapter 15. The Arrest of Ships

§1. Sources of Law

365. Arrests of ships in Germany are generally governed by the rules of the *Zivilprozessordnung* (ZPO; Civil Procedure Code) as contained in §§ 916–934 ZPO, out of which only two provisions contain special stipulations for the arrest of ships and new buildings registered in a Ship Register or Newbuildings Register respectively: § 930 ZPO insofar relates to ships or new buildings registered in a German Ship Register, § 931 ZPO for all other ships. Arrest proceedings are not part enforcement procedures, but part of contentious proceedings. In the latter respect they are special only insofar as they start as ex parte proceedings. Courts usually do not serve arrest applications on the opponent before rendering a decision, if time is of essence; the other party is usually only heard after the arrest order has been issued.

Germany has ratified the International Convention for the Unification of certain rules relating to the Arrest of seagoing Ships 1952, but the provisions of the Convention have not been incorporated into the Commercial Code or the Civil Procedure Code. As to the relevance of the Convention for arrest in Germany *see* § 4.

§2. Requirements for an Arrest under General Arrest Law

366. According to the general rules, an arrest requires a claim (§ 916 ZPO) and a reason for arrest (§ 917 ZPO). The main rule as laid down in § 916 ZPO is that the arrest is a remedy serving to secure enforcement into movable or immovable property for a monetary claim or a claim that may evolve to be kind of monetary claim. While generally German law requires a level of proof which excludes reasonable doubts, in arrest proceedings a lesser proof is sufficient, the overwhelming probability (cf. 'to the satisfaction of the court', §§ 920 (2), 294 ZPO).

367. A reason for arrest is given wherever there is the concern that without the arrest the enforcement of 'the judgment would be frustrated or be significantly more difficult' (§ 917 (1) ZPO. The provision itself accepts this to be the case 'if the judgment had to be enforced abroad and reciprocity has not been granted'. In particular the last two aspects have led to widespread debate and conflicting court decisions as to whether only German court decisions can be protected by an arrest, whether at least decisions of EU Member States are sufficient (this has meanwhile been confirmed by the European Court of Justice and made part of the law in § 917 (2) ZPO); whether awards either of German tribunals or tribunals anywhere in the world are sufficient, etc. For arrest in ships all this has become irrelevant, because in the course of the Maritime Law Reform a further sentence was added to § 917 (2) ZPO: 'No grounds for an arrest need be given if the arrest solely taking place for the purpose of securing the compulsory enforcement into a ship.'

368. Arrest proceedings being contentious proceedings, an arrest order itself is capable of being enforced. German law distinguishes, thus, between the arrest itself and its enforcement. The arrest is ordered generally in respect of property of the debtor, and it is a matter of enforcement whether the claimant attaches a ship of the debtor, which then is done through the action of a bailiff.

§3. Requirements for an Arrest of Ships

369. All the claimant has to do is to demonstrate to the satisfaction of the court that he has a claim against the shipowner (§ 916 ZPO). Since 2013 there is no more the need to show a reason for arrest. In particular, it is no more necessary to show that without the arrest enforcement would be more difficult. With the abolishment of the need for a reason for arrest also the limitations resulting from the debates on whether claims subject to foreign jurisdiction, or foreign arbitration awards, can be protected by an arrest in Germany, were set aside. All what is required now is that the claimant establishes his claim. As to limitations following from the Arrest Convention *see* below at § 4.

370. This possibility exists, however, only in respect of 'ships'. The ZPO does not itself what it means with the terms 'ship'. The general view is that the general definition of a ship applies as developed by the courts, namely that a ship is a vehicle of not only negligible size, which contains a hollow space and has the purpose and capability to carry goods or passengers on or under water.

§4. The 1952 Arrest Convention and the Relevance of Maritime Claims

371. Under German national law there are no limitations in respect of the grounds and types of claims for which an arrest can be sought into a vessel. In particular, the German national law does not require a claim to be a maritime claim of any kind in order to have it secured by an arrest in a ship. Maritime claims only are of relevance if an arrest is sought into a ship flying the flag of a Member State of the 1952 Arrest Convention. Article 2 of the Convention allows arrest of ships only in respect of maritime claims (Article 2). Maritime claims are defined in Article 1 (1) of the Convention and consists of the following claims:

(a) damage caused by any ship either in collision or otherwise;
(b) loss of life or personal injury caused by any ship or occurring in connection with the operation of any ship;
(c) salvage;
(d) agreement relating to the use or hire of any ship whether by charter party or otherwise;
(e) agreement relating to the carriage of goods in any ship whether by charter party or otherwise;
(f) loss of or damage to goods including baggage carried in any ship;

(g) general average;
(h) bottomry;
(i) towage;
(j) pilotage;
(k) goods or materials wherever supplied to a ship for her operation or maintenance;
(l) construction, repair or equipment of any ship or dock charges and dues;
(m) wages of Masters, Officers, or crew;
(n) Master's disbursements, including disbursements made by shippers, charterers or agent on behalf of a ship or her owner;
(o) disputes as to the title to or ownership of any ship;
(p) disputes between co-owners of any ship as to the ownership, possession, employment, or earnings of that ship;
(q) the mortgage or hypothecation of any ship.

Germany has declared reservations in respect disputes as to the title to or ownership of any ship (Article 1 (1) (o)) and disputes between co-owners of any ship as to the ownership, possession, employment, or earnings of that ship (Article 1 (1) (p)), so that those disputes do not qualify as maritime claims in Germany.

372. As mentioned above, the Arrest Convention applies to ships flying the flags of Convention States. The following states are Member States of the Arrest Convention:

> Algeria; Antigua and Barbuda; Bahamas; Belgium; Cambodia; Cayman Islands; Costa Rica; Dominica; Egypt; Falkland Islands; Germany; France; Gilbert Islands; Greece; Grenada; Guernsey; Haiti; Ireland; Italy; Lebanon; Luxembourg; Montserrat; Nigeria; Paraguay; Poland; Portugal; Solomon Islands; Spain; St. Helena; St. Kitts-Nevis-Anguilla; St. Lucia; St. Vincent; Switzerland; Syria; Tonga; Turks and Caicos Islands; United Kingdom; Vatican City State; Yugoslavia; Zaire.

The arrest in Germany of any ship flying the flag of those states, thus, requires that the claim, for which the ship shall be arrested, qualifies as a maritime claim. The seat and nationality of the claimant are as irrelevant as the seat and nationality of the shipowner. The exception of the case is that of a German claimant intending to arrest a ship flying the German flag. For these scenarios the Arrest Convention is not applicable (Article 8 (4)).

§5. Judicial Procedure

373. The procedure starts with an application of the claimant to the court. There are two courts with which such applications can be lodged. The first court with jurisdiction for an arrest order is the court which has jurisdiction for the claim as such. Such court may either have jurisdiction on basis of an agreement between the parties, or by the general rules applicable to jurisdiction of the court An arrest application with such a court can be served at any time. Neither is it a requirement that proceedings on the merits of the claim are already pending in court, nor is there a requirement that the ship is already in a port, let alone a German port. With such a court, thus, it is possible to have the judge consider the case without the time pressure otherwise occurring, if the application is only filed once the ship is in port. The only aspect which has to be observed is the statutory time for enforcement of the arrest order. Which court actually then is in charge of the matter, depends on the claim amount. If the claim is no more than EUR 5,000, the proper court will be the Local Court (*Amtsgericht*). For all other claims it will be the Regional Court (*Landgericht*).

374. Alternatively, the arrest application is filed in the court where the ship, into which the arrest shall be enforced, is physically present at the time of the arrest application (§ 919 ZPO). There is no possibility to file the application already in advance of the ship's arrival, because the jurisdiction of the court is dependent on the presence of the ship within the geographical jurisdiction of the particular court. Given the short periods of call in modern shipping, the time for obtaining and enforcing the arrest can be very short. What arrest applicants do in such situations is that they inform the court of their intention to file the arrest once the ship has arrived and keep the court posted of the ship's itinerary.

375. Generally the arrest application must address two different aspects, namely the claim for which the arrest is applied for, and the grounds for arrest. German law traditionally is reluctant in respect of grounds for arrest. § 917 ZPO stipulates that an arrest is an available remedy only wherever there is concern that without such arrest the enforcement of a claim would be frustrated or be significantly more difficult. What has been decided by the courts in respect of sufficient grounds for arresting a ship, however, is of no relevance anymore after the Maritime Law Reform of 2013. The Maritime Law Reform Act has amended § 917 (2) ZPO with a second sentence stating that no grounds for arrest are required if an arrest is obtained for the purpose of enforcing it into a ship. This has made arrest of ships in Germany much easier.

In the application for arrest the applicant has to identify and specify his claim. It is not necessary to bring full proof of the claim, but it is sufficient that the judge is satisfied that such a claim exists. This latter burden of proof takes into account that arrests usually are preliminary matters, that they have to be applied for quickly, if they shall have an effect, and that full evidence may not be available at such an early time.

As usually arrests in ships are matters of urgency and do not allow service of the arrest application on the opponent shipowner, the court decides on the arrest not by way of judgment (which would require an oral hearing), but by way of an order. If the court refuses to issue an arrest order, this is done by an order itself, which is not served on the opponent (§ 922 (3) ZPO). The shipowner, thus, usually does not become aware of an unsuccessful arrest application.

376. Once the arrest has been issued, the court delivers the order to the arrest applicant, who has to serve the arrest by himself. Service must be effected within one month, as afterwards no enforcement of the arrest order is possible anymore (§ 929 (2) ZPO). Service is done by instructing a bailiff, who serves the arrest order on the shipowner, represented by the master of the ship. As a matter of precaution, usually arrest applicants also apply to the court to serve the arrest order on the shipowner through diplomatic channels. This is done in order to avoid any discussion whether, under the applicable law, the master had authority for receiving the arrest order on behalf of the shipowner.

377. As the arrest court deals with the arrest application ex parte and as the arrest is served on the master of the ship usually at the time when the arrest order is enforced, the law has to provide for a remedy of the defendant shipowner against the arrest order. It does so by stipulating in § 924 ZPO that the shipowner can file an opposition against the arrest order. In his opposition he has to submit the grounds on which the arrest order should be set aside. The court will then schedule a hearing, in which both parties can plead their case. After the hearing the court renders judgment by which it either sets aside its original arrest order or confirms it as a whole or in part. Such a judgment is subject to an appeal to the next instance. The filing of an opposition does not suspend the enforceability of the arrest order (§ 924 (3) ZPO).

What the defendant shipowner also can do is to apply to the arrest court for an order that the arrest claimant has to commence substantive proceedings within a period to be determined by the court. Such an order cannot be enforced in a way that the arrest claimant actually has to commence substantive proceedings. But the legal consequence of not commencing substantive proceedings within the time determined by the arrest court is that the arrest order then has to be set aside upon application of the shipowner (§ 926 (2) ZPO).

§6. Protective Briefs

378. Prior to legislation introducing electronic exchanges with the courts in 2013, the Civil Procedure Code did not address anything like a protective brief (‘*Schutzschrift*’). Nevertheless it was an accepted means for a shipowner to try and avoid if not the arrest, then at least an ex parte decision on an arrest application. The protective brief was until 2013 to be delivered to the court where the shipowner expected an arrest. This was the court which had jurisdiction over the place where the ship was to be calling. If more than one German port was called, it was usual to deliver the protective brief with all respective courts.

Matter have become much easier with the introduction of § 945a ZPO into the Civil Code in 2013. In 2013 the German *Länder*, i.e., the various federal states in Germany, introduced a joint electronic Register of protective briefs. Since then it is only necessary to serve the brief in electronic form with this Register, to which all German courts have access. In the protective brief the shipowner sets out the details of the dispute with the potential arrest applicant and argues why no arrest should be granted, at least why it should not be granted ex parte. § 945a ZPO only stipulates that the courts have access to the Register but does not expressly state that the courts have to check the register for, and take notice of, the protective brief. However, it is settled that the constitutional right to a fair trial according to Article 103 of the Constitution requires the arrest court to check the Register for the existence of a protective writ.

The arrest applicant has no possibility to check the Register for the existence of a protective brief before he has filed his arrest application. Once he has filed it, the protective brief will be served on him.

§ 945a ZPO does not contain any language specifying the content of the brief. In particular it does not prevent a brief which is served after an arrest has been lifted against security. This may be meaningful, if the security was given '*in consideration of you refraining from arresting or rearresting*', in order to avoid a rearrest of the ship.

§7. Enforcement of the Arrest Order

379. When it comes to enforcement of the arrest order into a certain ship, the law distinguishes between ships registered in a German register of ships and any other ships. The starting point is the same for both situations: attachment of the ship follows the rules on the attachment of movable property (§ 931 (1) ZPO). Enforcement is inadmissible where the ship is travelling and not lying in a port (§ 930 (4) and § 931 (7) ZPO).

In case of a ship registered in a German Ship Register, the attachment is ordered by the arrest court as enforcement court, which will request the Ship Register to enter a priority notice in the register, such priority notice serving as to secure the lien (§ 931 (3) ZPO), which the attachment creates. Such lien avails the claimant, in relation to other rights on the ship, the same rights as a maritime lien (§ 931 (2) ZPO). Upon application of the claimant, the arrest lien can be entered into the ships register.

380. The Arrest order must be enforced within one month from the date it was issued (§ 929 ZPO).

§8. Security and Counter Security

381. It is more or less a standard practice that courts order arrests for enforcement into ships only against security. If the ship to be arrested is registered in a German Ship Register and, therefore, the attachment of the ship as enforcement of the arrest order is done by the court itself, the court will demand security before issuing the attachment order. In case of all other ships it is common practice for the courts not to make issuing of the arrest order dependent on the provision of security. Rather the courts will order that the arrest order is enforceable through a bailiff only once security is provided. Generally security is to be deposited with the court, but in view of the fact that arrest orders may have to be enforced at night time or through weekends and public holidays, arrest orders usual provide that the security may be handed over to the bailiff instructed with the attachment of the ship.

382. The amount of security is in the discretion of the court. What courts usually consider is what loss of income a ship of type in question is likely to incur due to the enforcement of the arrest order. Also the form of security is a matter of discretion by the court. It is a standard practice that courts accept guarantees by banks. This security can, depending on the order, either be posted with the court or handed over to the bailiff, whom the arrest applicant instructs with the enforcement of the arrest order.

383. What is also part of the arrest order is an express right of the defendant shipowner to avoid the arrest or have it lifted against provision of security. Usually the courts order security in the amount of the claim plus interest for two years and costs for two instances of court proceedings in respect of the main claim. Usually the courts will specify in which form such security has to be provided. Bank guarantees are always accepted. There is no published arrest order which would have allowed security to be put up by letters of undertaking by P&I clubs or insurers. However, it is up to the parties to agree against which foremost security the vessel will be released. In practice it is common for claimants to accept P&I club letters of undertaking or guarantees by insurers, in particular by hull insurers in collision cases.

§9. Subsequent and Repeated Arrest

384. Arrests cannot be obtained by only one claimant, but by a multitude of claimants. Each arrest application will be dealt with by the court separately, and separate arrest orders, if any, will be issued. Those arrest orders have to be served by the respective claimants on the defendant shipowner, and the arrest orders have to be enforced separately by attachment through a bailiff. As mentioned above, in case of a ship registered in a German Ship Register, the arrest court in its capacity as enforcement court will order the attachment of the ship and request the Ship Register to enter a priority notice in the register of ships (§ 931 (3) ZPO). The effect of this priority notice is that the ranking of the lien caused by the attachment is secured. Are more than one claimant obtaining arrests into a vessel, thus, their ranking as in between those claimants will depend on the order in which the arrest court attaches the ship and requests the entry of a priority notice in the Ship Register. In case of arrest of foreign ships, it is not the arrest court, which attaches the ship, but it is the bailiff. Here the ranking depends on the sequence of attachments made by the bailiff.

385. Arrests of ships are usually lifted against security, either provided by insurers, if they provide cover for the claim for which the ship has been arrested (e.g., hull insurers in respect of collision claims, salvage and general average contribution; P&I Clubs in respect of oil pollution, personal injury or cargo claims) or by the shipowner himself, if he has no cover in respect of such claim (e.g., claims for unpaid bunkers, provisions or uninsured losses). Once security is provided, the ship will be released from arrest and is therefore vulnerable to further arrests and rearrests of parties who already obtained security by way of an arrest. The German national law does not address the question directly, whether a rearrest of the same ship by the same claimant for the same claim is possible or not. But the basic provision of § 913 ZPO stipulates that arrest is a remedy serving to secure enforcement. If enforcement is already secured by way of a security provided upon a first arrest of the ship, there is no need for further security. If the arrest court in a further arrest application is aware of such security providing earlier, a rearrest would be denied, unless there are special circumstance, for example if after the first arrest the claim amount was established to be higher than originally estimated, so that the security provided upon the first arrest is not sufficient to cover the claim. Or the security from the first arrest has been provided a guarantor who subsequently becomes insolvent.

The Arrest Convention, which applies to arrest of ships flying the flags of a Convention state, deals with repeated arrests in Article 3 (3) that 'a ship shall not be arrested, nor shall bail or other security be given more than once in any one or more of the jurisdictions of any of the Contracting States in respect of the same maritime claim by the same claimant: and, if a ship has been arrested in any of such jurisdictions, or bail or other security has been given in such jurisdiction either to release the ship or to avoid a threatened arrest, any subsequent arrest of the ship or of any ship in the same ownership by the same claimant for the maritime claim shall be set aside, and the ship released by the Court or other appropriate judicial authority of that State, unless the claimant can satisfy the Court or other appropriate judicial authority that the bail or other security had been finally released before the subsequent arrest or that there is other good cause for maintaining that arrest'. The Arrest Convention, thus, generally prohibits rearresting of a ship by the same claimant for the same claim, but it is submitted that German courts would treat, for example, insufficiency of the security provided earlier as 'good cause' with the aforementioned context.

386. Independent from statutory provisions, rearresting maybe excluded by way of agreement between the parties either on occasion of or as part of the security provided upon the first arrest. Common wordings for arrest securities stipulate that security is given '*in consideration of you refraining from arresting or rearresting*'. If the arrest claimant accepts security with such a wording, it creates a contractual undertaking for him not to rearrest the ship. If the court handles a rearrest application ex parte and if no protective brief hat been filed with the Register of protective briefs, also showing the security with the mentioned wording issued, the court may not be aware of the wording of such security provided earlier with the consequence of the ship in fact being rearrested. But such rearrest would qualify as a breach of contract by the arrest applicant and, thus, be a wrongful arrest, which would expose him to a claim for damages.

§10. Lifting of the Arrest

387. The way in which an arrest is lifted depends on whether the ship arrested is registered in a German Ship Register or not. In the first case the arrest court, acting in its capacity as enforcement court, has to become active, because such ships have been arrested by attachment order of the court itself. It is only the court, thus, which can lift this order.

All other ships have not been attached by way of a court order, but through attachment by the bailiff. Here it is the bailiff, who can lift the arrest, which he will do upon respective instructions he receives from the claimant. This allows a flexible procedure even through night time, weekends or public holidays, because security can be posted by the defendant shipowner with the claimant, respectively his lawyers, who then can instruct the bailiff to release the ship from arrest.

§11. Remedies for Wrongful Arrest

388. Arrest applications in Germany are risky. § 945 ZPO provides for a liability of the arrest claimant should the arrest later prove to have been unfounded from the start. Such liability is strict, so that the claimant cannot escape from liability even by proving that he did not act negligently. The reason why the arrest is held to be unfounded from the outset is irrelevant. It may be a procedural reason (e.g., the ship was arrested while under way; the ship was in a port outside the jurisdiction of the arrest court), or it may be a substantive reason (the arrest applicant is not the proper claimant or the defendant shipowner not the proper debtor; the claim is unfounded; the claim is time-barred). The same strict liability is incurred, if the arrest court lifts the arrest upon an application the defendant shipowner for the reason that the arrest claimant did not commence substantive proceedings within the time limit fixed by the court (§ 926 ZPO).

Claims for damages under § 945 ZPO cannot be pursued as part of the arrest proceedings. Rather they are ordinary proceedings, in which the shipowner, now acting as claimant for damages, has to prove that the arrest order was unfounded from the start and that he has suffered damage from the arrest and attachment of the ship. Unlawful arrest under German law qualifies as a delict, which was committed at the place where the arrest was obtained. As a consequence, the court having jurisdiction over that place according to § 32 ZPO has jurisdiction also for claims for damages under § 945 ZPO. It is a matter of the claim amount whether the proper court will be the local court or the regional court, the latter having jurisdiction for claims in excess of EUR 5,000.

§12. Appeals

389. Ex Parte arrest orders or arrest judgments, rendered after an oral hearing, being ordinary court decisions in contentious proceedings, they are generally subject to the general rules on legal remedies. The remedies depend on whether an arrest order is challenged or an arrest judgment. If it is an order, then the legal remedy is the so-called immediate compliant (*sofortige Beschwerde*) according to § 567 ZPO, which has to be filed with two weeks after service of the order rejecting the arrest application or the arrest order (§ 569 (1) ZPO). The legal remedy against an arrest judgment is an appeal according to § 511 ZPO, which has to be filed within one month (§ 517 ZPO). If the first instance has been a Local Court (*Amtsgericht*), the court in charge of either the immediate complaint or the appeal will be the Regional Court (*Landgericht*). If the first instance court has been the regional Court, the court in charge of the legal remedy will be the Higher Regional Court (*Oberlandesgericht*).

Despite the proceedings being contentious proceedings, however, there is not the full range of legal remedies available. While generally there are two subsequent legal remedies against any court decision in Germany, for arrest proceedings this is limited to two instances. The court deciding on the legal remedy, thus, decides on the arrest finally.

§13. Costs

390. As arrest proceedings are contentious proceedings, they are subject to the general rules on costs for such proceedings. According to these rules the unsuccessful party bears all costs of the proceedings, § 91 ZPO, which includes the court fees as well as the lawyer fees of the successful party. If the arrest application is withdrawn before the court has rendered a decision, all costs are for the withdrawing applicant, § 269 ZPO. If the defendant shipowner had filed a protective brief, the lawyer fees payable by the shipowner for the brief are part of recoverable costs. If the arrest is ordered, costs will be ordered against the shipowner.

391. Both the court fees as well as the lawyer fees are subject to statutory tariffs. Lawyers are free to agree with their clients on hourly charges, and this is what is customarily done. But the law prohibits that the lawyer charges less than the statutory fees. The successful party can recover its costs only up to the statutory fees. Even the successful party may, therefore, be left with unrecoverable costs, if the fees on hourly basis exceed the statutory fees.

392. The court will order already in its decision on the arrest application, i.e., either in the order rejecting the application or in the arrest order, which party has to bear the costs. But the order will be as general as just mentioned. The actual costs recoverable are subject to a separate application to the court, on which usually the clerk of the court (*Rechtspfleger*) decides.

393. As the arrest procedure is a contentious procedure which is separate from the main proceeding on the merits of the claim, the costs consequences can be different in both proceedings. If the arrest application was successful and costs ordered against the shipowner, he will be left with this cost burden even if he is successful on the merits and the claim is rejected. On the other hand, if the arrest is lifted and costs ordered against the applicant, he will not be able to recover those costs even if he is later successful on the merits ion the main proceedings.

Chapter 16. Carriage of Passengers by Sea

§1. Introduction

394. German law on carriage of passengers prior to the Maritime Law Reform of 2013 was regulated in a rather peculiar way in an attachment to § 664 *Handelsgesetzbuch* (HGB; Commercial Code). In this attachment the majority of provisions as contained in the Athens Convention Relating to the Carriage of Passengers and their Baggage by Sea of 1974 were set out. Germany did not ratify the Athens Convention 1974, because the limits of liability provided by that Convention were considered to be too low.

The Maritime Law Reform Act completely reframed the German law on carriage of passengers and their baggage. This now forms Sub-chapter 2 (contracts for the carriage of passengers and their baggage) of Chapter 2 (transport contract) of the Fifth Book of the HGB and consists of §§ 536–552 HGB. Rather unusual for a German statute, the provisions start in § 536 HGB with rules on the scope of application. Subsection (2) stipulates that the provisions of the Sub-chapter do not apply (1) if the Regulation (EC) No. 392/2009, the so-called Athens Regulation, applies, or (2) were directly applicable measures contained in international conventions apply. Most relevant applicable convention are the Uniform Rules concerning the contract of international carriage of passengers by rail – CIV – which form Appendix A to the Convention concerning International Carriage by Rail (COTIF). Article 31 § 2 CIV deal with liability for personal injury of passengers where railway vehicles are carried by ferry.

395. While CIV only addresses very certain ways of passenger transport, the Athens Regulation has a very wide scope of application. The structure of the Athens Regulation is to set out the provisions of the Athens Convention 2002 as Annex 1 to the Regulation and then adds only a few amending provisions in the Regulation itself. The scope of application of the Athens Regulation is rather wide. Regardless of the size of the ship the Regulation applies to all international carriage, and also to national carriage in case of larger ships as per Classes A and B according to Article 4 (1) of Directive 98/18/EC. The Regulation applies, if the ship is flying the flag of or is registered in an EU Member State, or if the contract of carriage has been entered into in an EU Member State, or if the place of departure or destination, according to the contract of carriage, is in an EU Member State. This leaves only a rather narrow scope of application of the national German law, namely national carriage of passengers with smaller ships not belonging to Classes A or B under the mentioned Directive, or international carriage, subject to contractually agreed application of German law, without fulfilling the above-mentioned requirements for the scope of application of Article 2 (flag/registration/place of contract/places of departure or destination in an EU Member State).

§2. Statutory Provisions

396. Although rather uncommon for a German statute, § 537 HGB, the first substantive provision on carriage of passengers by sea, contains a number of definitions, all of which are relevant for the application of the subsequent provisions. It is noteworthy, however, that neither § 538 HGB nor any other provision of the HGB stipulates what the contract of carriage of passengers by sea is and what the respective rights and obligations of the parties are. For example, there is no provision in respect of the fare, which the passenger will have to pay under the contract of carriage. In so far the general rules of the Civil Code have to be applied. Under civil law a contract for the carriage of passengers qualifies as a contract for work according to § 631 *Bürgerliches Gesetzbuch* (BGB; Civil Code), so that the remuneration is subject to the provisions of § 632 BGB. Coming back to the definitions as contained in § 537 HGB, German law defines as follows:

- 'carrier' means a person by whom a contract of carriage by sea of a passenger (contract for the carriage of passengers) has been concluded;
- 'passenger' means:

  (a) a person carried under a contract for the carriage of passengers; or
  (b) a person who, with the consent of the carrier, is accompanying a vehicle or live animals that are being carried under a contract for the carriage of goods by sea;

- 'baggage' means any article being carried under a contract for the carriage of passengers, with the exception of live animals;
- 'cabin baggage' means any baggage that the passenger has in his cabin or that is otherwise in his possession; 'cabin baggage' shall include baggage that the passenger has in or on his vehicle;
- 'shipping incident' means a shipwreck, the capsizing, collision, or stranding of the ship, an explosion or fire in the ship, or a defect in the ship;
- 'defect in the ship' means any malfunction, failure, or non-compliance with applicable safety regulations in respect of any part of the ship or its equipment when used for any of the following:

  (a) escape, evacuation, embarkation or disembarkation of passengers;
  (b) the propulsion, steering, safe navigation, mooring or anchoring, arriving at or leaving berth or anchorage, or damage control after flooding; or
  (c) the launching of life-saving appliances.

§3. Liability and Limitation of Liability

397. German law distinguishes between liability for injury or death of a passenger and loss of or damage to baggage. For both liability attaches for occurrences in the course of the carriage. But what is 'carriage' is defined differently in respect of the passenger himself and his baggage. In respect of the passenger himself § 538 (3) HGB states that carriage is (1) the period during which the passenger is on board the ship, including the period during which he is embarking or disembarking and (2) the period during which the passenger is transported by water from land to the ship or vice versa, if the costs of this transport are included in the fare, or if the vessel used for this auxiliary transport has been made available for the passenger by the carrier. 'Carriage' does not cover the period which the passenger spends in a marine terminal or station, on a quay or in or on any other port installation.

For baggage, the law distinguishes in § 539 HGB between cabin baggage and other baggage. For both classes of baggage there are different definitions for carriage. As regards cabin baggage, carriage means the first two alternatives are similar to those of carriage of the passenger himself: (1) the period during which the cabin baggage is on board the ship, including the period during which the cabin baggage is transported onto or off the ship; (2) the period during which the cabin baggage is transported by water from land to the ship or vice versa, if the cost of such transport is included in the fare or if the vessel used for this auxiliary transport has been put at the disposal of the passenger by the carrier. But the definition differs in respect of terminals, etc. Here carriage of cabin baggage includes the period which the passenger spends in a marine terminal or station or on a quay or in or on any other port installation, if the cabin baggage has been taken over by the carrier or his servants or agents, and has not yet been redelivered to the passenger.

As regards baggage other than cabin baggage, carriage is essentially the same like the period of responsibility for carriage of goods, namely the period between the baggage having been taken over by the carrier on shore or on board and the time of its redelivery.

398. Liability for personal injury or death of a passenger generally requires fault. There is a significant difference in the burden of proof compared with carriage of goods. In carriage of goods there is an assumed fault, and the burden of proof that damage to or loss of the good could not have been avoided by the care of proven carrier rests with the carrier. In case of carriage of passengers the burden of proof of fault, as a matter of principle, rests with the passenger. The reason for the difference is that in case of carriage of goods usually the shipper has no influence and cannot protect the cargo once it is in the carrier's custody. In case of carriage of passengers, against that, passengers usually can freely move around on the ship, so that any accident they suffer from could also be from their own (mis-)behaviour.

The law provides for an assumed fault only in case of a shipping incident as defined above. The rationale behind this is that any of those shipping incidents usually do not involve carelessness and negligence of the passenger, but are rather in the scope of influence and responsibility of the carrier.

There is a peculiar way in which German law deals with certain courses of death or personal injury of a passenger. If a shipping incident is the consequence of hostilities, act of war, civil war, insurrection or natural phenomenon of an exceptional inevitable and irresistible character, then the carrier is relieved from the assumption of fault as per § 538 (2) HGB. But this does not mean that he is completely relieved from liability. Rather it is still open for the passenger to proof under § 538 (1) HGB that the carrier was at fault. An example would be that there is a malfunction of the ship (qualifying as a shipping incident) which was caused by an act of war, which was foreseeable when the ship was sent to the area, so that the carrier is at fault for the fact that the ship is in the war zone at all.

399. When it comes to fault, the carrier is not only liable for his own fault or neglect, but also for the fault and neglect of his crew and other servants, provided they were acting within the scope of their employment. He is also liable for any other person, including independent contractors, whose services he makes use of for the carriage, and in respect of these persons it is not even required that they were acting within the scope of their engagement.

400. The carrier's liability for death and personal injury is limited, and the limitation amount again is different for assumed fault and proven fault. For assumed fault the maximum liability is 250,000 SDR (§ 538 (2) HGB). If this amount is less than the damage caused, in case of proven fault of the carrier the maximum liability is 400,000 SDR (§ 541 (1) HGB). Finally, the carrier's liability is always subject to the so-called global limitation of liability as dealt with in §§ 611–617 HGB. § 611 declares the conventional limitation of liability for maritime claims of 19 November 1976, as amended by the Protocol of 2 May 1996 (LLMC 1996) applicable. Under LLMC 1996 the limitation amount is dependent on the carriage capacity of the ship. According to Article 6 (1) liability in respect of claims for loss of life or personal injury is limited to 2 SDR for a ship with a tonnage not exceeding 2,000 tons. For larger ships this amount is increased for each ton from 2,001 to 30,000 by 800 SDR, beyond that for each ton from 30,001 to 70,000 tons by 600 SDR and beyond that for each ton in excess of 70,000 tons by 400 SDR.

401. If more than one passenger loses his life or suffers personal injury, then the set amount of 250,000 SDR per passenger on each distinct occasion shall be replaced by the amount of 340 SDR million per ship on each distinct occasion, provided that the latter amount is lower and can be distributed pro rata amongst the injured parties, in proportion to the relative claims, as a single, non-current payment or as several partial payments.

All these limitations do not apply if the damage was caused by an act or mission of the carrier himself, done with the intent to cause such damage, or recklessly and with knowledge that such damage would probably result. Like in case of goods, thus, only qualified fault of the carrier himself bars limitation, but not qualified fault of a crew member or any other servant of the carrier.

402. In case of baggage the carrier is liable for loss of or damage of baggage and for delay in the delivery. As mentioned above, the law distinguishes between cabin baggage and any other baggage. In respect of such other baggage § 539 (1) HGB stipulates an assumption of fault for any loss of or damage to such baggage. In respect of cabin baggage such assumed fault is only available if loss or damage was caused by a shipping incident as defined above (paragraph 396). If cabin baggage was damaged or lost due to the other cause, the burden of proof of the carrier's fault rests with the passenger. For delay in redelivery of baggage § 539 (2) HGB stipulates that the carrier is liable for damage resulting therefrom, if the baggage has not been redelivered within a reasonable time after the arrival of the ship on which the baggage has been or should have been carried. There are certain exceptions from liability. The carrier is not liable for damage resulting from the loss of, damage to or delay in redelivery of monies, negotiable securities, gold, silver, gemstones, jewellery, artwork or other valuables, unless they had been deposited with the carrier for safe-keeping. And in respect of delayed delivery of baggage, there is no liability if the delay in the redelivery was caused by labour disputes.

Liability for loss of or damage to baggage or for delay in the delivery is limited. In respect of cabin baggage the limitation is 2,250 SDR per passenger and carriage. In case of the carrier's liability for loss of or damage to vehicles, including lugging in such vehicles, or delay in their redelivery the limit is 12,700 SDR per vehicle and carriage. For all other baggage the limit is 3,375 SDR per passenger and per carriage. The law allows the carrier to agree with the passenger on a deductible, which must not exceed 330 SDR in case of damage to a vehicle and 149 SDR in case of loss of, damage to or delay in redelivery of other baggage items (§ 542 (4) HGB).

403. § 549 HGB deals with notice of damage. No such notice is required if at the time of its receipt the condition of the baggage has been the subject of a joint surveyor inspection. If this has not been the case, and if the passenger does not give a notice in due time, there is a legal assumption that he has received the baggage undamaged. When such notice is due depends on the circumstances: in case of apparent damage to cabin baggage notice must be given at the time of disembarkation. In case of apparent damage to baggage other than cabin baggage, notice must be given at the time such baggage is redelivered to the passenger. If damage is non-apparent or if baggage was lost, notice must be given within fifteen days after disembarkation or after redelivery of the baggage respectively after the date on which the baggage should have been redelivered to the passenger. Any of the above notices must be made in text form.

404. In case of a passenger for death, personal injury or loss of, damage to or delay in redelivery of baggage become time-barred after two years (§ 606 No. 1 HGB). Such period starts to run in respect of claims for personal injury from the day of disembarkation; in respect of claims from death from the day when disembarkation should have taken place or, if the passenger died after this embarking, from the day of the passenger's death, but in no case later than one year after the passenger's disembarkation; in respect of claims resulting from the loss of, damage to or delay in redelivery of the baggage from the day of disembarkation or from day in which the passenger should have disembarked, whichever is later. The running of the limitation period is suspended as per § 608 HGB by declaration whereby the passenger asserts his claims. Such suspension continues until the carrier refuses to satisfy the claim. Apart from this commercial law suspension, also the civil law suspension under § 203 *Bürgerliches Gesetzbuch* (BGB; Civil Code) applies, according to which the running of the time limit is suspended during the time in which negotiations between the parties are pending. As a consequence of these suspensions considerable time may pass before the carrier actually knows whether he has to pay damages or not. This very fact is the reason for an exclusion contained in § 550 HGB. Claims for damages resulting from death of or personal injury to a passenger or from loss of or damage to or delay in redelivery of baggage, regardless of prescription, expire unless court proceedings are started either within three years from the date on which the claimant becomes aware of the death or personal injury or the loss, damage or delay in delivery (or from the date on which he should have become aware under normal circumstances), or within five years within the date of disembarkation or from the date when disembarkation should have taken place, whichever is later.

405. All the above dealt with contractual liability of the carrier. The law contains a number of further provisions dealing with liability in the context of passenger claims. One is that where carriage is performed, in whole or in part, by a third party who is not the carrier, then such third party, named by the law as performing carrier, shall be liable as if he were the carrier (§ 546 HGB). This concept is already known from carriage of goods. The performing carrier may rely on all objections at defences which the contractual carrier is entitled to raise under the contract for the carriage. And the carrier and the performing carrier are jointly and separately reliable.

If a claim is raised against one of the carrier's or performing carrier's servants, then such servants may avail themselves of the defences and limitations of liability available to the carrier or performing carrier, provided he was active under the scope of his employment. The same applies to crew members (§ 547 HGB).

Finally § 548 HGB determines that claims for death or personal injury to passengers or claims for loss of, damage to or delay in redelivery of baggage may only be pursued on basis of the provisions of the second subsection. This excludes, for example, claims in delict.

Part III. Other Transport

Chapter 1. Transport by Road

§1. Introduction

I. The CMR Convention and German Internal Law

406. The German law on carriage by road is contained in the Fourth Book of the *Handelsgesetzbuch* (HGB; Commercial Code). But Germany has ratified the CMR Convention (Convention on the Contract for the international Carriage of Goods by Road of 19 May 1956), which applies in Germany directly, i.e., without any transforming law. Where CMR applies, German law is superseded. CMR defines its scope of application in Article 1, which provides in subsection (1) that the Convention shall apply to every contract for the carriage of good by road in vehicles for reward, when the place of taking over of the goods and the place designated for delivery, as specified in the contract, are situated in two different countries, of which at least one is a contracting country. The places of residence and the nationalities of the parties are irrelevant. According to subsection (4) the Convention does not apply *inter alia* to furniture removal. Subject to these geographical and substantive regulations, German law applies to road transport. Transport of general goods is dealt within § 407–§ 449 HGB, carriage of furniture removal is covered by § 451–§ 451h HGB.

II. Compulsory Regulations

407. According to Article 40 CMR, any stipulation which would directly or indirectly derogate from the provisions of the convention are null and void. The question to what extent the German law on carriage by road is compulsory, is dealt within § 449 HGB. Subsection (1) stipulates that in so far as the contract for the carriage of goods is not for carriage of letters or similar items, deviation from certain liability provisions may only be made by way of individually negotiated agreements, but not by standard contract conditions. Individually negotiated agreements, however, do not have to be made for one individual contract only, but may have been made for several similar contracts between the same parties. But § 449 (2) HGB leaves room for deviation by standard contract conditions in respect of two areas of law, namely the limitation of liability per kilogram of gross weight lost and for the shipper's liability under § 414 HGB. The standard weight limitation according to § 431 HGB is 8.33 SDR per kg. § 449 (2) HGB allows to agree on any other amount per kilogram in a corridor between a minimum of 2 SDR and a maximum of 40 SDR. As regards shipper's liability, § 414 HGB stipulates an unlimited no fault liability of the shipper for damage, cost or expense costs to the carrier by insufficient packing or labelling of the goods, inaccuracy or incompleteness of information in the confinement note, failure to disclose dangerous nature of the goods. What § 449 (2) HGB allows is to agree by way of standard contract conditions on a limitation of the shipper's liability. Different from the carrier's liability, here no corridor is stipulated by the law.

§2. The Scope of Application of the German Internal Law

408. The scope of application of the German internal law is determined by the definition of a contract for the carriage of goods as contained in § 407 HGB. According to this definition there is a contract for the carriage of goods if one party, namely the carrier, takes over the obligation to carry goods to their destination and to deliver them there to the consignee (subsection 1). There must be consideration from the consignor, which subsection 2 provides as the consignor's obligation to pay the agreed freight. Without an obligation to pay freight, thus, there exists no contract of carriage, so that none of the provisions of the Fourth Chapter of the Commercial Code apply to such an agreement.

409. What kinds of goods are carried is generally irrelevant. The only goods the law deals separately with are removal goods, which are subject to the special provisions contained in § 451 to 451h; *see* insofar paragraph 477. Where it is illegal, though, to carry certain goods, no valid contract of carriage can be concluded. In case of prohibited transport of goods any contract concluded for their carriage would be void according to § 134 *Bürgerliches Gesetzbuch* (BGB; Civil Code). This is, e.g., the case if goods are listed on sanction lists and if their transport is prohibited under sanction legislation. Apart from this situation, there is only one class of goods which is dealt with especially by the law, namely removal goods. Contracts for carriage of removal goods are also subject to all the provisions on contracts of carriage as dealt with in the First Sub-chapter of the Fourth Book of the HGB (§§ 407–450 HGB), but the Second Sub-chapter (§ 451–451h HGB) contain special provisions for removal goods, which partly amend and partly alter the general provisions contained in the First Sub-chapter and which in any event have priority over those provisions. As regards dangerous goods, the law contains a number of special provisions for them, but they form part of the general provisions on carriage of goods.

410. In order for there to be a contract for carriage, the carrier must take over the obligation to carry goods. It is settled that the distance of such carriage is irrelevant. It can be an extremely small distance. If a separate contract is added into, e.g., for the discharge of goods from a truck to a storage place, then such contract is a contract of carriage, even if the distance over which the goods are carried may only be a few metres.

411. What kinds of carriage are embraced by § 407 HGB is dealt with in § 407 (3) HGB. This stipulates that the provisions of the First Sub-chapter apply whenever the goods are to be carried over land, on inland waterways or by aircraft. Interesting enough, the first two alternatives do not link the application of the law to special transport means, but to the location, on which the carriage is performed: over land and on inland waterways. In the third alternative, against that, the law does not refer to air transport, but to transport by aircraft. The difference looks more relevant than it actually is, because the definition of aircraft as contained in § 1 (2) *Luftverkehrsgesetz* (LuftVG; Air Traffic Act) is wide enough to include any means which are used for commercial transport.

As mentioned, in respect of carriage over land and on inland waterways the law does not limit the application to certain transport means. Accordingly, transports by motorcars or trucks, by motorbikes or by bicycle fall under § 407 HGB just as transports by pedestrians or even by pipelines. There is, indeed, no need for any transport means at all. It is settled that the movement of herds of animals also qualifies as carriage on land according to § 407 (2) HGB.

412. Just as the means of land transport are irrelevant, the means of transport on inland waterways are irrelevant as well. Most notably, the law does not refer to inland craft, so a distinction between inland craft and seagoing ships is irrelevant. As a consequence, transport by an inland craft over sea (be it allowed or not) is not governed by § 407 HGB, because this is limited to transport on inland waterways. On the other hand, transport by a seagoing ship on inland waterways (e.g., on the rivers Rhine, Weser or Elbe) is subject to the application of §§ 407 et seq. HGB, and not subject to the provisions on contract of carriage by sea, which is governed by §§ 481 et seq. HGB. As many rivers in Germany are navigable for seagoing ships, the law needs to clarify which provisions apply to contracts providing for carriage partly on inland waterways and partly on the sea. The Commercial Code deals with this in § 450 HGB, which stipulates that if the contract of carriage obliges the carrier to carry the goods, without transhipment, both on inland waterways and by sea, maritime law and carriage goods by sea applies to the contract if either a bill of lading has been issued or if the distance by sea is longer than that on inland water ways.

§3. Rights and Obligations of the Carrier, the Consignor and the Consigneeunder National Law and CMR

I. General

413. Under German law the contract for carriage of goods is a contract entered into between two parties, the carrier and the consignor, for the benefit of the third party, the consignee. German law acknowledges only contracts for the benefit of a third party, but not to its detriment. The contractual parties, thus, cannot burden the consignor with any obligation. In particular, there is no obligation of a consignee to take delivery of the cargo from the carrier. What the law accepts, however, is that obligations for the consignee arise if he elects to make use of the benefits availed to him under the contract. One of the major examples is that the consignee becomes liable for the payment of the freight as soon as he makes use of his right to claim delivery of the goods to him.

Contracts of carriage of goods do not create personal obligations, which the parties could only fulfil *in persona*. To the contrary the parties, in particular the carrier, are entitled to perform the transport either himself or through a subcarrier which he engages. Such sub-carriage can be either for part of the carriage only or for the whole carriage. Such subcontracts are contracts of carriage themselves. In practice, whole chains of contracts are made, with the main carrier and the subcarriers in many cases not performing all or not even any part of the contract, until the chain reaches the final subcarrier, who actually performs. To the extent that a subcontract for carriage provides for the delivery of the goods to the (original) consignor, all these contracts are for the benefit of one and the same consignor. After a change of the jurisprudence of the German Federal Court of Justice in 2007, actually rendered in a CMR case, it is now settled law for such constellations that the consignor in case of loss of or damage to the goods or delay in delivery is entitled to make use of his consignor's rights against the main carrier any of the (sub-) contracts.

414. Contracts of carriage have to be distinguished from forwarding contacts. While a carrier takes over the obligation to perform the carriage of the goods, a forwarder only takes over the obligation to arrange for the dispatch of the goods, § 453 (1) HGB. A forwarder, thus, only promises to make arrangements for the carriage of the goods, but he does not promise to carry himself, either personally or through a subcarrier. The most relevant distinction between the obligations of a carrier and the obligations of a forwarder rest in the area of liability. The forwarder is responsible for carriage without loss of or damage to the goods and without delay in delivery, while the forwarder only is responsible for due diligence in selecting the carrier. The legal regime for forwarders, thus, is considerably less burdensome when compared with that of carriers. The Commercial Code contains three special types of forwarding contracts, however, under which the forwarder has the rights and liabilities of a carrier, despite the fact that the obligation he took over was not to carry the goods but only to arrange for carriage. Those three special cases are:

(a) Performance of a carriage by the freight forwarder himself. § 458 HGB provides that a freight forwarder is entitled to perform the carriage of the goods himself, but if he does so, he has the rights and duties of a carrier (or a sea carrier respectively in case of self-performance of a sea carriage).
(b) More relevant is the arrangement of carriage of different goods for different consignors by way of a collective consignment. § 460 HGB allows the freight forwarder to arrange for the dispatch of the goods together with the goods of other senders by way of one contract for carriage of goods, which covers all the goods of his different customers as one collective consignment. Also in this case the forwarder has the rights and obligations of a carrier (or sea carrier).
(c) Most relevance has § 459 HGB. This stipulates that if a fixed amount is agreed as remuneration of the forwarder, which includes the costs for the carriage, then again the freight forwarder has the rights and obligations of a carrier (or sea carrier). In practice this is the way German forwarders do their business. Only in

extremely rare cases forwarders do not act on fixed costs, so that it is a legal and commercial reality that even if a forwarding contract has been concluded, the forwarder usually has the rights and liabilities of a carrier.

II. The Consignment Note

415. The Commercial Code deals with the consignment note in §§ 408, 409, 414 and 421 HGB, the CMR in Articles 5–9. The contract of carriage is a consensual contract, which does not require the issuing of a consignment note for its validity (in this regard expressly Article 4 CMR). Nevertheless the Commercial Code and the CMR deal in great detail with the consignment note, because a consignment note can provide various kinds of proof, which is important for the application of other provisions of the Commercial Code. Proof is the main purpose of the consignment note. In so far it must be clearly distinguished from the consignment bill, which is dealt with in §§ 443–448 HGB. According to § 448 HGB the consignment bill is a document of title, so that the issue and first handing over of the consignment bill to the consignee designated therein has the same effect, in terms of the acquisition of rights to the goods, as a physical handing over of the goods. A consignment note has no such effect. Apart from this major difference in the function of a consignment note compared with the consignment bill, the consignment note is issued by the consignor (§ 408 HGB), while the consignment bill is issued by the carrier (§ 443 HGB). The consignor has to issue a consignment bill, if the carrier so requests. In contrast, the consignor has no statutory right that the carrier issues a consignment bill (while the shipper in a contract of carriage by sea can demand from the carrier issuing a bill of lading, § 513 HGB). But the parties to the contract of carriage obviously can agree that the carrier has to issue a consignment bill.

416. The Commercial Code deals with the content of the consignment bill in § 408 HGB and with its evidentiary effect in § 409 HGB. The CMR Convention contains comparable, but slightly different rules in Article 6 and Articles 8 and 9. According to § 408 (1) HGB the consignment note shall have the following particulars:

(1) place and date of issue;
(2) name and address of the Consignor;
(3) name and address of the Carrier;
(4) place and date of taking over of the goods and place designated for delivery;
(5) name and address of the consignee and notify address, if any;
(6) description in common use of the nature of the goods and the method of packaging, and, in the case of dangerous goods, their description as required by the regulations concerning dangerous goods, or, in the absence of such requirement, their generally recognized description;
(7) number of cargo units and their special marks and numbers;
(8) the gross weight of the goods or their quantity otherwise expressed;
(9) the freight owed on delivery and any costs to be incurred up to the time of delivery, as well as a statement concerning payment of the freight;
(10) any amount of 'cash on delivery charges' to be collected on delivery of the goods;

(11) instructions relating to customs and other official processing;
(12) any agreement concerning carriage in an open uncovered vehicle or on deck.

Out of this list, freight still owed on delivery is rarely entered into consignment notes.

417. Under German national law the consignment note is issued in three originals, all of which have to be signed by the consignor. Reproductions of the personal signatures by means of printing or stamp are sufficient. While the carrier can demand that the consignor issues a consignment bill, once this has happened, the consignor can demand that the carrier countersigns it. As a consequence, there may exist consignment notes which only carry the signature of the consignor, but also consignment notes which also carry the signature of the carrier. The latter is the usual constellation. Under CMR Article 5 requires always signatures by the consignor and the carrier.

418. The evidentiary value of a consignment note signed only by the consignor under German national law is limited. It is not dealt with in the Commercial Code at all but follows the general principles of documentary evidence. It proves nothing more than that the consignor has made the respective declarations, but it does not extend to the question whether those statements are correct or not. The only further relevance such a consignment note has is in context with the consignor's no fault liability under § 414 HGB (*see* in detail at paragraph 436). One of the liability scenarios there is the inaccuracy or incompleteness of information in the consignment note. Obviously in this respect the consignment note as such proves its content and in so far is a means of proof for the carrier if he wants to pursue claims for damages against the consignor.

419. For consignment notes signed by the consignor as well as the carrier, § 409 HGB contains a number of evidentiary rules. First, until proof to the contrary, the consignment note serves as prima facie evidence of the conclusion of the contract of carriage (§ 409 (1) HGB). As regards the goods, such a consignment note also gives prima facie evidence that the carrier has taken over the goods (§ 409 (1) HGB). According to § 409 (2) HGB such a consignment note establishes a legal presumption that the apparent condition of the goods and their packaging were in order at the time the carrier took them over and that the number of units, their marks and numbering were those as specified in the consignment note. This is a presumption only, but it has the effect that the burden of proof shifts to the carrier, if he wants to rely on an unsound condition of the goods upon taking them over or on discrepancies as regards units, marks and numbers. The carrier can avoid such legal presumption, however, if he enters a reservation in the consignment note stating that he had no reasonable means of checking the accuracy of the information. A typical case would be that the consignor hands over a pallet on which cartons are secured by straps and shrinking foil, so that the carrier cannot verify the number of cartons handed over to him.

420. Finally the consignment note may be of relevance in respect of the consignee's obligation to pay freight. According to § 421 (2) HGB this obligation is triggered only upon the consignee requiring the carrier to deliver the goods to him (§ 421 (1) HGB). If this happens the consignee becomes liable to pay freight, but only up to the amount specified in the consignment note according to § 408 (1) No. 9 HGB. If no such amount is mentioned in the consignment note, this does not mean, that the consignee does not become liable for the payment of the freight. It only means that the limitation to such amount does not apply, but that the consignee is liable for any freight actually still unpaid.

III. The Carrier

421. The carrier's obligation under a contract of carriage is to carry the goods from the agreed place of shipment to the agreed place of delivery. His most important obligation at this respect is, obviously, to carry and deliver the goods in their entirety, without damage and without delay. If the carrier breaches any of these obligations, he will be liable for damages. This is dealt with in paragraph 442. But there are a number of other obligations of the carrier, which have nothing to do with liability for damages. The obligations start with the loading process. Here the obligations are shared by the consignor and the carrier. While the consignor has to load the goods onto the transport means and secure them in a way that they can withstand an ordinary transport, the carrier is obliged in respect of a loading and securing which allows the safe operation of the transport means (§ 412 HGB). Loading must take place during a certain time, the loading time. Unless it is agreed between the parties, in the absence of another agreement, it is assessed based on the time which is reasonable under the circumstances (§ 412 (2) HGB). If the loading time elapses without the cargo being fully loaded or without any cargo being loaded, the carrier cannot simply stop waiting and either commence the transport with what is on board or leave the loading place. Rather he has to set a reasonable time for the Consignor within which to load and stow the cargo, or to hand it over for carriage (§ 417 (1) HGB). During such time the carrier is entitled to a reasonable remuneration, called *Standgeld* (demurrage; *see also* paragraph 430). Only if the additional time has also elapsed, the carrier may carry out the transport with what is as cargo on board, or he may terminate the contract of carriage.

422. Sometimes transports cannot be carried out as intended by the parties. It may happen, therefore, that extraordinary measures are required in order either to deliver the goods at the intended place of delivery, or to bring the contract to an end in another orderly way. Such situation would also arise if the consignee refuses to take delivery of the cargo. Such measures usually result in additional costs, which were not calculated as part of the agreed freight. The law must, therefore, provide for mechanisms for such unforeseen developments and their financial consequences. German law does so by stipulating in § 419 (1) HGB that the carrier must ask for instructions if it becomes evident, after the goods have been taken over, that the transport of the goods or their delivery cannot be performed in accordance with the contract. The carrier must seek such instructions from the proper party. Seeking from and following instructions of the wrong party qualifies as a breach of contract and can make the carrier liable towards those entitled. Prior to arrival at the place of delivery proper party for instructions generally is the consignor (§ 419 (1) 2 HGB). But if subcontracts of carriage exist, there are necessarily different consignors under the different contracts. In such cases the identity of that consignor must be determined separately for each contract of carriage. Under the head contract of carriage, entered into between the first carrier and the first consignor (the original consignor), this original consignor is the only party entitled to the instructions to the main carrier. If the main carrier has entered into a subcontract of carriage with a subcarrier, under such contract it is the main carrier, who is the consignor, but not the original consignor. If such subcarrier during performance of his transport is confronted with a situation which prevents him from fulfilling what has been agreed in his subcontract of carriage, he must not seek instructions from the original consignor, but from the consignor under his contract of carriage, i.e., the main carrier. The main carrier insofar has a double role: on one hand he is consignor under the subcontract of carriage; on the other hand he is carrier under the main contract of carriage. If his subcarrier informs him of an obstacle for performance, this obstacle usually is an obstacle also for fulfilment of his own carrier's obligations under the main contract of carriage. This means that the main carrier himself then has to seek instructions, in this case from the original consignor. In contract chains, thus, seeking of instructions will go up the chain of subcontracts until they reach the consignor, who will then give instructions which go down the chain of subcontracts until they reach the carrier who actually performs the carriage.

423. Interference of the consignor with cargo in the course of transit may cause problems under the underlying contract of sale, under which the buyer/consignee may want to be protected against any alteration of the intended transport by the consignor. One way to do so would be to let the carrier issue a consignment bill, because where such a consignment bill has been issued, the only person entitled to give instructions to the carrier is the rightful holder of the consignment bill (§§ 419 (1) 1, 446 HGB). A buyer/consignee, who is in possession of the consignment bill, thus, is protected from interventions of the consignor. Another, less stringent, way is to enter a remark into a consignment note that instructions may be given by the consignor only upon presentation of the original consignment note. This protects the buyer/consignee, if he has obtained possession of a consignment note so especially claused. But it makes handling of such unexpected situations more difficult, because the consignee would have to send the consignment note to the consignor, so that he could present it to the carrier when giving instructions. Consignment notes claused this way, therefore, are rare in practice.

424. The right of the consignor to give instructions is lost once the goods reach the place of delivery. At this moment it is the consignee who is entitled to give instructions; but again if a consignment bill has been issued, the consignee must be in possession of the bill in order to give instructions himself. If it is not possible to locate the consignee or if the consignee refuses to accept delivery, in the absence of a consignment bill the right to give instructions falls back to the consignor. Should a consignment note have been claused to request production of the consignment note, in this particular situation the consignor may give instructions even without having the consignment note. If a consignment bill has been issued but is not presented to the carrier, he must not follow instructions of the consignor or the consignee, but has to take such appropriate steps as he has to take if he does not get instructions at all (*see* below).

425. If an obstacle prevents the carrier from continuation or completion of the transport or from delivery to the consignee, he has to describe such obstacle in his request for instruction in a way allowing the party entitled to give instructions to form a view of the situation. Insofar the information given must be sufficiently accurate. The carrier then has to wait a reasonable time for instructions. What is reasonable depends on the situation. If the instructing party has additional questions, the carrier must answer such questions to the best of his ability. If finally instructions are given, the carrier has to follow and execute them. It depends on the question in whose sphere the obstacle arose, whether the carrier is entitled to claim indemnification for costs incurred and additional remuneration. If the obstacle arose in his own sphere, e.g., if the truck used for transport suffers an engine damage, then the carrier is not entitled to expenses and additional remuneration. In all other situations, i.e., in situations where the obstacle arose in the sphere of the consignor (e.g., insufficient packing of the cargo), but also in cases where the obstacle was neither in the consignor's nor the carrier's sphere – the so-called *neutral zone* –, the carrier is entitled to reimbursements of costs incurred and to additional remuneration, which reflects additional time needed for fulfilment of the contract.

426. If the carrier is unable to obtain instructions within reasonable time he is entitled, and obliged, to take such measures as seem to be in the best interest of the party having the right to give instructions (§ 419 (3) HGB). The law sets out possible activity, but the alternatives mentioned in § 419 (3) HGB are not conclusive and final, but just examples. For instance, the carrier may unload the goods and store them, in latter case he may entrust them to a third party for storage. If he does so, his only liability in respect of such storage is for exercising due diligence in choosing a third party. The carrier also may return the goods to the place of shipment. He may sell them if they are perishable or if the condition warrants such a measure, or if the costs to be incurred otherwise would be out of proportion to the good's value. Finally, he is also entitled to destroy goods which cannot be sold. It is settled that out of all these alternatives the carrier has to choose the one which places the least burden on the party entitled to give instructions. If, for example, the goods still have a value and can be returned to the place of shipment, the carrier is obliged to do so and not entitled either to sell them, even less to destroy them.

427. Special rights are availed to the carrier in case of carriage of dangerous goods. The dangerous nature of the goods may be an obstacle for the further transport of the goods. Had the Carrier been properly advised of the danger, such situations fall under § 419 HGB, so that the carrier has to seek instructions from the party entitled to give such instructions (paragraphs 422 et seq.). But if the carrier had not been advised of the danger, he does not have to seek instructions. Rather he may, according to § 410 (2) HGB to the extent necessary unload, store, or return dangerous goods or, destroy them or render them harmless without thereby becoming liable in damages to the Consignor, and he may claim reimbursement from the Consignor of any costs or expenses necessitated by the measures taken. Maritime law contains in § 483 (1) 2 HGB a further rule. It allows the sea carrier to act in the same manner even if he had been aware or informed of the dangerous nature of the goods. The only difference is that he then cannot take action at any time, but only if the goods are actually likely to become a danger to the ship or its cargo, and only if such danger was not due to the Contractual Carrier's fault or neglect. A comparable provision was part of the maritime law also prior to the Maritime Law Reform. While in other aspects the lawmaker has amended also the general transport law when reforming the maritime law, here the difference was kept.

428. There can be additional obligations of the carrier if he accepts a cash on delivery agreement in the contract of affreightment. This is dealt with in § 422 HGB. This provision does not itself define the content of such agreement but presupposes it by stating that if the parties have agreed that the goods are to be delivered to the consignee only on a cash on delivery basis, it is presumed that the amount is to be collected in cash or in a form equivalent to cash. Obviously the parties can agree otherwise but if they do not, the carrier is obliged to collect cash. Apart from this legal presumption, the provision regulates two further aspects. In § 422 (2) HGB it is stipulated that in relation to creditors of the carrier, the amount received by the carrier is deemed to have been transferred to the consignor. The purpose of this provision is to protect the consignor from an insolvency of the carrier or from attachment steps taken by creditors of the carrier. By stipulating that the amount received is deemed to have been transferred to the consignor, the cash received is deemed to be not the carrier's but the consignor's money, so that in a case of insolvency it is not part of the insolvency estate, and in case of attachment it is not debtor's property so it cannot be attached. Should the cash have been paid into a bank account of the carrier if the carrier falls into an insolvency prior to payment to the consignor, the consignor can demand from the public receiver the full amount received. Equally, if the bank account has been attached by a creditor of the carrier, the consignor can demand release of the amount from the attached bank account.

If the carrier delivers the goods to the consignee without collecting cash from the consignee, according to § 422 (3) HGB he is liable to the consignor for damage caused thereby. But this liability is limited up to the cash on delivery amount.

429. As the law stipulates that freight is payable only upon delivery of the goods (§ 420 (1) HGB), the carrier has to fulfil his contractual duties before he receives his remuneration. Therefore, the carrier needs to be protected against non-payment of the freight. The law does so by availing the carrier a lien on the cargo carried. This lien does not only cover freight, but also any other monetary claim of the carrier under the contract, e.g., claims for reimbursements of costs and additional remuneration which he is entitled to after following instructions (§§ 418, 419 HGB). Such lien is not limited to goods owned by the consignor. If this were the case, in many situations the carrier would not be properly protected. In particular under subcontracts of carriage the consignor, being the preceding carrier, generally is not the owner of the goods. Subcarriers, thus, would not at all be protected if the lien existed only on cargo owned by the carrier. Instead the law provides that also goods owned by third parties are subjected to the lien if they had consented to the carriage of the goods. This does not require consent to a particular contract of carriage, but merely to the carriage as such. But the law goes beyond that. It avails the carrier a lien on goods owned by the consignor for all other undisputed claims which the carrier has under other contracts he has concluded with a consignor for the carriage of goods, for the carriage of goods by sea, for freight forwarding or for warehousing.

Generally the lien is a possessory lien, i.e., it exists as long as the carrier has possession of the goods, which includes possession by right of disposal by means of the bill of lading, a consignment bill or a warehouse warrant. But there is an extension of the existence of the lien, which goes beyond a strictly possessory lien, because according to § 440 (3) HGB the lien continues to exist for further three days after delivery if during these three days the carrier asserts the lien by way of a court action. But there is one limit provided by the law. At the time of submitting the application to the court within the mentioned three days the goods still must be in possession of the consignee. If the consignee has transferred possession of the goods to a third party at the time of submitting the application to court, there is no further protection of the carrier by a lien.

IV. The Consignor

430. The consignor's main obligation is to pay freight and demurrage payable according to § 412 (3) HGB if the contractual carrier waits beyond the time for loading or unloading on the basis of contractual agreement or for reasons which lie outside the sphere of the carrier's risk. Freight is only payable upon delivery of the goods, which means that the carrier has to fulfil his obligations before the consignor has to fulfil. The obligation to pay freight falls away if the carriage is impossible. It is only impossible if the goods cannot be brought to the place of delivery. If there are merely obstacles, which can be overcome by adapting the transport upon instructions sought by the carrier given from the entitled party (cf. paragraphs 422 et seq.), the transport is not impossible and the obligation to pay freight does not fall away. Rather, additional obligations in respect of disbursements of the carrier or additional remuneration may arise. The obligation to pay freight also continues to exist if the transport becomes impossible for reasons within the sphere of risk of the consignor or as a time when the consignor is in default of his obligation to accept performance by the carrier.

431. However, the consignor is also under various other obligations. One obligation has already been discussed above (paragraph 415): Upon request of the carrier the consignor is obliged to issue and sign a consignment note, the statutory content of which is stipulated in § 408 HGB. If the goods to be shipped are of dangerous nature, and if a consignment note is issued, according to § 408 (1) No. 6 HGB the consignor has to enter the description as required by regulations concerning dangerous goods. The most relevant regulations in this area are contained in the IMDG Code, which gives a certain code number for each dangerous cargo listed in the Code. But there are further requirements in respect of dangerous goods, which go beyond just quoting the correct code in the consignment note. § 410 (1) HGB requires the consignor to inform the carrier in a timely manner of the precise nature of the danger and, to the extent necessary, of any precautionary measures to be taken to count as such dangers. This extra information must be given in text form which, according to § 126b of the *Bürgerliches Gesetzbuch* (BGB; German Civil Code) means that the declaration must be made in a document or in another manner suitable for its permanent reproduction in writing. The last alternative applies to the most relevant form of communication nowadays, e-mails.

Not only for dangerous cargo, but for any kind of cargo, the consignor is under an obligation to package cargo, which in view of its nature and the carriage agreed requires packaging, to package them in such a way that it is protected against loss and damage and in such a way that the carrier suffers no loss or damage. These two obligations are of different quality. The first obligation is one which is meant to protect the consignor himself for loss or damage. If he does not fulfil it, the consequences resulting therefrom have to be borne by himself.

If goods are lost or damaged due to insufficient packaging, the carrier is released from liability according to § 427 (1) No. 5 HGB (*see also* paragraph 453). A carrier who realizes that packaging may not be insufficient in view of the nature of the goods and the carriage agreed, may be under an obligation to inform the consignor of this fact, but he is not entitled to refrain from carrying such goods, because the consequences of such insufficient packaging would only be borne by the consignor. The situation is different with the second alternative, where the insufficiency of packaging could lead to loss or damage of the carrier. If this actually happens, the consignor is liable according to the general provision for breach of contractual obligations under § 280 BGB. Such liability may be reduced under the principle of contributory negligence as laid down in § 254 BGB, if the carrier realized the insufficiency of packaging but nevertheless performed the transport. If the carrier realizes the insufficiency of the packaging, he is entitled to withhold his own obligation (§ 320 BGB), i.e., he can refrain from commencing the transport until the packaging is sufficient.

Just as the consignor has to care for proper packaging of the goods, he is obliged to label or mark the goods insofar as their contractually agreed handling so requires. The main purpose of this rule is to avoid that goods of similar outer appearance are mixed up and wrongly delivered. Here, usually no damage to the carrier occurs so that the consequences of inferior labelling or marking hit the consignor only: According to § 427 (1) No. 5 HGB the carrier is released from liability for loss of or damage to the goods or for delay in delivery, if same was caused by insufficient labelling or marking.

432. Unless the circumstances or customary practice require otherwise or unless the parties to the contract have agreed otherwise, the consignor is obliged to load, stow and secure the goods in a way they can be safely transported. This includes the physical movement of the goods onto or into the transport means and the protection of the goods in the transport means against movement. The law cannot be more precise because different goods and different transport means as well as different ways of carriage require different methods of stowing and securing. What the consignor is not obliged to do is to ensure that the loading and stowage does not impair the safe operation of the vehicle. The consignor's obligations are restricted to the preservation and protection of the cargo during (ordinary) transport. It is a matter for the carrier to make sure that his vehicle can be safely operated in the way the cargo is loaded, stowed and secured by the consignor (*see also* paragraph 421).

433. As the contract of carriage under German law is a contract for the benefit of a third party (cf. paragraph 413), the law cannot put an unconditional obligation on the consignee to unload the cargo. What would have been possible, however, would be a conditional unloading obligation, conditional in the sense that it arises only after the consignee has requested delivery of the cargo to him. This is the way the law deals with unpaid freight, which arises for the consignee according to § 421 HGB once he requests delivery of the goods to him. As regards unloading, the law has followed a different way. According to § 412 (1) HGB it is the consignor who must unload the cargo. Except in situations where a consignor sends cargo to his own premises where he can unload the cargo with his own personnel, usually the consignor will not be present at the place where the cargo is to be unloaded. Rather the consignor will have to agree with the consignee on who unloads the cargo from the transport means. Such an agreement can either be that the unloading is performed by the carrier (this requires a respective clause also in the contract of carriage, making the carrier responsible for unloading in deviation from § 412 (1) HGB) or the consignor and the consignee agree that the consignee unloads the cargo. This is an agreement outside the contract of carriage, but as regards § 412 (1) HGB such an agreement makes the consignee a servant of the consignor whom he employs to fulfil his obligation to unload the cargo. The consequence is that the consignor is liable for any fault of the consignee in respect of careless unloading, with the consequence that the consignor would be liable for damage suffered by the carrier according to §§ 280, 278 BGB.

434. The scenario, in which difficulties arise for the carrier in respect of performing the agreed transport, have already been discussed above. In these scenarios, the carrier is obliged to seek instructions from the party entitled to give such instructions (for details *see* above paragraph 422). Such scenarios may arise, however, also before the carrier realizes them, or situations may arise which do not affect the transport as such, but which make the transport as agreed less useful or even useless for the consignor. For both situations, the law gives the consignor the right to change what had originally been contractually agreed. This effect, the change of the content of the contract, is not really apparent from the words chosen by the lawmakers. § 418 HGB is headed *Nachträgliche Weisungen* (subsequent instructions). The first sentence of subsection 1 does say no more than that the right of disposal in relation to the goods is with the consignor. Then follow certain examples of this right under which the consignor may give certain instructions to the carrier who has to follow them according to the third sentence. What is not directly visible from the wording of the law, but what is settled in German law, is that such instructions actually do change the content of the contract. As long as such 'instructions' remain within the limits provided for by the law, the contract is changed merely by the consignor making such instructions. This leads to certain difficulties, which are still awaiting final clarification by the German Federal Court of Justice, when instructions are not directly given to the carrier, but for example to the carrier's driver who appears with the truck at the consignor's premises in order to take over the cargo. In order for instructions to change the contract, there must be declarations of will and they must be received by the counterparty. The counterparty is the carrier and not the driver. It is, therefore, in dispute whether instructions given merely to the driver can change the contract, as drivers usually do not have sufficient authority to change contracts of affreightment. This applies even more if instructions are given to the driver of a subcarrier, who by no means has authority to change the contract of the main carrier.

435. The right to give instructions is a right in relation to the goods. It follows that the right is limited to the goods as agreed in the contract of carriage. Neither can the consignor replace the contractually agreed goods with other goods nor can he change the quantity of goods to be carried. But in relation to the goods to be carried the law allows him to instruct the carrier to stop the goods in transit, to deliver them to another destination, to deliver them to another place of delivery at the destination or to deliver them to another consignee. To the extent that the law then states that the carrier is obliged to comply with such instructions, this actually means that the carrier is obliged to fulfil the contract in its amended or altered content. But also these rights are not unlimited. The law states that the carrier is not obliged to comply with instructions insofar as this cannot be done without the risk of prejudice to his business or damage to the consignors or consignees of other shipments. If this is the case, not only is the carrier not obliged to follow the instructions, but it is settled that in such scenarios the consignor's instructions do not effectively change the content of the contract. The right of the consignor to change the contract does not come for free. Rather the carrier may claim from the consignor reimbursement of the costs and expenses incurred as a result of having carried out the consignor's instructions. If the transport means is used for a longer time than it would have been used on basis of the original contract of carriage, the consignor is also obliged to pay the carrier a reasonable remuneration.

436. While generally liability under German law is fault based, § 414 HGB contains special cases, in which the carrier is liable irrespective of his fault: he has to indemnify the carrier for damage, costs or expenses caused by insufficient packaging or labelling or marking of the goods (obligation according to § 411 HGB), inaccuracy or incompleteness of any information in the consignment note (obligation according to § 408 HGB) or failure to disclose the dangerous nature of the goods (obligation according to § 410 HGB).

437. Prior to the Maritime Law Reform of 2013, this no-fault liability of the consignor was limited to 8,33 SDR for each kg of the goods. The German shipping law prior to the Maritime Law Reform also contained a no-fault liability of the shipper in comparable cases, but this liability was unlimited. In the course of the Maritime Law Reform, the lawmaker, aiming at harmonizing maritime transport law and general transport law, had to decide either whether to introduce limitation of liability into the maritime law or to abolish it in general transport law. The decision was in favour of abolishing limitation of liability in general transport law, which is now an unlimited liability. This creates a significant burden for consignors and has shifted risks very much on consignors. If the consignor himself has packaged and marked the goods, and if he has the necessary knowledge in respect of potential dangers resulting from the goods, unlimited no-fault liability is indeed justified. But many transports nowadays involve forwarders. In many of these cases the forwarders neither package nor mark the goods nor are they aware of the dangerous nature of the goods. For a forwarder, thus, an unlimited no-fault liability creates an almost incalculable risk, in particular in view of the fact that liability insurance in the market is available only for limited amounts.

438. Finally, in case of loss of or damage to the goods or delay in delivery the consigner is entitled to claim damages from the carrier (§ 421 (1) HGB).

V. The Consignee

439. The main right of the consignee is to demand from the carrier delivery of the goods once the goods have arrived at the place designated for delivery (§ 421 (1) HGB). This right is not unconditional. Rather the consignee, who demands delivery, has to perform certain obligations under the contract. One of these obligations is especially dealt with in § 421 (2) HGB: a consignee who executes his rights must pay any freight still due. The law limits this liability to pay freight up to the amount specified in the consignment note (§ 408 (1) No. 9 HGB), but in practice such remarks are rare so that the consignee in such a situation is actually liable for the full freight still unpaid. According to § 421 (3) HGB the payment obligation of the consignee extends to demurrage, but to demurrage arisen during the transport or already at the time of loading only to the extent he has been informed of such demurrage at the time of delivery of the goods

440. But the consignee has certain rights even before he has demanded delivery of the goods and by that created own obligations for him. By virtue of § 418 (2) HGB the right of disposal over the goods, which is originally vested in the consignor, expires at the moment the goods arrive at the place designated for delivery. From this moment on the right of disposal is vested in the consignee. This right is not dependent on the consignee demanding delivery. As a consequence, the consignee is in a position to alter the contract of affreightment by giving instructions to the carrier without being subjected to the obligations he is exposed to when demanding delivery. But if the consignee so alters the contract, resulting costs or expenses incurred by the carrier as well as a possible reasonable remuneration will be payable by the consignee (§ 418 (2) 2 HGB). Amongst the rights transferred from the consignor to the consignee upon arrival of the goods at the place of delivery is the right to instruct delivery to another consignee (§ 418 (1) 1 HGB). If the consignee makes use of this right, effectively he puts someone else in the position of the consignee. This new consignee then is the consignee with all the statutory rights vested in a consignee by the law. This would mean that such new consignee, again, would have the right to instruct the carrier to deliver to another consignee. But this is what the law does not allow. It is the only restriction which a new consignee has: he may give all instructions allowed for a consignee, but he can no more instruct to deliver to another, now a third, consignee (§ 418 (3) HGB).

441. Finally the consignee who has demanded delivery of the goods to him, is entitled to claim damages from the carrier in case the goods have been delivered damage or late or have been lost (§ 421 (1) 2 HGB).

§4. Liability and Limitation of Liability of the Carrier

I. The Basis for Liability

A. The Starting Point: Liability Based on Custody

442. As mentioned before, the German law is generally fault-based in the sense that, absent special statutory regulation, liability attaches only in case of fault. The grades of fault under German law traditionally have been negligence, gross negligence and intent. The main liability provision in transport law is § 425 (1) HGB which stipulates that the carrier is liable for any damage resulting from the loss of, or damage to, the goods occurring between the time the goods have been taken over for carriage and the time of their delivery, or resulting from delay in delivery. There is no reference to fault in this statutory provision, this being the reason for the wide spread term of *Obhutshaftung* (custodial liability). Judging just from this statutory provision, the liability appears to be strict and not dependent on any grade of fault. But § 425 HGB must be read together with § 426 HGB, which provides that the carrier is released from liability in so far as the loss of, or damage to, the goods or the delay in delivery was due to circumstances which the carrier could not avoid even by exercising the utmost diligence and the consequences of which he was unable to prevent. This provision, thus, introduces a subjective element of fault into the law in the carrier's liability. The reason for providing, in the first instance, for custodial liability without any requirement of fault and then, in the second instance, to release the carrier from liability under certain fault-based scenarios, is the burden of proof. Under German burden of proof principles the burden of proof for a certain fact rests with such person which would benefit from proof of the respective fact. If fault, and even at the high level as provided for in § 426 HGB, were a requirement for liability, it would be on the claimant – the consignor or the consignee (§ 421 (1) HGB) – to prove this fault. The way the law is structured, however, the claimant now only has to prove loss of or damage to goods or delay in delivery while the cargo is in the custody of the carrier. Lack of fault now is a defence, so that under the general principles the burden for lack of fault rests with the carrier, as he would benefit from such lack of fault.

443. § 425 HGB deals in its first alternative with a liability for loss of the goods. While it is relatively simple for a consignee or consignor to establish that goods were damaged at the time they were delivered, proof of loss of the goods is much more difficult. The mere fact that they are not delivered at the delivery time is no such proof, as the goods might just be delayed and still on the way. But even disregarding this, mere non-delivery of goods may also be caused by the fact that the goods had been left in a warehouse during transshipment, and are still safely stored there. The law is aware of these difficulties in respect of burden of proof, and helps the claimant by a presumption of loss, which is dealt with in § 424 HGB. This stipulates that the claimant may consider the goods lost if delivery has taken place neither within the delivery period nor within a further period that is equal to the length of the delivery period, but not shorter than twenty days, or in cases involving international transport not shorter than thirty days. In order to calculate this time, thus, the delivery period must be determined. This is done by § 423 HGB, which provides that the carrier is obliged to deliver the goods within the agreed period, or in the absence of an agreement, within such a period as reasonably be conceded to a diligent carrier with regard to the circumstances. The presumption of § 424 HGB does not step in with the expiry of the delivery period, but with the expiry of a further period of the same length. With this presumption at hand, the claimant no more has to prove actual loss, but simply can await the expiry of the mentioned period and then treat the goods as lost. The law also deals with the question what has to happen if the goods are found after the claimant has been indemnified for their loss. This depends on whether the claimant has demanded, at the time he is indemnified, to be informed if the goods are found. If he has demanded this, within one month after respective information the claimant is entitled to demand that the goods be delivered to him in return for the reimbursement of the compensation. If no demand in respect of information has been made and the goods are found after the claimant had been indemnified, the carrier has the right of free disposal of the goods.

444. § 425 HGB deals in its first alternative with a liability for loss of the goods. While it is relatively simple for the consignee or consignor to establish that goods were damaged at the time they were delivered, proof of loss of the goods is much more difficult. The mere fact that they are not delivered at the delivery time is no such proof, as the goods might just be delayed and still on the way. But even disregarding delay scenarios, mere non-delivery of goods may also be caused by the fact that the goods had been left in a warehouse during transshipment, and are still safely stored there. The law is aware of these difficulties in respect of burden of proof, and helps the claimant by a presumption of loss, which is dealt with in § 424 HGB. This stipulates that the claimant may consider the goods lost if delivery has taken place neither within the delivery period nor within a further period that is equal to the length of the delivery period, but not shorter than twenty days, or in cases involving international transport not shorter than thirty days. In order to calculate this time, thus, the delivery period must be determined. This is done by § 423 HGB, which provides that the carrier is obliged to deliver the goods within the agreed period, or in the absence of an agreement, within such a period as reasonably be conceded to a diligent carrier with regard to the circumstances. The latter alternative allows differing views of what should be reasonably conceded, so that differing views can result on when the time has expired after which the claimant may consider the goods lost. The presumption of § 424 HGB does not step in with the expiry of the delivery period, but with the expiry of a further period of the same length. With this presumption at hand, the claimant no more has to prove actual loss, but simply can await the expiry of the mentioned period and then treat the goods as lost. The law also deals with the question what has to happen if the goods are found after the claimant has been indemnified for their loss. This depends on whether the claimant has demanded, at the time he is indemnified, to be informed if the goods are found. If he has demanded this, within one month after respective information the claimant is entitled to demand that the goods be delivered to him in return for the reimbursement of the compensation. If no demand in respect of information has been made and the goods are found after the claimant had been indemnified, the carrier has the right of free disposal of the goods.

445. In the second alternative, § 425 HGB give the claimant a right of damages against the carrier for damage to the goods. Damage to goods requires a change in the physical characteristics of the cargo, which must have a reduction in value as a consequence. The test is an objective one. It is irrelevant whether the actual consignor or consignee can or cannot use the goods for certain, special purpose, but decisive is alone the perspective of a neutral third party. Situations may arise in which the marketability of goods is affected despite the fact that it later turns out that they are not physically damaged at all. German courts had to deal with two different scenarios. The first one is where, under the circumstances of the transport, there is a suspicion that damage might have arisen. Typical cases are transports of sophisticated machinery, for which shock recorders show that the goods have been exposed to shocks. If the defined limits of acceptable shocks are exceeded, such equipment may need testing in order to verify whether damage actually occurred. Such testing methods may not be available at the place of delivery of the goods, but may only be available at the premises of the manufacturer. In order to verify whether damage arose, thus, in such cases it is necessary to transport the goods back to the manufacturer and test them there. If damage is detected, the case turns out to be an ordinary cargo claim. But if the tests reveal no damage, then the requirement for a claim under § 425 HGB is not fulfilled: there is no physical damage. Nevertheless, the courts have decided that these cases are to be dealt with under § 425 HGB. This has positive effects for both sides. The claimant gets the benefit of the custodial liability of the carrier, but the carrier can rely on the statutory defences.

446. The approach is different where the marketability of goods is excluded despite the fact that there is no proven damage to the cargo. Typical cases are those of transport of foodstuff, in particular vegetable oil. Here regulations provide that such oil may only be carried in containers in which for the last preceding voyages no mineral oils were carried. If these regulations are not observed and oil is carried in a container in which mineral oil had been carried before, then the vegetable oil is not marketable, even if tests prove that the vegetable oil is not contaminated. In these cases, the application of § 425 HGB has been rejected. This does not mean that the carrier is free from liability. Rather he is liable according to the general rule of § 280 BGB, but only for ordinary negligence and not the much higher standards of the 'ideal carrier' (cf. paragraph 449). On the other hand, such liability is not limited by the limitations of the HGB. For example, under the circumstances of the transport, suspicion can arise that damage might have occurred. Typical cases are transports of sophisticated machinery, for which shock recorders have been placed in the cargo, which show that the goods have been exposed to shocks. If a defined limit of such shocks is exceeded, such equipment may need testing in order to verify whether damage actually occurred. Such testing methods may not be available at the place of delivery of the goods, but may only be available at the premises of the manufacturer. In order to verify whether damage arose, thus, in such cases it is necessary to transport the goods back to the manufacturer and test them there. If damage is detected, the case turns out to be an ordinary cargo claim. But if the tests reveal no damage, then the requirement for a claim under § 415 HGB is not fulfilled: there is no physical damage. Nevertheless the courts have decided that these cases are to be dealt with under § 425 HGB. This has positive effects for both sides. The claimant gets the benefit of the custodial liability of the carrier, but the carrier can rely on the statutory defences.

447. Custodial liability of the carrier applies between the time the goods have been taken over for carriage and the time of their delivery. Taking over of the goods by the carrier requires a respective readiness of the carrier. If the consignor just leaves the goods at the doorstep of the carrier, this does not qualify as taking over of the goods. Difficulties may arise if the carrier is already in possession of the goods, e.g., because they had been stored with him already. In such a case the time of taking over of the goods actually depends on the agreement between the consignor and the carrier. In this context it is relevant that the law requires that the goods are taken over *for carriage*. As a consequence, not too much time may pass by until carriage actual begins. In cases like these designation of the exact point in time when liability under § 425 HGB commences is usually heavily in dispute and depends on the circumstances of each individual case.

As to delivery, also here the readiness of the consignee to take delivery is required. Just as the consignor cannot cause the custodial liability to commence by bringing the goods to the carrier's premises against his will, the carrier cannot bring the custodial liability period to an end by leaving the goods with the consignee without the consignee's readiness to accept the goods. It has been discussed above that a consignee is not obliged to take delivery of goods under a contract of carriage (cf. paragraph 413). It has also been discussed that a denial to accept delivery by the consignee qualifies as an obstruction, which requires the carrier under § 419 HGB to obtain instructions from the consignor what to do now with the goods (cf. paragraph 422). In the context of delivery, and therefore in the context of the custodial liability period, it must be observed that in such a scenario the period of responsibility under § 425 HGB is extended. In result, thus, the carrier remains liable for a longer period than originally contractually agreed. This may seem surprising, but on the other hand the carrier is protected by being entitled to disbursements he incurs in the interest of the cargo, and possibly also by reasonable remuneration for his extended services (cf. paragraph 427).

448. Liability for delay in delivery requires a certain delivery period. This is dealt with in § 423 HGB. The delivery period is either a period agreed in the conflict of carriage or, in the absence of such an agreement, a period as should reasonably be conceded to a diligent carrier, having regard to the circumstances. Delay in delivery as addressed in § 425 HGB is given if this delivery period, either contractual or statutory, is exceeded.

B. General Exceptions

449. The law contains two general exceptions. According to § 426 HGB the carrier is released from liability insofar as loss of or damage to the goods or delay in delivery was caused by circumstances which the carrier could not avoid even by exercising utmost diligence, in the consequences of which he was unable to prevent. This places a significantly higher burden on the carrier than the law places on an ocean carrier according to § 499 HGB (cf. paragraph 230). The carrier is released from liability only if loss, damage or delay could not have been avoided by an 'ideal' carrier who has all available knowledge and all available means to avoid damage or delay. There is a certain overlap with the special exclusions contained in § 427 HGB (cf. paragraph 453) because in many of the situations addressed these special exclusions even an ideal carrier with utmost due diligence may not be able to prevent the damage. In such scenarios carriers will always rely on the special exclusions of § 427 HGB, then try to prove with utmost care according to § 426 HGB because under § 427 HGB the burden of proof situation is much more favourable for the carrier (for details *see* paragraphs 452 et seq.). Similar to the situation in maritime law (paragraph 399) when it comes to fault, the carrier is not only liable for his own fault or neglect but also for the fault and neglect of his crew and other servants, provided they were acting within the scope of their employment. According to § 428 HGB he is also liable for any other person, including independent contractors, whose services he makes use of for the carriage, and in respect of these persons it is not even required that they were acting within the scope of their engagement.

450. Within § 426 HGB certain scenarios are discussed. One of these scenarios is strikes. It is settled that under § 426 HGB the carrier cannot be held liable if his employees go on strike, as otherwise the carriers' position as an employer in labour disputes would be significantly affected. Commercial law of carriers' liability, though, must not have any influence on labour disputes. But what a carrier is required to do is to carefully consider possible strike scenarios and take every reasonable step for being able to fulfil his carriers' obligations despite a strike.

As regards theft, misappropriation and fraud, it is settled that utmost care of the carrier requires that he constantly controls his employees in respect of their personal honesty. Vehicles and warehouses must be best possible protected against theft. Vehicles must not be left unattended or unguarded so that theft can occur with normal criminal activity.

Deficiencies of vehicles will usually lead to the carrier's liability. The carrier will escape such liability only upon proof that the deficiency could not have been detected even upon application of the highest standard of care. Requirements are particularly high in respect of damage caused by defective tires. As a general rule, the carrier will escape liability on basis of § 426 HGB only in case of external damage caused to the tire because carriers who apply utmost care are expected to change the tires of their vehicles regularly. It is accepted, however, that a new tire which fails upon a production failure does not lead to liability of the carrier.

451. A second general exclusion is contained in § 425 (2) HGB. This deals with cases where conduct on the part of the consignor or consignee or a particular defect of the goods have contributed to the damage. These cases are discussed under paragraph 455.

C. Special Exceptions

452. The special exceptions to the carriers' liability are contained in § 427 HGB. Subsection 1 enumerates six different scenarios, in which the carrier shall not be liable. For three of these scenarios subsections 3, 4 and 5 contain further special rules. Subsection 2 stipulates a certain legal assumption.

453. The special exclusions as contained in § 427 (1) are as follows:

(1) Use of an open, unsheeted vehicle or loading on deck if such mode of carriage had been agreed or was customary. This exclusion, however, is further qualified by § 427 (3) HGB, which provides that the carrier may rely on these defences only to the extent that the loss of or damage to the goods or the delay in delivery was not due to the carrier failing to comply with any specific instructions made by the consignor for the carriage of the goods.
(2) Insufficient packaging by the consignor.
(3) Handling, loading or unloading of the goods by the consignor or consignee.
(4) Nature of the goods which makes them particularly susceptible to damage, especially by breakage, rust, internal spoiling, drying out, leakage or normal wastage. Also here there is a qualification, which is contained in § 427 (4) HGB. There it is stipulated that in case the carrier has agreed in the contract of carriage to protect the goods, particularly from the effects of heat, cold, temperature

variations, humidity, vibrations or similar effects, then he may avail himself of the mentioned defences only if he has taken all measures which can be expected from them in the given circumstances, in particular in respect of the choice, maintenance and use of specific equipment, and only if he has complied with any specific instructions given to him.

(5) Insufficient labelling or marking of cargo by the consignor.

(6) Carriage of live animals. Also here, there exists a qualification, which is contained in § 427 (5) HGB. The qualification is similar to the one contained in the preceding subsection in respect of nature of goods insofar as the carrier can rely on the exception for damage to live animals only if he has taken all of the measures which can be expected from him under the circumstances, and if he has complied with any specific instructions given to him. What is missing here, in contrast to subsection 4, is that the carrier must take all the mentioned measures even without respective agreements contained in a contract of carriage. In case of carriage of live animals, thus, there is no need for particular agreements in the contract of carriage.

454. Under the general rules of burden of proof in German law the carrier would have to bring full proof that damage was caused by an accepted peril as enumerated in § 427 (1) HGB. § 427 (2) HGB, however, gives the carrier a legal assumption at hand. If loss or damage has occurred, which, given the circumstances, may have been caused by one of the risks set out in subsection 1, then it is presumed that such loss or damage has in fact been so caused. This means that the carrier no more has to bring full proof of causation by only proof that under the prevailing circumstances the loss could have been proved by such risk. This assumption is not a final one. If the carrier has brought the respective proof, claimants still are in a position to prove the contrary, i.e., that actually the risks enumerated in § 427 (1) HGB did not cause the damage. But this proof again would be full proof, which means that the judge would have to be convinced of the causation, not only of a balance of probabilities and even less of the possibility only.

D. Concurrent Causes

455. Concurrent causes are dealt with in two different provisions. There is a general provision contained in § 425 (2) HGB. If conduct of the consignor or consignee or a particular defect of goods has contributed to the damage, then the carrier's obligation to pay compensation, and the amount of such compensation, depend on the extent to which such circumstances have contributed to the damage.

Concurrence of causes is also addressed with reference to the special exceptions contained in § 427 HGB because in the opening words of subsection 1 it is stated that the carrier is released from liability *insofar* as loss, damage or delay was due to one of the enumerated risks in subsections 1–6. But also here the difference in burden of proof must be observed. In order to invoke contributory causation under § 425 (2) HGB the carrier must bring full proof of such contribution. Within the scope of § 427 HGB, against that, the carrier only has to bring proof that either all or at least part of the damage may have been caused by one of the enumerated risks.

II. The Limitations of Liability

A. General

456. The general concept under German civil law in respect of damages is that the liable party must compensate in full. § 249 (1) *Bürgerliches Gesetzbuch (BGB;* Civil Code) stipulates that a person who is liable in damages must restore the position that would exist if the circumstance obliging him to pay damages had not occurred. § 252 BGB adds that the damage to be compensated for also comprises lost profits.

Transport law, in contrast, provides an array of regulations which partly frame the way damage is calculated and to be rectified, by this excluding certain kinds of damage from rectification, and partly then limits the generally recoverable damage to certain amounts.

B. Loss

457. § 429 HGB standardizes the indemnification a carrier liable for loss of goods has to pay. What he has to pay is the value which the goods had at the place and at the time they were taken over for carriage. The same concept applies also for maritime transport, but with the difference that § 502 HGB links the value not to the place and time where the goods were taken over for carriage, but to the place of the agreed destination and the time when they should have been delivered. The difference can be substantial, bearing in mind that goods may be existing in abundance at the place of shipment but may have an expensive market at the agreed destination.

The law also contains rules on how to determine the value at the place and time of shipment. § 429 (3) HGB stipulates that such value shall be determined by reference to the market price of the goods or, if there is no such market price, the normal market value of the goods of the same kind and characteristics. To make valuation even easier, the second sentence of this provision contains a rebuttable assumption: If the goods were sold immediately prior to being taken over for carriage, the purchase price as shown in the seller's invoice, including any costs of carriage contained therein, shall be presumed to be their market price. This assumption, however, is subject to counter-proof. A carrier can prove that the claimant did a bad deal and bought the goods above their real market value, as well as a claimant can prove that he did a good deal and that their real market value was above his purchase price. The burden of proof for either of these options rests with the party pleading it.

The value of the goods at the time and place where they were taken over for carriage is both the maximum and minimum amount payable by the carrier. The claimant is barred from proving a loss higher than the value at the place and time of taking over for carriage, as the carrier is barred from proving that the claimant's actual loss is lower than this value.

The effect of the standardization is also that there is no indemnification for consequential losses. Such consequential losses may, for example, be caused by an interruption of production as a result of the lack of raw materials which are required for production. Such losses of production can by far exceed the value of the lost goods, which usually is the case if the goods have a rather low value but are used for production of high value and products.

458. Liability in excess of the mentioned value only exists where the law itself expressly stipulates so. This is the case for costs for assessing the damage resulting from loss of cargo. In essence these are the costs necessary to determine the value at the time and place of taking over the goods and, in case or partial loss, the costs required to determine which part of the cargo was lost. The scope of application, thus, is rather limited. It is settled that it does not extend to costs incurred in order to determine the cause of the loss.

Also payable beyond the value of the goods are freight, public levies and other charges incurred in connection with carriage of the goods (§ 432 HGB).

459. The liability so assessed is then subject to a limitation which is linked to the weight of the goods. This weight-based limitation, however, only limits liability according to § 429 HGB (value of the goods) and § 430 HGB (costs of assessing the damage), but not of § 432 HGB (liability for certain other costs), the latter being payable on top of the limitation amount.

The applicable limit according to § 431 (1) HGB is calculated by multiplying each kilogram of the goods' gross weight with 8,33 SDR. To give an example: If goods with the weight of 1,000 kg and a value of EUR 10,000 are lost, the maximum liability of the carrier amounts to EUR 8,330 SDR. The weight limitation is a pure limitation and does not lead to an increase of liability. To give another example: If goods with a weight of 1,000 kg and a value of EUR 5,000 are lost, the carrier's liability is no more than EUR 5,000. The limitation amount of 8,333 SDR, which is the result of calculations made under § 431 (1) HGB does not lead to an increase of liability but only leads to the ineffectiveness of the weight limitation.

If the goods consisted of several cargo units and only some of them are lost, then the limit of liability shall be calculated on basis of the weight of the entire cargo if the entire cargo has been depreciated in value, or of the part of the cargo that has depreciated in value if only a part of the cargo has depreciated in value. Two examples for both scenarios: Two chairs of a rococo ensemble of furniture, consisting of four chairs and a table, are lost. The remaining two chairs and the table, now being incomplete, are affected in their remaining value as well. Here the full weight of all four chairs and the table are used for calculating the weight limitation. If, in contrast, forty mobile phones out of a full consignment of one hundred phones are lost, the remaining sixty mobile phones are not affected in their value by the loss of the other mobile phones. Here, only the weight of the fifty lost mobile phones is relevant for the weight calculation.

C. Damage

460. With some alterations only, the concept on valuation and limitation just described for loss of cargo also applies also to damage to cargo. As regards valuation, § 429 (2) HGB stipulates that compensation payable shall be the difference between the value of the undamaged goods at the place and time they were taken over for carriage and the value that the damaged goods would have had at the place and time they were taken over for carriage. For the first of those two values, the value in sound condition, the rules and the legal assumption contained in § 429 (3) HGB apply, i.e., the goods are deemed to have had the value expressed in the seller's invoice, this assumption being open to rebuttal by both the carrier and the claimant. The assessment of the value of the goods in damaged condition is far more difficult. The seller's invoice shows the value only in sound condition, and generally market prices also exist only for sound, but not for damaged goods. Assessment of the value in damaged condition is even more difficult due to the fact that, different from the similar situation in maritime transport, where § 502 HGB requires determination of the damaged value at the place of destination, in general transport this assessment must be made for the place of taking over of the cargo, while the damaged goods are actually at the place of destination. In order to ease these difficulties, the law also here contains a legal presumption. According to § 429 (2) HGB the costs necessary to mitigate or remedy the damage are presumed to be equal to the difference between sound and damaged value of the goods. Again, this is a presumption only which can be rebutted by full proof of a different value brought either by the carrier or by the claimant.

In all other respects liability and limitation of liability for damage to goods follows the same concept as that for loss of the goods.

D. Delay

461. As regards delay, economical loss resulting only from delay must be distinguished from physical damage or even total loss, resulting from delay. A typical example for the second alternative is that carriage of fruit is so heavily delayed that the fruit is completely decayed when it finally reaches the destination. The law deals with this exclusively under the rules of loss of or damage to goods. The rules on liability for delay in delivery apply only to damage which is the consequence of the delay as such, but not the consequence of physical loss or damage. Both classes of damage can occur parallel: Goods can arrive in a partly damaged condition and delayed, and the damage can consist of the reduced value of the goods plus additional economical damage merely resulting from the delay in delivery, e.g., a reduced time for bringing the goods to the market.

Also in the area of liability for delay and delivery the law differs from the civil law principle of full indemnification. Whereas in principle in case of loss or damage to goods the liability is linked to the value of the goods or the difference in value between sound and damaged condition, the limitation for liability and delivery has no connection whatsoever to the damage caused by the delay. Like many other laws, also German law links the carrier's liability for delay and delivery to the freight paid for the carriage of the goods and stipulates in § 431 (3) HGB that the carrier's liability is limited to an amount equal to three times the freight. Also in this area, general transport law deviates from maritime transport law. Maritime law does not contain any particular rules on liability for delay in delivery. In particular, there is no mandatory liability for delay in delivery in maritime transport. As a consequence, there neither exist rules on limitation of liability. If delay in delivery occurs in maritime transport, thus, the general civil law applies, under which the liable carrier may well be called to indemnify the claimant for all losses resulting from the delay, if the respective requirements under the civil law are met. It is fair to say, however, that due to the absence of mandatory liability for delay and delivery in practice this liability usually is excluded so that the principally unlimited liability under civil law has no real practical relevance.

E. *Other Pecuniary Loss*

462. Finally, the law contains one further provision on limitation which applies if the carrier is liable for damage resulting from the breach of a contractual obligation in connection with a performance of the carriage of goods if the damage is not the result of loss of or damage to the goods or the result of delay in delivery. If, in such a situation, damage is pure financial loss, i.e., if it does not consist of physical damage or damage to persons, the carrier's liability is limited to three times the amount which he would have been liable for if the goods, forming the subject of the contract of carriage, had been lost. Here the law, thus, follows a concept different from when dealing with damage resulting from delay in delivery. In that case, the limitation is linked to the freight, and the limitation amount is three times the freight. In case of the pecuniary losses dealt with in § 433 HGB, in contrast, the link is to the liability for loss of the goods, and the amount is three times of that liability.

F. *Interest*

463. There do not exist any special interest provisions in German transport law. Rather the general provisions of the *Bürgerliches Gesetzbuch* (BGB; Civil Code) apply. § 288 BGB provides that in case of default, default interest of 5% points above the basic rate of interest is payable. The basic rate of interest is published from time to time by the German Federal Bank. Default requires after due date of a payment obligation a warning notice by the claimant to the liable party (§ 286 BGB)

G. *Extra-contractual Claims*

464. All the above limitations form part of the law of the contract of carriage. Insofar they relate to contractual claims. But the carrier may also incur liability outside the framework of the contract of carriage, in particular on the basis of tort law. If limitation of liability of the carrier were only available for contractual claims, claimants would be invited to pursue non-contractual claims rather than contractual claims, if such non-contractual claims lead to unlimited liability. But German law prevents such an escape into the non-contractual law by stating in § 434 (1) HGB that exemptions from and limitations of liability provided for by the provisions of contract law apply equally to any non-contractual claims which the consignor or the consignee may have against the carrier for loss of or damage to the goods or for delay in delivery. While this provision deals with non-contractual claims, it still has not left the framework of the contract of carriage because it deals with non-contractual claims of contractual partners, namely the consignor or the consignee. Insofar, the provision is well-placed amongst the regulations on contract of carriage in the Commercial Code.

465. The framework of the contract is left when § 434 (2) HGB deals with non-contractual claims of third parties, i.e., claimants who are neither consignor nor consignee under the contract. When allowing the carrier to avail of limitations of liability founded in the law of contract of carriage also in respect of claims by parties who have no contractual relationship with the carrier, the law leaves the contractual area. In substance, thus, § 434 (2) HGB is not a provision of contract law, but a provision of non-contractual law, i.e., tort law. It could well have formed part of the tort law as contained in the civil code, but the lawmaker had decided to place it into the Commercial Code because it refers to limitations as provided for in the law on contract of carriage. What the law allows in the first place is that the carrier relies on all exemptions from and limitations of liability as provided for by contract law. But there are three scenarios in which those limitations are not available for the carrier:

(1) The contractual limitation on which the carrier intends to rely is based on an agreement with a consignor which deviates to the detriment of the consignor from the statutory provisions.
(2) The third party which pursues non-contractual claims for loss, damage or delay in delivery had not consented to the carriage of goods, and the carrier was either aware of this lack of consent or his unawareness of a lack of consent is based on the carrier's gross negligence.
(3) Prior to being taking over for carriage by the carrier the goods had been lost or stolen or otherwise gone missing.

All three exemptions are meant to protect third parties from limitations they do not have to expect: They neither have to expect that the consignor has availed the carrier wider exemptions or limitations than provided for by the law; he does not have to expect any limitation on basis of contractual defences if he did not even agree that his goods are being carried; and he does not have to expect such defences if the goods had been lost from his own custody.

III. Unlimited Liability

466. The aforementioned exemptions from the limitations of liability are available to the carrier only in cases where loss of or damage to the goods or delay in delivery was not caused by severe fault. The standards generally are the same as in maritime transport. Exemptions and limitations do not apply if damage was caused by an act or omission done with the extent to cause such damage, or recklessly and with knowledge that such damage will probably result (§ 435 HGB). Different from maritime transport where only intent or recklessness of the carrier itself excludes exemptions and limitations, in non-transport law also intent and recklessness of those persons referred to in § 428 HGB lead to unlimited liability of the carrier. These persons are the carrier's servants, provided the servants where acting within the scope of their employment, and any other persons whose services the carrier makes use of for the carriage of the goods (paragraph 449).

467. The German Federal Court of Justice has defined recklessness as going beyond gross negligence and requiring a particularly severe breach of obligation in which the carrier or those for whom he is liable disregard grossly the security interests of the contractual partner. In respect of the required knowledge that damage would probably result the Court accepted that this is a subjective requirement but that objective facts may be sufficient to conclude that under the circumstances and in view of the reckless behaviour the carrier must have had this knowledge. As regards probable damage, there is no requirement for knowledge of the particular way damage could develop, neither must there be knowledge of any particular damage, even less the damage actually occurred, but knowledge that any kind of damage probably will occur is sufficient. As regards the probability of damage, the Federal Court of Justice has rejected the idea to determine percentages of probability. The Court even has held that a probability of less than 50% may be sufficient. Generally, all facts have to be taken into account.

IV. Time Limits for Complaint and Action

468. Transport law aims at an early determination of claims. For this reason the law contains provisions on notice of damage and limitation of claims. According to § 438 HGB, loss of or damage to goods which is apparent must be notified to the carrier latest on delivery of the goods. The notice must describe the loss or damage in sufficiently clear terms. If no notice is given at all or if the notice does not sufficiently clarify the loss or damage, then there is a legal presumption that all the goods carried were delivered in undamaged condition. This presumption is rebuttable for cargo interests.

Obviously notification is not possible upon delivery if at that time damage was not apparent. For this situation, the law could stipulate that notice must be given once loss or damage become apparent. But the law does not so. Rather the law stipulates a period of seven days after delivery within which the notice must be given. In essence this forces the consignee to check the goods for completeness and damages within seven days. Where this is not possible, the legal presumption will apply regardless of any fault or even possibility to carry out the mentioned investigation on the part of the consignee.

469. If no cargo is delivered at all, § 438 HGB and its provisions on notification do not apply because by their very wording they presuppose that there is a delivery. In case of a total loss of the complete consignment, thus, there exist no legal presumptions in case of non-notification that the carrier delivered the cargo in its entirety.

470. Delay in delivery is treated by the law in an entirely different way. The first difference is that the notification period in this case is twenty-one days after delivery. The relevant time, thus, is not the time when delivery ought to have been performed, but when it is actually performed. The major difference to notification of a loss or damage, where non-notification or insufficient notification merely create a legal presumption for proper delivery, in case of delay and delivery expiry of the twenty-one days leads to the extinguishment of the claim for damages. Also here, fault is irrelevant so that the claim does not even survive if the consignee could show that he cannot be blamed for the non-notification.

471. As regards prescription, the period provided for in the commercial code is shorter than the general prescription period of three years according to § 195 *Bürgerliches Gesetzbuch* (BGB; Civil Code). According to § 439 (1) HGB, the prescription period is one year. It does not only apply to contractual claims under the contract of carriage, but to any claim, including tort claims, as long as they are in connection with a carriage which is subject to the provisions on contract of carriage in the HGB. In line with § 435 HGB which deals with unlimited liability § 439 (1) HGB stipulates that in cases of intent or recklessness the prescription period shall be three years.

472. While the general limitation period of three years under civil law commences at the end of the year in which the claim arose and the claimant obtained knowledge of the circumstances giving rise to the claim and of the identity of the liable party (or would have obtained such knowledge if he had not shown gross negligence), the limitation periods under § 439 HGB commence on the expiry of the day the goods were delivered or, if they were not delivered, the day they should have been delivered. In practice often there is not only one carrier involved in a transport, but more carriers. One carrier, the main carrier, may have contracted with the consignor and then subcontracts all or part of the transport with a subcarrier who may himself involve further subcarriers. If there was no special provision on prescription of recourse claims, such recourse claims, also qualifying as claims for damages under a contract for the carriage of goods, would be subject to the same time limit as the claim of the consignor against the main carrier. In order to avoid this, § 439 (2) HGB contains a special provision for recourse claims. Here the limitation period commences on the day on which a judgment against the recourse claimant becomes final and binding or, if there is no final and binding judgment, on the day on which the recourse claimant has satisfied the claim. This means that recourse claims can become time-barred considerably later than one or three years after delivery. Negotiations on claims may take long time, and the time until there is a final and binding judgment may be even longer. This creates the risk that potential recourse debtors who may be not aware of proceedings pending against the recourse claimant or negotiations held between the original claimant and the recourse claimant, may get into a disadvantageous position as regards securing of evidence. In order to avoid these disadvantages, § 439 (2) HGB stipulates that the extension of the prescription period just described does not apply if the recourse debtor was not informed of the damage within three months after the recourse claimant became aware of the damage and of the recourse debtor's identity. For a potential recourse claimant, thus, it is vital that he informs a potential recourse debtor within those three months of the claim. Frequently these three months will commence at the time of delivery or at least shortly thereafter because usually notice of damage is given by the consignee so that the carrier is aware of the damage. If the recourse debtor is a subcarrier of the recourse claimant, he is also aware of his identity. This provision, thus, forces the recourse debtor to notify the subcarrier of a potential recourse possibly long before a claim actually has been presented to him by the claimant.

473. Failure to give such notice leads to the application of the one- or three-year prescription periods commencing to run upon delivery of the goods. A potential recourse claimant, who has failed to notify his potential recourse debtor of the respective claim, thus, may find himself in a position that at the last day of the prescription period he is not aware whether he has been sued, but still has to start proceedings himself in order to avoid prescription of his recourse claim. The only alternative to proceedings in such a situation is to agree with a potential recourse debtor on a time extension.

474. Such time extensions are possible for all prescription periods addressed above. The only requirement is that the extension is granted by and in favour of the correct party, i.e., by the debtor to the claimant. But the law provides for two different ways to suspend the time without an agreement on extension. One of these provisions forms part of the Commercial Code, the other part of the Civil Code. Both operate independently of each other, have different requirements and different effects. § 439 (3) HGB stipulates that prescription is suspended by the consignor or consignee asserting their compensation claims with the carrier. Such assertion must be made in text form, which according to § 126b *Bürgerliches Gesetzbuch* (BGB; Civil Code) requires that the declaration is made in a document or in another manner suitable for its permanent reproduction and writing. This includes telefaxes and e-mails. Suspension in the meaning of § 439 (3) HGB means that the prescription period is stopped from running at the moment the claimant's declarations received by the carrier. The suspension ends when the carrier refuses to satisfy the claim. Also, this refusal must be made in text form and the suspension ends when the refusal is received by the claimant. It is almost a standard practice at least for German carriers to reject claims immediately after they have been received. The main purpose for this rejection is not to end discussions but to avoid suspension of the prescription period. It may be that the claimant re-asserts his claims and sends a new declaration to the carrier, but according to § 439 (3) HGB such a further declaration does not result in an additional suspension of the prescription period. Usually, thus, suspension under § 439 (3) HGB is a matter of days only.

475. Suspension under Civil Law follows an entirely different concept. According to § 203 BGB, prescription is suspended if negotiations are in progress between the claimant and the debtor in respect of the claim or in respect of the circumstances given rise to the claim. There is, thus, no need for the assertion of a claim in text form. Even if no claim has been raised, but the parties just correspond for example on the cause of a damage, suspension under § 203 BGB takes place. Civil law then distinguishes between the termination of the suspension and the actual time bar. Description is suspended until one party or the other refuses to continue the negotiations. This means that from this moment on the remaining time of the prescription period continues to run. If this remaining time exceeds three months, no peculiarity arises. However, if the remaining time is less than three months, then the claim does not become time-barred after expiry of this remaining time. Instead, § 203 second sentence BGB stipulates that the time bar will occur at the earliest three months after the end of the suspension.

As mentioned, § 203 BGB declares the end of the suspension to take place if one or the other party refuses to continue the negotiations. The courts are rather strict when testing this. They require a 'double no': The claim must be rejected and the debtor must refuse to continue the negotiations. A mere rejection of the claim, thus, does not mean that the suspension comes to an end. But in real life not always such clear declarations are made. As a matter of fact, there are many cases in which the negotiations 'fall asleep' – an expression actually used by German courts. For such situations, the Federal Court of Justice has held that the suspension ends at the moment in which the other side reasonably should have continued the negotiations. What moment in time this is depends on the facts of each individual case. Negotiations may start with weekly messages sent, but then may slow down to a sequence of two weeks, one month, two months or even longer. Even in case of rather long periods between messages, negotiations would still be deemed pending so that in practice at least the time between the last two communications must expire before the suspension will be treated as ended.

V. Jurisdiction of Courts

476. Starting, all over, with the general rules on jurisdiction under German law, according to § 17 *Zivilprozessordnung* (ZPO; Civil Procedure Code) legal persons can be sued in their general venue. This general venue is defined by their registered seat which, unless anything to the contrary is stipulated elsewhere, is deemed to the place at which the legal person has its administrative centre. If a contract has been entered into by a branch office of the carrier, then § 21 ZPO allows commencement of an action also in the court which has jurisdiction over the location of such branch office. To the extent that claims are based on delict, § 32 ZPO allows commencement of an action in the court which has jurisdiction over the place where the delict was committed. Finally, § 30 ZPO deals with jurisdiction in cases of contract of carriage. This provision only amends the jurisdiction of other courts mentioned before and does not set them aside. The provision had previously been part of the commercial code as § 440 HGB old version. § 30 (1) ZPO deals with carriage of goods, § 30 (2) with carriage of passengers and their baggage by ship. As regards carriage of goods, § 30 (1) ZPO stipulates that also those courts have jurisdiction, which are in charge of the place where the goods have been taken over or delivered. It is further stipulated that an action against an actual carrier can also been commenced in the court which has jurisdiction for claims against the carrier. Vice versa, an action against the carrier can also be commenced in the court which has jurisdiction over the actual carrier.

§5. Carriage of Removal Goods

477. As stated above, the carriage of removal goods is subject to special regulation, contained in § 451–451h HGB. § 451 HGB clarifies that carriage of removal goods is also subject to the general provisions of §§ 407–450 HGB, but that those provisions only apply to the extent that the special provisions of § 451a–451h do not have deviating provisions. The most relevant special provisions are:

- § 451a: The duties of the Contractual Carrier include dismantling and reassembling the furniture, as well as the loading and the unloading of the removal goods.
- § 451b: The consignor is not obliged to issue a consignment note. If removal goods are dangerous, the consignor must inform the carrier only in a general form, and in no particular form.
- § 451d: Further and above the special exclusion of § 427 HGB, the carrier is not liable for carriage of precious metals, jewels, precious stones, money, stamps, coins, securities or documents.

- § 451e: Liability is not subject to a limitation of 8.33 *SDR* per kilogram, but by EUR 620 per cubic meter of the loading space required for the performance of the contract.
- § 451f: Notification of apparent loss or damage must be made within one day after delivery, notification of not apparent loss or damage must be made within fourteen days after delivery.
- § 451g: Limitations of and exemptions from liability are not available to the carrier, if the carrier, at the time the contract was concluded, did not inform the Consignor of the provisions relating to liability and to advise him that a more far-reaching liability could be agreed upon or that the goods could be insured.

According to § 451h HGB, the provisions of § 451–451g HGB apply mandatorily, if the consignor is a consumer.

§6. Carriage of Passengers by Road

478. Liability of the carrier for personal injury or death of the passenger or damage to his baggage in case of carriage by route is not covered by the commercial code, but by a special law, the *Personenbeförderungsgesetz* (PBefG; Passenger Carriage Act). The act mainly deals not only with licensing aspects but also contains a few provisions on liability. § 14 PBefG stipulates that the carrier is liable for death or personal injury of the passenger and for damage to baggage according to the general provisions. The most relevant provision in this respect is § 7 *Straßenverkehrsgesetz* (StVG; Road Traffic Act). This provision stipulates a no- fault liability of the keeper of the motor vehicle for death or personal injury of a passenger or loss of or damage to the passenger's baggage. § 8a StVG contains a special provision for carriage of passengers against remuneration and stipulates that the liability according to § 7 StVG for death or person injury may neither be limited nor excluded. Liability for loss of or damage to baggage is not addressed in § 8a StVG. This dealt with in the second sentence of § 14 PBefG, where it is stipulated that the carrier is liable for physical damage in aspect of each person carried up to a maximum of EUR 1,000. This limitation does not apply if the physical damage was caused by intent or gross negligence of the carrier.

Chapter 2. Transportation by Rail

§1. Introduction

479. In the past, transport by rail was exclusively in the hands of the state-owned German Railways (*Deutsche Bundesbahn)*, which was a public company owning and operating all railway cars and the rail structure as such. The previous *Deutsche Bundesbahn* was incorporated as a stock company under the name *Deutsche Bahn AG*. This now owns the railcars previously owned by *Deutsche Bundesbahn*. The infrastructure was transferred to another stock company, *DB Netz AG*. Both Deutsche Bahn AG and DB Netz AG are still 100% owned by the Federal Republic. Neither company is listed at the stock market, although since years preparations are made list at least Deutsche Bahn AG.

§2. Statutory Provisions: Legislation

480. After privatization of the sector, transportation by rail is now governed by the *Allgemeines Eisenbahngesetz* (AEG; General Railroad Act. The Act distinguishes between railway operating companies and railway infrastructure companies. Both may be either public or private companies. Security of rail transport is in charge of the *Eisenbahnbundesamt* (Federal Railway Office). According to § 10 AEG, public rail carriers engaging in passenger transport are bound by law to carry any passenger, if the conditions of carriage are observed and if carriage is possible with the regularly used rail cars. Railway operating companies and railway infrastructure companies must take out insurance for the liability for personal injury and damage to goods (§ 14 AEG). The minimum sum insured per incident is EUR 20 million, which must be available at least for two incidents per cover period (§ 14b AEG). The AEG does not deal with aspects of liability for personal injury or property damage.

481. Prior to the reform of the general transport law in 1998, liability for damage to goods during carriage by rail was not dealt with in the *Handelsgesetzbuch* (HGB; Commercial Code) but in special the legislation in respect of railways. One of the main reasons for the law reform was to bring most of the means of carriage under the application of one and the same set of rules. As a consequence the provisions on carriage of goods in §§ 407 et seq. HGB now apply to carriage over land, on inland waterways or by aircraft.

§3. The CIV Convention (Passenger and Their Baggage)

482. Germany is Member State of the Convention concerning International Carriage by Rail (COTIF) of 1980 as amended in 2006. This Convention deals with liability in respect of death or injury of passengers and loss of or damage to baggage in the Uniform Rules concerning the Contract of International Carriage of Passengers by Rail (CIV), which form Appendix A of COTIF.

I. Scope of Application

483. According to Article 1 § 1 the provisions of the CIV apply to every contract of carriage of passengers by rail, whether for reward or free of charge, when the place of departure and the place of destination are situated in two different Member States. The domicile or the place of business and the nationality of the parties to the contract of carriage are not of relevance. The CIV applies mandatorily. Any agreement which derogates from the rules of the CIV to the disadvantage of the passenger is void (Article 5).

II. Liability of the Passenger

484. The CIV deals with liability of the passenger in Article 53. The provision is complex and refers to a number of other provisions, which stipulate obligations for the passenger. If the passenger has not complied with the formalities required by customs or other administrative authorities (Articles 10, 14 CIV) or if he has not properly marked his registered baggage (Article 20 CIV), if he has not fulfilled his obligations resulting from special provisions for the carriage of vehicles, contained in the General Conditions of Carriage, or the Regulation concerning the International Carriage of Dangerous Goods by Rail (RID), which form Annex C to the COTIF Convention, passenger is liable to the carrier for any loss or damage. Different from the national German law, which stipulates in § 414 HGB a no-fault liability, if he proves that the loss or damage was caused by circumstances that he could not avoid and the consequences of which he was unable to prevent, despite the fact that he exercised the diligence required of a conscientious passenger. This liability is per se unlimited. But as Article 5 CIV allows deviations from the CIV which are in favour of the passenger, clauses limiting the passenger's liability are permitted and valid.

III. Liability for Death and Personal Injury and Damage to Baggage or for Delay in Delivery

485. Basic provisions are found in Article 26 CIV, according to which the carrier is liable for loss or damage resulting from death of or personal injuries or any other physical or mental harm to a passenger, which is caused by an accident arising out of the operation of the railway and which is happening while the passenger is in the vehicle, entering it or getting off the vehicle. The liability is not a no-fault liability, but the carrier is relieved from liability if the accident was caused by circumstances which are not connected with the operation of the railway and which the carrier, despite having applied the care required under the circumstances, could not avoid and the consequences of which he could not prevent. The carrier is also relieved from liability if the accident was due to the fault of the passenger. But here Article 26 § 2 b CIV provides that the carrier is only relieved 'to the extent' that the accident is due to the fault of the passenger. If the fault of the passenger merely contributed, the carrier will be relieved only to the extent of this contribution.

486. In case of death of a passenger, persons for whom he had a legal duty to maintain and who are, by the death of the passenger, deprived of this support, have a right to be compensated for such loss (Article 27 § 2 CIV). The carrier is also liable to bear necessary costs, in particular the costs of transport of the body and funeral expenses (Article 27 § 1 a CIV). According to Article 28 CIV in case of personal injury the carrier is liable for all necessary costs, in particular costs of treatment and transport, and for compensation of financial losses due to total or partial incapacity to work, or in respect of increased needs. Article 30 § 2 CIV limits liability to 175,000 special SDR per passenger, either as a lump sum or as an annual annuity corresponding to that sum.

487. According to Article 33 § 2 CIV, the carrier is liable for total or partial loss of or damage to hand baggage and animals, if such loss or damage is caused by the carrier's fault. Liability for loss or damage is generally unlimited and limited only if it occurs in the context of death of or personal injury to the passenger. In this case Article 34 CIV limits the carrier's liability to 1,400 SDR per passenger. Liability is excluded if the loss or damage arose from the fact that the passenger did not conform to customs or other administrative formalities (Article 35 CIV).

Regarding registered baggage, Article 36 CIV provides for a no-fault liability of the carrier for loss or damage for the time between taking over by the carrier and the time of delivery and for delay and delivery. He is relieved of such liability to the extent that loss, damage or delay were caused by fault of the passenger himself. He is also relieved if loss or damage was caused by certain special risks, namely inadequate packing, the special nature of the cargo or if the consignment consists of articles which are excluded from carriage as baggage. The carrier bears the burden of proof if he wants to rely on fault of the passenger. In respect of the other circumstances referred to above it is sufficient if the carrier establishes that the loss or damage could have arisen from one or more of the special risks (Article 37 CIV).

The burden of proof for loss or damage within the above-mentioned liability period rests with the passenger. Article 20 § 1 CIV contains a legal assumption that baggage is deemed lost if it is not delivered within fourteen days after request of delivery (Article 40 § 1 CIV).

488. Liability for loss of baggage is the amount of damage, once proven, but no more than 80 SDR per kilogram or 1,200 SDR per piece of baggage. If the amount of damage is not proven, the carrier is liable for liquidated damages of 20 SDR per kilogram or 300 SDR per piece of baggage.

489. Liability for delay and delivery of baggage is linked to the time of delay and amount in respect of the delayed baggage. According to Article 43 CIV in case of delay in respect of each whole twenty-four hour period after delivery the carrier must pay, but for no more than fourteen days, compensation of any damage established up to a maximum amount of 0.8 SDR per kg or 14 SDR per piece of baggage. If loss is not proven, the passenger is entitled to liquidate damages of 0.14 SDR per kilogram or 2.8 SDR per piece of baggage. Special rules apply to loss of or delay in delivery of vehicles. In case of loss of vehicles the carrier's liability is limited to 8,000 SDR (Article 45 CIV), in case of delay and delivery it is limited to the amount of the charge payable for the carriage.

490. The aforementioned limitations of liability do not apply if it is proved that the loss or damage has resulted from an act or omission of the carrier which was committed with intent to cause such loss or damage, or recklessly and with knowledge that such loss or damage would probably result (Article 48 CIV).

§4. CIM Convention (Carriage of Goods by Rail)

491. The CIM Convention forms part of the COTIF Convention as Appendix B. As Germany has ratified the COTIF Convention, the CIM Convention applies in its scope of application.

I. Scope of Application

492. According to Article 1 § 1 CIM applies to every contract of carriage of goods by rail, but different from international passenger contract by rail only in case of carriage for reward, if the place of taking over of the goods and the designated place of delivery are located in two different Member States. The place of business and the nationality of the parties to the contract of carriage are irrelevant. The provisions of the CIM apply mandatorily. Any derogation from the convention is void, but the carrier may assume a greater liability than provided for in the CIM rules (Article 5 CIM).

II. Liability of the Consignor

493. According to Article 8 CIM the consignor is liable for costs, loss or damage suffered by the carrier by irregular, incorrect or incomplete entries by the consignor in the consignment note, and by the consignor omitting to make the entries prescribed by the regulations concerning the International Carriage of Dangerous Goods by Rail (RID), which form part of COTIF as Appendix 10. The RID is a very detailed set of provisions, covering almost 1,000 pages. The mentioned liability is unlimited and does not require any fault of the consignor.

III. Liability for Loss of or Damage to Goods or for Delay in Delivery

494. According to Article 23 CIM the carrier is liable for loss of or damage to the goods between the time of taking them over and the time of their delivery, as well as for loss or damage resulting from delay in delivery, which is described here as an exceeding of the transit period. The liability is not a no-fault liability, but the carrier can exonerate himself in certain situations, namely (a) to the extent that loss or damage was caused by the fault of the claimant, (b) that it was caused by an order of a person entitled to give such an order (unless given as a result of the fault of the carrier), (c) if caused by an inherent defect of the goods like decay, wastage, etc. or, (d) by the general defence that it was caused by circumstances which the carrier could not avoid and the consequences of which he was unable to prevent (Article 23 § 2 CIM).

Article 23 CIM then goes on in § 3 to deal with special risks and relieves the carrier from liability to the extent that loss or damage has arisen from such special risks. The first of these risks is carriage in open wagons, either on basis of general conditions of carriage or on basis of an express agreement, which is entered into the consignment note. The carrier is also relieved from liability in case of absence or inadequacy of packaging if the goods by their nature required this. He is also relieved of liability if loss or damage is caused by loading of the goods by the consignor or unloading by the consignee as well as for loss or damage as a result of the nature of goods which exposes them to loss or damage, especially by breakage, rust, decay, desiccation or wastage. Furthermore, there is no liability resulting from irregular, incorrect or incomplete description or numbering of packages. Finally, there is no liability in respect of carriage of live animals and neither any liability for damage which could have been averted by an accompanying attendant if consignor and carrier had agreed that the goods would be accompanied by an attendant.

495. The burden of proof that loss or damage occurred during the carrier's period of responsibility is not particularly dealt with and rests, under the general rules of burden of proof, with the claimant. If the carrier wants to rely on the defences of Article 23 § 2 CIM, according to Article 25 (1) CIM he has to prove the respective facts. The burden of proof is reduced in respect of the defences under Article 23 § 3 CIM. According to Article 25 (2) CIM here the carrier only has to prove that the damage could have arisen for one or more of the special risks. Once this proof is brought, it is assumed that this actually was the cause but this assumption is not irrefutable. Rather the claimant has the possibility to prove that the loss or damage was not attributable to any of those risks. As regards proof of loss, Article 29 § 1 CIM provides that loss is assumed if the goods are not delivered within thirty days after the expiry of the transit periods. Transit periods are regulated in detail in Article 16 CIM. They are expressed in hours, the number of hours depending on the distance on which the goods had to be carried and the fact whether the cargo had been tendered as wagon-load consignment or as less than wagon-load consignment.

496. Liability for loss or damage is limited in various ways. First, the liability is limited to the market price of goods lost (Article 30 § 1 CIM). It is limited to a maximum of 17 SDR per kilogram (Article 30 § 2 CIM). Regarding wastage of goods, which by reason of their nature are generally subject to wastage and transit by the sole fact of carriage, the carrier is liable only to the extent that the wastage exceeds certain allowances, regardless of the length of the route. For liquid goods or goods consigned in a moist condition, this allowance is 2% of the mass, for dry goods it is 1%. In case of damage to goods the carrier is liable to compensate the loss and value of the goods (Article 32 CIM), liability for delay and delivery is limited to four times the carriage charge (Article 33 § 1 CIM). It is expressly stipulated that in case of total loss there is no additional liability for delay and delivery (Article 33 § 2 CIM).

497. Limitations of liability as described above are lost if it is proved that the loss or damage results from an act or omission of the carrier which he has committed either with intent to cause such loss or damage or recklessly and with knowledge that such loss or damage would probably result (Article 36 CIM).

§5. DOMESTIC CARRIAGE OF PASSENGERS AND BAGGAGE BY RAIL

498. German law regulates domestic rail carriage of passengers found in the *Eisenbahn-Verkehrsordnung* (EVO; German Rail Traffic Ordinance). But with Germany being an EU Member State, domestic rail carriage of passengers is primarily governed by the Regulation (EC) No. 1371/2007 of the European Parliament and the Council of 23 October 2007 on Rail Passengers' Rights and Obligations. Subject to any greater liability provided in national laws of EU members, in its Article 11 the Regulation effectively makes the provisions of the CIV on liability applicable to national transport within the EU. For details, please *see* therefore paragraphs 482 et seq.). The EVO does not provide for greater liabilities than the Regulation, so that the liability regime of the Regulation (which incorporates the liability regime of CIV) is conclusive and final.

A peculiarity only exists as regards carriage of baggage. For this § 25 EVO stipulates that a passenger can hand over his baggage for carriage, but that such baggage must be packed as required for carriage. § 26 EVO stipulates that the rail carrier is entitled to reject any baggage which is not sufficiently packed, which is unsuitable for carriage, which shows obvious signs of damage or which is not properly marked. If the rail carrier nevertheless accepts such baggage for transport, he may make respective remarks in the baggage document. If the passenger accepts a document containing such remark, he accepts the condition of the baggage as described in such document. As regards delivery of baggage handed over to the carrier for transport, § 29 EVO obliges the rail carrier only to delivery against any payment of any still unpaid costs.

§6. DOMESTIC CARRIAGE GOODS BY RAIL

499. As mentioned above (paragraph 411), the general transport law as contained in §§ 407 et seq. HGB also applies to carriage of goods by rail. There is, thus, no special law regarding liability for carriage of goods by rail anymore. For this reason paragraphs 413 et seq. is referred to.

Chapter 3. Inland Navigation

500. Prior to the general transport law reform, inland navigation was governed by the *Binnenschifffahrtsgesetz* (BSchG; Inland Navigation Act). This included very detailed rules on contracts for carriage of goods on inland waterways and lakes, which were governed by §§ 27–76 BSchG. Those provisions were repealed when the general transport law was reformed. The consequence is that since then the general transport law on carriage of goods as contained in §§ 407 et seq. HGB also applies to carriage of goods on inland waterways and lakes. Insofar reference is made to paragraphs 413 et seq.. But the provisions of the BSchG remain in force for all non-contractual aspects of inland navigation. As regards international inland waterway transport, Germany has ratified the Budapest Convention on the Contract for the Carriage of Goods by Inland Waterway of 26 May 2000 (CMNI) and the European Agreement concerning the International Carriage of Dangerous Goods by Inland Waterways of 26 May 2000 (ADN). In respect of limitation, the rules for international transport are contained in the Strasbourg Convention on the Limitation of Liability in Inland Navigation of 4 November 1988 (CLNI 1988), which Germany has ratified. Germany has also signed, but not yet ratified, the Strasbourg Convention of 2012 on the Limitation of Liability in Inland Navigation of 27 September 2012 (CLNI 2012), which is yet not in force. The national law on limitation of liability is contained in the BSchG.

§1. Carriage of Goods by Inland Waterways

I. River Craft: Definition

501. Just as the Commercial Code (HGB) does not contain any statutory definition of an (ocean-going) ship, neither do the HGB nor the BSchG contain a definition of a river craft. Widely in use is the definition developed by the Federal Court of Justice as broadened by the legal literature: a ship is a vehicle of not only negligible size, which contains a hollow space and has the purpose and capability to carry goods or passengers on or under the water. German courts will use this definition also for international inland navigation, because also the CMNI does not define the term ship. When it comes to limitation in international transport, Article 1 (2) of the Strasbourg Convention defines a ship to be an inland navigation vessel including hydrofoils, ferries and small craft, but not air-cushion vehicles. Also as ships shall be considered dredgers, cranes, elevators and all other floating and mobile appliances or plant of a similar nature. But this definition is more valuable to exclude or include certain craft, rather than giving a comprehensive definition of a ship.

II. Owner's Legal Liability

502. The owner of a vessel in navigation is, first of all, like any other person liable under the general German tort law. This is contained in the German *Bürgerliches Gesetzbuch* (BGB; Civil Code), which contains two basic provisions. According to § 823 BGB a person who, intentionally or negligently, unlawfully injures the life, body, health, freedom, property or another right of another person is liable to make compensation to the other party for the damage arising from this. § 831 BGB contains a provision for vicarious liability according to which a person using another person to perform a task is liable to make compensation for the damage that the other person unlawfully inflicts on a third party when carrying out the task. There is a possibility of exoneration by the principal showing that he exercised reasonable care when selecting the person employed and properly supervised.

But just as maritime law, also inland navigation law contains a further provision on statutory liability of the ship owner. This is contained in § 3 BSchG, which stipulates that the owner is liable for damage caused to a third party by the fault of a member of the ship's crew or a pilot on board in the course of exercising their tasks. Different from § 831 BGB, here the owner cannot escape liability by showing that he properly selected and supervised the crew.

III. Charter Parties and Carriage of Goods

503. As mentioned above, there does not exist any particular national law on carriage of goods by inland navigation anymore. Rather § 26 BSchG refers to the general transport law provisions contained in the *Handelsgesetzbuch* (HGB; Commercial Code), i.e., §§ 407 et seq. HGB. This is introduced in detail in paragraphs 413 et seq. § 27 BSchG then contains two references to the maritime law as contained in the Fifth book of the HGB. In § 27 (1) BSchG, refer to §§ 553–556 HGB as regards rent of an inland navigation vessel. These provisions are explained in paragraphs 186, 191 and 196. § 27 (2) BSchG contains a reference to the provisions on time charters in §§ 557–569 HGB, which are explained in paragraphs 190 and 195.

IV. Limitation of Liability

504. Limitation of liability of an owner of an inland navigation vessel is governed by §§ 4 et seq. BSchG. The provisions follow the structure of the CLNI Convention, so that for ease of reference the respective articles of the Convention are shown in brackets. § 4 (1) BSchG, Article 1 CLNI allow an owner to limit his liability for claims for damages in respect of injury and physical loss caused on board or in direct connection with the operation of the ship or with its salvage or wreck removal. Such claims are subject to limitation regardless of their legal basis, regardless whether they are of private or public law nature and regardless of whether they are pursued on basis of a contract or by way of an indemnity claim. Liability for wreck removal expenses is expressly subject to limitation, but the limitation right does not affect the right of a contractual wreck removal in respect of his contractual remuneration. Claims which are subject to remuneration and counter-claims of the owner against the claimant are set off against each other so that limitation only applies after set-off (§ 5a BSchG; Article 5 CLNI). Limitation is excluded if the damage is attributable to an act or omission of the owner himself, done with the intent to cause such damage or recklessly and with knowledge that such damage would probably result (§ 5b BSchG; Article 4 CLNI). The right to limit, thus, is not lost if a member of the ship's crew or any other employee or person engaged by the owner has caused the damage.

505. Limitation is effected by way of maximum liability for amounts dealt with in detail by § 5e–5k BSchG, Articles 6 and 7 CLNI. It can either be relied on by way of institution of a limitation fund in a contracting state of the CLNI Convention, or by way of a defence in proceedings pursued by the claimant (§ 5d (1) and (2) BSchG (Articles 10 and 11 CLNI)). If a fund is instituted, the institution, the limitation proceedings and the distribution of the fund will be subject to the provisions of the *Schifffahrtsrechtliche Verteilungsordnung* (SVertO; Shipping Law Limitation Procedure Ordinance). For details *see* paragraphs 174 et seq.

The limitation amounts depend on the one hand on the type of vessel, on the other hand on the kind of damage. According to § 5e BSchG, Article 6 (1) (a) CLNI the maximum amount for personal injuries are:

(1) Passenger Ships: 200 SDR per cubic meter water displacement at the highest permitted draft, in case of ships with own propulsion plus 700 SDR per kilowatt of the engine.
(2) Cargo ships: 200 SDR per ton deadweight, in case of ships with own propulsion plus 700 SDR per kilowatt of the engine.
(3) Tugs and pushing boats: 700 SDR per kilowatt of the engine. In case of a push boat which is, at the moment of the incident, connected to a push barge, the limitation amount is increased by a further 100 SDR per ton deadweight of the push barge. In turn, however, the maximum liability in such situation for the connected push barge is reduced by the same amount.
(4) Dredgers, cranes, elevators or other floating and movable installations: The value of such installation at the time of the incident.

The minimum limitation, however, is at least 200,000 SDR, unless it concerns barges which are exclusively used for transshipment in ports.

506. In case of personal injury of passengers who are carried by the ship on basis of a passage contract or in case of persons who attend, with the consent of the carrier, vehicles or live animals carried by the ship, according to § 5 k BSchG, Article 7 CLNI a separate limit of liability applies, which is only available to these persons. It amounts to 60,000 SDR, multiplied by the number of passengers which the ship is authorized to carry according to the ship's certificate. If there is no number of passengers which the ship is authorized to carry as prescribed in the ship certificate, then the number of passengers actually carried by the ship at the time of the occurrence is decisive. The limit of liability is at least 720,000 SDR and at the most 12 million SDR. The provisions in CLNI are more detailed and define in Article 7 (1) sublimits of maximum liabilities for different sized ships, namely max. 3 million SDR for ships of a carrying capacity of up to 100 passengers and 6 million SDR for ships of a passenger capacity of more than 100 and up to 200. The 12 million SDR as stipulated by the German law as maximum, applies under CLNI only for ships with a passenger capacity of more than 180.

507. The maximum liability for property damage amounts to half of the aforementioned maximum liabilities for personal injury § 5f BSchG, Article 7 (1) b) CLNI. Claims in respect of damage to harbour works, harbour basins, waterways, logs, bridges and aids to navigation have priority over all other claims for damage to property.

508. If the limit of liability calculated for personal injury is insufficient to pay the respective claims, the limit of liability for property damage is available for payment of the unpaid balance of personal injury claims. In such case the unpaid balances for personal injury claims have the same ranking as property claims. In such scenario, thus, there is no priority for claims in respect of harbour works, etc. (§ 5g BSchG (Article 7 (1) c) CLNI).

509. Under the German law a special limit exists for claims for damages caused by dangerous goods carried by the ship, which is not reflected in CLNI and, thus, does only apply to German national inland waterways transport. For such claims § 5h BSchG stipulates that there shall be a separate limitation of liability which is only available for satisfaction of this class of claims. Dangerous goods in this sense are all goods which are either completely banned from transport or which are allowed for transport under the conditions prescribed by the European agreement concerning international carriage of dangerous goods by inland waterways (AND) or by the *Gefahrgutverordnung Straße, Eisenbahn und Binnenschifffahrt* (GGVSEB; Dangerous Goods Ordinance on Road, Railway and Inland Navigation). The limitation of liability for all personal injury resulting from the same incident is three times the amount otherwise applicable for personal injury (*see* paragraph 505 above), but in any event not less than 5 million SDR. As regards property damage, also here limitation of liability for all property damage resulting from an incident is three times the amount otherwise applicable to property damage, and in no case less than 5 million SDR. Also here, claims in respect of damage to harbour works, etc. have priority. Similarly, if the limitation amount is not sufficient to cover all personal injury, the limit of liability for property damage is available for payment of the unpaid balance of claims, with such personal injury claims having the same rank as property claims, and without priority of claims for damage to harbour works, etc.

510. Special limits of liability apply for salvors and pilots onboard of an inland navigation ship. In respect of personal injury their maximum liability is 200,000 SDR and in respect of property damage 100,000 SDR (§ 5i BSchG). Article 6 (3) CLNI stipulates this in connection with Article 6 (1) (d) CLNI only for salvors, but not for pilots, who are not addressed in CLNI at all.

511. A special rule also exists in respect of limitation for claims of wreck removal. According to § 5j BSchG these claims are subject to a separate limitation amount which amounts to half of the amounts applicable to property damage. This limit of liability is available only for claims for wreck removal.

V. Towage and Pushing

512. Under national German law contractual towage and pushing of barges is considered as contractual carriage, which is subject to the general provisions of §§ 407 et seq. HGB. A carrier who damages barges towed or pushed is, thus liable to the barge owner on basis of § 425 HGB. This is different with international inland navigation which is subject to the provisions of CMNI (paragraph 516). Article 7 No. 1 CMNI stipulates that the term 'Goods' does not include either towed or pushed vessels.

513. If a pushboat and a barge, which is pushed by this boat, cause damage to third parties due to a nautical mistake by the pushboat master, it has been held by the German Federal Court that the owner of the pushboat and the barge pushed is liable also with his barge for damage caused by the pushboat master. As the reason the Court stated that despite performing his duty only on the pushboat, the pushboat master must be conserved as part of the crew of the barge as well, so that the barge owner would be liable for the master's nautical error according to § 3 BSchG. The Court did not have to decide whether this would be different if the barge and the pushboat were owned by different parties, but indicated that in such scenario the proper solution would be an analogous application of § 3 BSchG.

VI. General Average

514. In the past the Inland Navigation Act used to deal with general average in considerable detail in §§ 78–91 BSchG. After the Maritime Law Reform, the BSchG contains only two provisions of substance in § 78 (1) and (2) BSchG and otherwise refers in subsection 3 to the rules on general average in maritime law as contained in §§ 589–592, 594 and 595 HGB. Still being dealt with in the BSchG is a basic provision of what constitutes general average and how it works. § 78 (2) BSchG in this respect stipulates that if the ship, the fuel, the cargo or several of these items are intentionally damaged or voluntarily sacrificed upon the master's orders in order to preserve them from common peril, or if any expenses are incurred to this end upon the master's orders – this scenario is legally defined to be general average –, then the resulting damage, costs or expenses are to be borne jointly by the parties to the adventure. The parties to the adventure are largely the same in inland navigation as in maritime law to the extent that they are the owner of the ship and of the fuel. They are different as regards cargo and freight. In maritime law, it is the party at risk at the time of the general average incident (*see* paragraph 293 above), in inland navigation law it is the owner of the cargo and the party entitled to claimed freight, i.e., for all practical purposes the carrier.

The only other substantive provision in the BSchG is § 78 (2) which stipulates that the parties entitled to general average allowances shall have a lien on the ship according to §§ 102–115 BSchG.

For all other elements of general average please refer to paragraphs 275–283.

VII. Freight Market Regulation

515. The freight market in Germany is largely unregulated, freight can be freely negotiated between the shipper and the carrier. Only demurrage is dealt with in the *Verordnung über die Lade- und Löschzeiten sowie das Liegegeld in der Binnenschifffahrt* (BinSchLV; Ordinance on Loading and Discharging Times and Demurrage in Inland Navigation). This Ordinance is referred to in § 412 (4) HGB where the general transport law, which applies also to contracts of carriage by inland navigation, deals with loading and unloading and stipulates that the Federal Ministry of Justice and Consumer Protection is empowered to determine by regulation not only the prerequisites for the commencement and duration of laytime in time for discharge in inland navigation, but also for the amount of demurrage. The BinSchLV distinguishes between dry and liquid cargos. In both cases demurrage depends on the deadweight of the ship. In case of dry cargo it amounts to EUR 0.05 per ton deadweight (tdw) and each waiting hour commenced for ships of up to 1,500 tdw, and for larger ships EUR 75 plus EUR 0.02 for any ton dead weight in excess of 1,500 tdw. For liquid cargo, the demurrage differs between size and type of ships. For single hull ships it amounts to:

- EUR 25 for ships of up to 500 tdw.
- EUR 54 for ships between 500 and 1,000 tdw.
- EUR 75 for ships between 1,000 and 1,500 tdw.
- EUR 75 plus EUR 10 for each further commenced 500 t for ships of more than 1,500 tdw.

For double hull ships, the amounts are raised to:

- EUR 60 for ships of up to 500 tdw.
- EUR 80 for ships between 500 and 1,000 tdw.
- EUR 100 for ships between 100 and 1,500 tdw.
- EUR 100 plus EUR 20 for each commenced 500 t for ships beyond 1,500 tdw.

§2. International Inland Navigation, Treaty Law

516. As referred to above, Germany has ratified the Budapest Convention on the Contract for the Carriage of Goods by Inland Waterway of 26 May 2000 (CMNI) as well as the Strasbourg Convention on the Limitation of Liability in Inland Navigation of 4 November 1988 (CLNI 1988) and the ADN. Germany has also signed, but not yet ratified the Strasbourg convention of 2012 on the limitation of liability and inland navigation of 27 September 2012 (CLNI 2012), which is not yet in force.

I. Budapest Convention on the Contract for the Carriage of Goods by Inland Waterway of 26 May 2000 (CMNI)

517. Liability for damage to cargo in an international inland waterway transport is covered by CMNI. While the German inland navigation law on contract of carriage is now subject to the general transport law as contained in §§ 407 et seq. HGB and, thus, only contains very few provisions special for carriage with a ship, CMNI is a typical shipping convention. According to Article 2 it is applicable to any contract of carriage according to which the port of loading or the place of taking over of the goods and the port of discharge or the place of delivery of the goods are located in two different states, of which at least one is a state party to CMNI. As carriage on inland waterways is not necessarily limited to inland waterways, but may, without transshipment, take place both on inland waterways and on waters to which maritime regulations apply, a provision is necessary to delineate maritime law from inland waterways law. This is done by Article 2 (2) CMNI which stipulates that CMNI is applicable in such cases unless a maritime bill of lading has been issued in accordance with the applicable maritime law or the distance to be travelled in waters to which maritime regulations apply is the greater.

518. CMNI places obligations on the shipper in Article 6 which includes furnishing the carrier particulars concerning the goods, including dimensions, number or weight and stowage factor of the goods, marks, nature, characteristics and property of the goods. This is fairly comparable with § 408 HGB which deals with the respective information in the context of the issuing of a consignment note. Dangerous goods are separately dealt with in Article 7 CMNI where it is stipulated that if dangerous or polluting goods are to be carried, the shipper shall inform the carrier clearly and in writing of the danger and the risks of pollution inherent to the goods and of the precautions to be taken. This is very similar to § 410 HGB. Article 8 CMNI goes on to stipulate a no-fault liability of the shipper in respect of all damages and costs incurred by the carrier in respect of the information referred to above. This is comparable to § 414 HGB. Under both provisions there is no limit for this no-fault liability of the shipper. But the Convention and the national law handle the question whether limitation may be agreed contractually differently. While Article 25 CMNI which deals with the mandatory application of the Convention only prohibits contractual agreements which exclude, limit or increase the carrier's liability and do not at all address agreements on the shipper's liability, § 449 (1) HGB generally declares also the shipper's liability according to § 414 HGB mandatory, but allows in subsection (2) that the liability may be limited, even by standard contract terms. Despite the different technique, thus, both the Convention and the national law allow agreements on limitation of the shipper's liability.

519. As regards the carrier's liability, this is regulated in Article 16 CMNI and provides that the carrier shall be liable for loss resulting from loss or damage to the goods caused between the time when he took them over for carriage and the time of their delivery, or resulting from delay in delivery. It differs from §§ 425, 426 HGB in respect of the standard of care. While under national law the inland navigation carrier is released from liability only if loss or damage could not be avoided even by exercising the utmost diligence and if he was unable to prevent the consequence – a standard of care well beyond due diligence (*see* paragraph 449 above) –, under Article 16 (1) CMNI he only has to show that the loss was due to circumstances which a diligent carrier could not have prevented and the consequence of which he could not have averted. Most noteworthy, Article 16 (2) CMNI leaves liability for loss or damage before loading or after discharging to national law. If German law applies, this means that different standards of care are applicable to an inland navigation carrier. Until loading and after discharge he has to exercise utmost diligence according to § 426 HBG, while from loading until discharge he only has to act like a diligent carrier.

520. The CMNI contains in Article 18 special exonerations from liability. They are generally comparable with the German national as contained in § 427 HGB but contain one additional exoneration, namely in respect of loss, damage or delay caused in the course of rescue or salvage operations or attempted rescue or salvage operations on inland waterways (Article 18 (1) (g) CMNI).

Like the German national law, CMNI does not contain an exclusion for error in navigation or fire. But Article 25 (2) CMNI allows contractual stipulations according to which the carrier shall not be liable for losses for acts or omissions by the master, the pilot or any other person in the service of the vessel during navigation and for losses arising from fire or explosion on board of the vessel. German national law does not allow such contractual stipulations so that according to § 449 HGB the carrier is liable for error in navigation and for fire. Article 25 (2) CMNI is somewhat similar to § 512 HGB which contains the German maritime law. As explained above (paragraphs 210 et seq.) also in German maritime law there is no statutory exemption for error in navigation and fire, but such exemptions may be contractually agreed, even by way of standard contract terms. But there remains a difference between Article 25 CMNI and § 512 HGB. In German national maritime law the carrier is not liable for error in navigation even if the act or omission of the master or other crew member resulted from their intention to cause damage or from their reckless conduct with the knowledge that such damage would probably result. Article 25 (2) CMNI does not allow to exclude liability in these scenarios. As regards fire, German national maritime law allows to exclude liability for fault or neglect of his servants or crew members in respect of loss or damage resulting from fire or explosion on board of the ship. While Article 25 (2) (b) CMNI, like German maritime law, allows exclusion of liability where it is not possible to prove that the fire or explosion resulted from a fault of the carrier (this is identical to § 512 which anyhow refers to a carrier's servants and crew members only), it does not allow and exclusion of liability in case of fault of the carrier's servants or agents or in case of a defect of the vessel. Under CMNI, thus, a contractual agreement to exclude liability for fire or explosion is not allowed in case of negligence of servants, and not even in case of a defective ship, even if there was no fault of the carrier in respect of such defect.

521. Comparable with § 429 HGB in national German transport law, also under CMNI compensation is based upon the value of the goods lost or damaged. Different from § 429 HGB, but in line with § 502 HGB for maritime transport, the decisive value is the value at the place and on the date of delivery. § 429 HGB insofar refers to the place and time the goods were taken over for carriage.

522. The close relationship between CMNI and traditional maritime conventions, in particular the Hague-Visby Rules, is also visible in the stipulations on maximum limits of liability in Article 20. Here it is said that the carrier shall under no circumstances be liable for amounts exceeding 666,67 SDR per package or any other shipping unit, or 2 SDR per kg of goods lost or damaged, whichever is the higher. Under German national law, § 431 stipulates a maximum liability of 8.33 SDR per kg. There is no alternative limitation per package or unit. One cannot generally say that the carrier is exposed to a higher liability under German national law. If a huge number of units, each having high value but little weight only, is damaged, the unit-based limit of liability, which multiplies every unit with 666,67 SDR, will be considerably higher when multiplying the little weight of the total consignment with 8.33 SDR per kg.

But CLNI contains one particular feature of limitation on containers which finds no counterpart in the German national law. Article 20 (1) CMNI says that if the package or other shipping unit is a container and if there is no mention in the transport document of any package or shipping unit consolidated in the container, the limitation amount shall not be calculated on basis of 666,67 SDR, by the amount of 1,500 SDR for the container without the goods it contains and, in addition, the amount of 25,000 units of account for the goods which are in the container.

523. The standards for the loss of the right to limit liability are, in principle, the same as under German national law. The carrier is not entitled to rely on exonerations or limits of liability provided for in CMNI or on a contract of carriage if it is proved that the damage was caused by an act or omission, either with the intent to cause such damage or recklessly and with the knowledge that such damage would probably result. This is the same test as in § 435 HGB. But CMNI also proves here the proximity to the Hague-Visby Rules by stipulating that the carrier loses his right only if he himself has caused damage in such a way. Under German national law any intent or recklessness by servants or other persons made use of for the carriage of goods is attributed to the carrier (*see* paragraph 466 above).

II. Strasbourg Convention on the Limitation of Liability in Inland Navigation of 4 November 1988 (CLNI 1988)

524. As mentioned above, the German national law on limitation of liability for owners of navigation vessels is largely modelled after the Strasbourg Convention. For details *see* paragraphs 500–511.

Chapter 4. Air Transport

§1. Introduction

525. Under national German law, carriage of cargo on the one hand and carriage of passengers and their baggage on the other hand are regulated by different acts. As mentioned above in paragraph 411, carriage of cargo by air is subject to the German general transport law as contained in §§ 407 et seq. of the *Handelsgesetzbuch* (HGB; Commercial Code). Carriage of passengers and their baggage, against that, is subject to the provisions of the *Luftverkehrsgesetz* (LuftVG; Air Traffic Act). The LuftVG also contains provisions on the non-contractual liability of the air carrier to its third parties. As regards international transport, Germany has ratified the Montreal Convention which covers carriage of cargo as well as of passengers and their baggage.

§2. German National Law

I. Carriage of Cargo by Air

526. As regards carriage of cargo by air, this is subject to the general provisions of §§ 407 et seq. HGB which apply according to § 407 (3) HGB whenever the goods are carried, *inter alia*, by aircraft. The HGB does not contain a definition on aircraft, but it is settled that the definition contained in § 1 (2) LuftVG applies also for carriage under HGB. It includes any mode currently used for the carriage of cargo or passenger, including helicopters, airships and gliders, regardless of whether they are manned or unmanned. Drones, thus, qualify as aircraft under German law and carriage of cargo by drones is subject to the provisions on general transport law as contained in the HGB. For details on this law please refer to paragraphs 413–463.

II. Carriage of Passengers and Their Baggage by Air

527. National law on carriage of passengers and their baggage is contained in the Air Traffic Act (LuftVG). Those provisions are of a limited relevance. According to Article 44 LuftVG they only apply (a) to national air transport and (b) unless Council Regulation (EC) No. 2027/97 of 9 October 1997 on Air Carrier Liability in the Event of Accidents, as amended by Regulation (EC) No. 889/2002 of the European Parliament and of the Council of 13 May 2002 does not apply. According to Article 3 of the Regulation it applies to community air carriers, which are defined in Article 2 (b) of the regulation as air carriers with a valid operating licence granted by a Member State in accordance with the provisions of Regulation (EEC) No. 2407/92, and for those carriers the application of the Montreal Convention is declared. As a consequence, national air transport is subject to the Montreal Convention, if the carriage is performed by a carrier with an EU operating license. This leaves room for application of the national air carriage law as contained in the LuftVG only in the following cases: (a) the carriage is performed by carrier licensed outside the EU, or (b) the Montreal Convention does not apply for other reasons than their territorial scope. As the Montreal Convention applies also to gratuitous carriage (Article 1 (1) of the Convention), this leaves essentially only air carriage by others than air transport undertakings, which actually leads to air carriage by private persons. The most relevant aspect of air carriage, however, is that of commercial carriage of passengers. As explained, this is subject to the Montreal Convention even for national transport. The liability regime of the Montreal Convention is explained in more detail in paragraphs 543–563.

528. The provisions on liability are contained in the second sub-chapter of the second chapter of the LuftVG in §§ 44–51. The basic liability provision is § 45 LuftVG. It provides for a no-fault liability and stipulates that the air carrier is liable to indemnify a passenger for damage suffered due to an accident on board an aircraft or during boarding on or leaving of an aircraft. This liability is in principle unlimited. For two scenarios, however, subsection 2 provides for a limitation per passenger of 113,100 SDR: either the damage was not caused by an illegal and at least negligent act or omission of the carrier or his servants, or it was exclusively caused by the illegal and at least negligent act or omission of a third party. While subsection 2 creates the impression that the limit of 113,100 SDR is available for each passenger, according to subsection 3 this is not the case. If more than one passenger suffers a personal injury, all claims of all passengers injured are added up and each claimant only receives pro rata that part of the 113,100 SDR which represents his share of the total amount of damages.

529. If delay occurs in carriage of a passenger, the carrier has to indemnify the passenger for all losses resulting therefrom, but subject to a limit of 4,694 SDR per passenger. For two scenarios there exist alterations, one leading to a full liability, the other to a total exclusion of liability. The limit does not apply with the consequence of full liability of the carrier, if the damage was caused by the carrier or his servants either with intent or with gross negligence. Liability is completely excluded if the carrier and his servants have taken all reasonable measures to avoid the loss or have not been able to take such measures at all.

530. Damage to baggage is regulated very detailed in § 47 LuftVG. The law distinguishes between baggage which is checked in and baggage which the passenger carries with him. As regards checked baggage, the carrier is liable for loss of all damage if the damage occurs on board of the aircraft or otherwise in the carrier's custody, unless the damage was caused by the nature of the baggage or its inherent vice. If checked baggage is delayed, the carrier is obliged to indemnify the passenger for resulting losses, unless the carrier and his servants have taken all reasonable measures to avoid the damage by not have been able to take such measures.

As regards baggage which was not checked in but which the passenger has taken with him into the cabin, the carrier is liable for loss or damage only if this loss or damage was caused at least negligently by the carrier or his servants.

For both classes of baggage, liability is limited to 1,131 SDR per passenger, but liability is unlimited if the damage was caused by the carrier or his servants with intent or gross negligence.

531. Finally, § 47 (6) and (7) LuftVG contain time limits for notification of damage and provide for consequences if no timely notification was made. In case of damage to checked baggage or delay in its delivery, claims can only be raised if the passenger gives written notice to the carrier without undue delay after it has been detected, in case of damage to baggage latest within seven days after delivery, in case of delayed delivery latest within twenty-one days after the passenger had received the baggage. None of this applies if the carrier has acted deliberately. Acceptance of damaged baggage does not lead to a loss of the right to claim damages but it leads to a legal assumption that it had been delivered without damage. Such damage is refutable so that the passenger can bring proof of damage prior to delivery to him.

In case of the loss of checked baggage, claims can only be pursued once the carrier has acknowledged the loss or once twenty-eight days have expired since the day on which the baggage should have arrived.

532. Like § 434 HGB in general transport law, § 48 LuftVG contains provisions to secure that the limitations of liability as contained in the LuftVG do not only apply to contractual claims against the carrier but to any other legal basis. It is expressly stipulated that in principle third parties remain fully liable under the law applicable to them, but that servants of the carrier who have acted in execution of their obligations can rely on the requirements for and limitations of liability under the LuftVG. It is further provided that if the carrier and servants are both liable, their joint liability is limitation amounts apply to their joint liability, so that the amounts are available only once.

533. The LuftVG also contains provisions on cases where more than one carrier is involved in the carriage. The law distinguishes two different situations: the involvement of more than one carrier without one contract covering the whole of the carriage and the involvement of more than one carrier under one contract of carriage. The first situation is dealt with in § 48a LuftVG. Here the law distinguishes between personal injury and loss of or damage to baggage. If the carriage of a passenger is performed by successive carriers and if during such carriage the passenger is either killed, injured or his carriage delayed, only that carrier is liable for damages which has carried out the part of the carriage in the course of which the accident or the delay occurred, unless the first carrier has accepted full liability for the complete carriage. As regards loss of or damage to baggage or delay in its delivery in case of involvement of successive carriers, the first carrier, the last carrier and that carrier are liable during which the loss, damage or delay occurred. All these carriers are liable jointly and severally.

534. When in the course of the general transport law reform the concept of actual carrier was introduced in the Commercial Code, also the LuftVG was amended. § 48b LuftVG now provides that the actual carrier is jointly and severally liable with the contractual carrier, but only for damage which is caused on that part of the overall carriage which he performs. It is well in line with the general principles in the HGB (§ 428 HGB) that the contractual carrier is liable for acts or omissions of the actual carrier and the actual carrier's servants. However, § 48b (3) LuftVG contains a very peculiar rule, alien to any other German transport law, which stipulates that the actual carrier is also liable for acts or omissions of the contractual carrier and his servants. The provision is modelled after Article 41 (2) Montreal Convention. Also like under the Montreal Convention this liability is limited to the amounts stipulated in §§ 45–47 LuftVG (*see* above paragraphs 528–529). As a consequence, the contractual carrier may be liable without limitation if the respective requirements under §§ 45–47 LuftVG are given, but the actual carrier in any case is liable only within the statutory limits.

535. Claims for damages must be pursued within a period of two years, commencing with the day on which the aircraft reached its designated place of arrival or on which it should have reached this place or on which further carriage was given up. If this period expires, claims are extinguished.

536. If the air carriage is performed either against remuneration or as part of a business, the carrier's liability is mandatory and cannot be excluded or limited in advance. Any agreement to the contrary is null and void, but the remainder of the contract remains valid.

537. According to § 50 LuftVG the carrier is obliged to take out liability insurance for damage he is liable for. This applies to contractual carriers as well as to actual carriers. The minimum cover limits are provided in the fifth chapter of the *Luftverkehrszulassungsordnung* (LuftVZO; Air Traffic Licensing Ordinance). § 103 LuftVZO stipulates a minimum amount of 250,000 SDR per person for death and personal injury. The liability insurance for damage to cargo is that within § 104 LuftVZO. If the liability is subject to the Montreal Convention (*see* paragraphs 543 et seq. below), the liability insurance must cover liabilities under the Montreal Convention. The minimum cover limit must be 19 SDR per kg cargo carried if the carrier operates the aircraft himself. If the carrier does neither operate nor steer the aircraft, the minimum limit is EUR 600,000 per incident. An annual aggregate for liability under the insurance policy may be agreed. This must at least be twice the statutory minimum amounts.

III. Non-contractual Liability of the Air Carrier

538. First of all, the air carrier, like any other person, is liable for death or personal injury or damage to things under the general German tort law according to § 823 *Bürgerliches Gesetzbuch* (BGB; Civil Code). § 831 BGB contains a provision for vicarious liability according to which a person using another person to perform a task is liable to make compensation for the damage that the other person unlawfully inflicts on a third party when carrying out the task. There is a possibility of exoneration by the principal showing that he exercised reasonable care when selecting the person employed and properly supervised.

But just like maritime law and inland navigation law, also air transport law contains a special provision on non-contractual liability. § 33 LuftVG stipulates the liability of the keeper of an aircraft to indemnify damage caused by death or personal injury of a person or damage to property. § 62 No. 7 LuftVZO defines who is the keeper of an aircraft: The person who has the unrestricted power of control required to operate an aircraft.

The liability is a no-fault liability. There exist no exclusions from liability, but § 34 LuftVG declares § 254 Civil Code (BGB) applicable if behaviour of the injured person has contributed to the occurrence of the damage. In case of damage to property it is clarified that it is not the behaviour of the owner of such property which is of relevance, but the behaviour of such person who has the actual control of the property. By reference to § 254 BGB claims against the carrier can be reduced on basis of contributory causation of the injured party.

539. The no-fault liability is a limited liability only. According to § 37 LuftVG the maximum amount of liability depends on the gross take-off mass of the aircraft. It amounts to:

- 0,750,000 SDR for up to 500 kg.
- 1.5 million SDR for up to 1,000 kg.
- 3 million SDR for up to 2,700 kg.
- 7 million SDR for up to 6,000 kg.
- 18 million SDR for up to 12,000 kg.
- 80 million SDR for up to 25,000 kg.
- 150 million SDR for up to 50,000 kg.
- 300 million SDR for up to 200,000 kg.
- 500 million SDR for up to 500,000 kg.
- 700 million SDR in excess of 500,000 kg.

Within those limits there is a limit of EUR 600,000 or EUR 36,000 for an annuity in case of personal injury. If both personal injury and physical damage were caused, two thirds of the abovementioned maximum amounts are reserved for personal injury, the remaining one third for property damage. If more than one person is entitled to damages and if the amounts they are each entitled to in combination exceed the abovementioned maximum amounts, the available maximum amount is distributed to all claimants pro rata their claim. But also here two thirds of the maximum amount are reserved for personal injury.

540. If damage was caused by more than one aircraft, each keeper of the aircrafts involved will be liable with respective maximum amount for his aircraft. Internally, as between the keepers of the aircrafts involved, damage is allocated pro rate their contributory causation of the incident.

541. Claimants have to notify their claims within three months after they obtained knowledge of the liable person. If claims are not notified in such way, the right to claim damages is extinguished.

542. The LuftVG does not provide for unlimited liability. Even in case of gross negligence and intent of the keeper of an aircraft, liability under § 33 LuftVG remains limited to the amounts stipulated in § 37 LuftVG. But this does not mean that the keeper of the aircraft in the end will only be liable for limited amounts. § 42 LuftVG expressly stipulates that liability under other provisions of federal law remains unaffected. In case of fault, thus, the keeper of an aircraft will be liable for damages according to § 823 BGB without any limitation.

§3. The Montreal Convention

543. Germany has ratified the Montreal Convention and amended its national law in many ways to bring national aviation law in line or at least close to what the Montreal Convention provides. Apart from that, Article 3 of Regulation No. 2027/97, as amended by Regulation No. 889/2002, extends the application of the Montreal Convention also to national transport by EU licensed carriers within the EU as regards carriage of passengers and their baggage.

I. Scope of Application

544. The Montreal Convention applies to all international carriage of passengers, baggage or cargo for reward. In case of such reward, it is irrelevant whether the carriage is performed by an air transport undertaking or by a private person. But reward is not necessarily required for the application of the Convention. It applies equally to gratuitous carriage if such carriage is performed by an air transport undertaking.

II. The Ticket and the Air Waybill

545. The Montreal Convention deals with documentation for carriage in Articles 3–11. What is commonly referred to as the ticket for carriage of passengers, is addressed under Article 3 as an individual or collective document of carriage. The ticket is to be issued by the carrier and shall mention the places of departure and destination and the fact that the carriage is subject to the provisions of the Convention which may limit the liability of the carrier in respect of death or injury and for destruction or loss of or damage to baggage and for delay. As regards baggage, the carrier has to provide the passenger with a baggage identification tag for each piece of checked baggage.

546. In respect of cargo, Article 4 provides for delivery of an air waybill or a cargo receipt which according to Article 5 shall name the places of departure and destination and the weight of the cargo. Different from national German transport law, the Montreal Convention does not require that the air waybill contains details on dimensions, packing, quantity, volume or condition of the cargo. Usually, however, such information is entered in the waybill because this can be of evidentiary value according to Article 11 (*see* paragraph 547 below). According to Article 7 it is not the carrier, but the consignor who issues the waybill in three originals. The first original is to be marked 'for the carrier' and is signed by the consignor. The second is marked 'for the consignee' and is signed by both the consignor and the carrier. The third original is signed by the carrier for handing over to the consignor after the cargo has been accepted.

547. According to Article 11 the air waybill or the cargo receipt does not only provide prima facie evidence on the conclusion of the contract, the acceptance of the cargo and the conditions of the carriage mentioned in the waybill or cargo receipt, but Article 11 (2) contains detailed rules on further evidentiary value and thereby distinguishes between statements relating to the weight, dimensions and packing of the cargo as well as number of packages on one hand and statements in respect of quantity, volume and condition of the cargo on the other hand. In respect of the first group, statements in the air waybill provide prima facie evidence. Any party relying on such statements, thus, can bring proof simply on basis of the air waybill. Such evidence, however, is not conclusive, but a party denying the correctness of the statements bears the burden of proof in this respect. In respect of the second group of statements, Article 11 (2) stipulates that only a statement in respect of the apparent condition of the cargo constitutes evidence against the carrier. In all other respects (quantity and volume) the air waybill constitutes evidence only if both have been checked by the carrier in the presence of the consignor and if this is stated so in the air waybill.

III. Liability in Case of Carriage of Passengers or Baggage

548. Basic provision is Article 17, stipulating the liability of the carrier. Exoneration is dealt with in Article 20 and limitation of liability in Article 21.

The carrier's liability for death and injury of passengers as per Article 17 is a no-fault liability and requires only that the accident which caused the death or injury took place on board of an aircraft or during embarking or disembarking of the aircraft. As regards loss of or damage to baggage, the Convention distinguishes between checked and unchecked baggage. For checked baggage, Article 17 (2) provides for a no-fault liability of the carrier for any loss or damage taking place on board of the aircraft or during any period within which the checked baggage was in the charge of the carrier. There is no liability, however, for damage caused by inherent defect, quality or vice of the checked baggage. As regards unchecked baggage, the liability is not a no-fault liability but the carrier is liable only if the damage resulted from his own fault or the fault of his servants or agents.

549. Exoneration from liability by Article 20 of the Convention is limited to causation or contribution of the damage by negligence or other wrongful act or omission of the passenger or those claiming for the loss of life of a passenger. If such negligence or wrongful act or omission has only contributed to the damage, the carrier is partly exonerated to the extent that such negligence or wrongful act or omission has contributed to the damage.

For damage up to 113,100 SDR per passenger there is no further possibility for the carrier to escape liability, In contrast, to the extent that damage per passenger exceeds 113,100 SDR, according to Article 21 (2) the carrier is not liable if he proves that such damage was not due to his own negligence or other wrongful act or omission or due to negligence or wrongful acts or omissions of his servants or agents. Neither is the carrier liable for damage in excess of 113,100 SDR if he proves that such damage was solely caused by negligence or by another wrongful act or omission of a third party. Two aspects deserve underlining: The possibilities of exoneration only apply to damage in excess of 113,100 SDR. This means that also in case where the damage per passenger exceeds 113,100 SDR, for the first part of the damage up to 113,100 SDR no exoneration is possible. Secondly, causation by a third party is only of relevance if only such third party has caused the damage. Contribution by negligence of the carrier or his servants or agents eliminates this possibility of exoneration.

550. The carrier's liability in respect of baggage, regardless of whether checked or unchecked (Articles 22 (2), 17 (4) of the Convention), the carrier's liability for loss or damage is limited to 1,131 SDR per passenger unless the passenger has declared a higher value and, as applicable, has paid an additional supplementary sum. The limitation to 1,131 SDR per passenger does not apply in case of intent or recklessness with knowledge that damage would probably result from the carrier or his servants or agents if they acted within the scope of their employment (Article 22 (5) of the Convention).

IV. Liability in Case of Carriage of Goods

551. The Convention deals with damage to cargo in Articles 18, 20 and 22. Article 18 (1) provides for a no-fault liability for loss or damage and requires only that the event which has caused the damage took place during the carriage by air, which according to Article 18 (3) does not only mean the time during which the cargo is in an aircraft, even less only the time when the aircraft is in the air, but the period during which the cargo is in the charge of the carrier. Article 18 (4) contains detailed rules to delineate Convention liability. It is expressly stated that the period of carriage by air does not extend to carriage by land, by sea, or by inland waterway, even if in the charge of the carrier, if this is performed outside an airport. However, if such mentioned carriage is performed as part of a contract of carriage by air for the purpose of loading, delivery or transship, there is a legal presumption, subject to proof of the contrary, that the damage was caused during the period of carriage by air. It is then on the carrier to prove that the damage occurred outside of an airport. The application of the Convention is extended even further if a carrier, contrary to the agreed carriage by air, performs carriage by another mode of transport without the consent of the consignor. Such practice is rather widespread because to an air carrier it may seem more economical to carry smaller parcels of cargo on the first or last leg of a transport by truck rather than aircraft. Article 18 (4) stipulates for such situation that regardless of the transport mode, such carriage is deemed to be carriage by air with the consequence that the Convention applies in respect of damage to the cargo.

552. The carrier has various possibilities of exoneration from liability. According to Article 18 (2) he is not liable to the extent he proves that the damage resulted from inherent defect, quality or vice of the cargo, from defective packing if the carriage was performed by a person other than the carrier or its servants or agents, from an act of war or an armed conflict or from an act of public authority. Apart from that, in respect of damage to cargo, the carrier is exonerated by Article 20 in the same way as he is exonerated in respect of personal injury: There is no liability of the carrier for damage to cargo to the extent that he proves that the damage was caused by negligence or a wrongful act or omission by the claimant.

553. If the carrier is liable and not exonerated from liability, his liability for loss of or damage to cargo is limited to 19 SDR as per Article 22 (3) of the Convention. This limitation is unbreakable. Even in case of recklessness of the carrier with knowledge that damage will probably result and even in case of intent to cause damage the carrier is not liable for more than 19 SDR per kg. There has been a discussion in Germany whether such a legal stipulation would be in breach of the ownership guarantee as contained in Article 14 of the German Constitution, under which the state is obliged to protect property of the owner. The way out has been a reference to the possibility to contract out of Article 22 of the Convention so that limitation can be broken in case of intent or recklessness. Should there be any monopoly situations which, as a matter of fact, do not give the cargo owner a realistic chance for contractual unlimited liability, it has been suggested to treat the unconditional limited liability as in contradiction with German public policy and to allow unlimited tort claims under § 826 of the German Civil Code.

V. Liability for Delay

554. The carrier is liable for damage caused by delay in the air carriage of passengers and their baggage as well as cargo. Different from liability for personal injury and loss or damage, however, the carrier can avoid liability by proving that he and his servants and agents took all measures reasonably required to avoid the damage, or by proving that it was impossible for him to take such measures (Article 19). If the carrier is liable, his liability is limited in respect of each passenger to 4,694 SDR (Article 22 (1)). If the carriage of baggage is delayed, liability is limited to 1,131 SDR per passenger (Article 22 (2)). The carrier's liability is unlimited if the damage resulted from an act or omission of the carrier or his servants or his agents done with the intent to cause damage or done recklessly and with knowledge that damage would probably result (Article 22 (5)).

VI. Liability of the Consignor

555. The liability of the consignor is linked to the correctness of particulars and statements he has made, either by way of inserting them in the airway bill or in any other way. The liability, which is laid down in Article 10 (2) of the Convention, does not require any fault of the consignor and is unlimited.

VII. Successive and Actual Carriers and Combined Transport

556. Successive carriage and combined carriage can occur in one and the same transport, but they do not necessarily have to. Successive carriers require that more than one carrier accepts passengers, baggage or cargo. Article 1 (3) of the Convention, which generally deals with the scope of application of the Convention as such stipulates that if the carriage is to be performed by several successive carriers, then such carriage is treated as one undivided carriage if it has been regarded by the parties as a single operation. This is regardless of whether a single contract or a series of contracts has been entered into. Once this is given, according to Article 36 each carrier is deemed to be a party to the contract of carriage in respect of that part of the carriage which he carries out or supervises. The rights of the injured party depend on whether claims for personal injury or claims for loss of or damage to baggage or cargo are pursued. In the first case, the claimant generally can only pursue claims against the carrier who performed that part of the voyage during which the accident or the delay occurred. Claims against the first carrier are only possible if the first carrier, by agreement, has assumed liability for the whole of the carriage (Article 36 (2)). The claimant has more options in respect of baggage and cargo. If loss or damage is caused or if delivery is delayed, according to Article 36 (3) the claimant can pursue his claims against the first carrier, the last carrier or the carrier who performed that part of the transport during which loss, damage or delay occurred.

557. An actual carrier, which the Convention deals with in great detail in Articles 39–48, is given if the person who has entered into the contract of carriage with the passenger or cargo owner – defined by Article 39 as 'contractual carrier'– engages another carrier for performing whole or part of the carriage. This other carrier then is defined as 'actual carrier'. Article 39 requires an authority by the contracting carrier for the actual carrier, but at the same time presumes such an authority.

If an actual carrier is involved in the carriage, he and the contractual carrier have a joint liability. The contractual carrier's liability then is for the whole of the carriage, the actual carrier's liability is limited to the part of the carriage he performs. To the benefit of the claimant, Article 41 stipulates that act and omissions of the actual carrier and of its servants and agents are deemed to be also acts or omissions of the contracting carrier. This is in line with the German general transport law, which contains a similar provision in § 428 HGB. Article 41 (2) of the Convention, however, contains a provision which, vice versa, makes the actual carrier responsible also for acts or omissions of the contractual carrier or his servants or agents although only in respect of the part of the carriage performed by the actual carrier. Such a provision is alien to German national law, under which generally only acts or omissions of an agent or a subcontractor are attributed to the principal or the head contractor, but not the other way round.

As regards the joint liability, Article 44 secures that the involvement of an actual carrier and the liability of both the contractual and the actual carrier do not lead to a doubling of the maximum liability. The amount recoverable for the claimant shall not exceed the highest amount which could be awarded either against the contracting carrier or the actual carrier. As regards the proper addressee of claims, § 45 stipulates that the claimant has the option of pursuing his claims either against the contractual or against the actual carrier or against both. If he decides to pursue his claims only against one of them, this carrier has to right to require that the other carrier be joined in the proceedings.

558. While successive carriage according to Articles 1 (3), 36 of the Convention presupposes that the successive carriers are all air carriers, combined carriage as dealt with in Article 38 does not deal with the involvement of more than one carrier but with the involvement of different modes of transport. If carriage by air is combined with carriage by any other mode of transport, Article 38 of the Convention declares the Convention applicable, but only to that part of the carriage which is performed by air. The only exception to this rule is Article 18 (4), which has been explained in more detail above (paragraph 551). If the carrier, in breach of the contract, performs (all or a part of) the carriage by other modes of transport than by aircraft, the Convention also applies to the carriage with such other modes of transport.

VIII. Time Limits

559. The Convention deals with time limits in two provisions. Article 31 deals with notice of complaints and applies only in respect of baggage or cargo. If the complaints are not made within the times stipulated by Article 31 (2) (seven days from the date of receipt in case of checked baggage, fourteen days from the date of receipt in case of cargo; in respect of delay twenty-one days from the date baggage or cage have been made available), then the claim for damage is extinguished. If this happens, the exclusion period dealt with in Article 35 of the Convention is of no more relevance because exclusion according to Article 35 is only possible in respect of claims which have not already been extinguished due to the lack of timely notice of complaint. Article 35, thus, only applies to claims in respect of baggage and cargo which have been properly notified and in respect of personal injury to passengers. It stipulates that the right to damages is extinguished if an action is not brought within a period of two years. This period commences at the date of arrival at the destination or at the date at which the aircraft ought to have arrived or at the date at which the carriage stopped. The method of calculating this period is left to the law of the court which determines the case.

IX. Jurisdiction of Courts, Procedure and Arbitration

560. The Montreal Convention contains various provisions on jurisdiction. With Germany being an EU member, European law generally confines Germany to the provisions contained in the Regulation (EU) No. 1215/2012 of the European Parliament and of the Counsel of 12 December 2012 on Jurisdiction and the Recognition and Enforcement of Judgments in Civil and Commercial Matters, the so-called Brussels 1a Regulation. International conventions to which EU Member States have acceded may have provisions and jurisdictions which differ from the Brussels 1a Regulation. The Regulation takes this into account and stipulates in Article 71 that it shall not affect any convention to which EU Member States are parties and which govern jurisdiction. The provisions on jurisdiction in the Montreal Convention are, thus, also applicable to Germany.

561. Article 33 finally stipulates which courts have jurisdiction for claims under the Convention. The general rules as per Article 33 provide for four options for all actions for damages: (a) the courts of the domicile of the carrier, (b) the courts of the carrier's principal place of business, (c) the courts where the carrier has a place of business through which the contract had been made or (d) the courts at the place of destination. There are more options on jurisdiction in respect of damage for death or personal injury of a passenger. According to Article 33 (2), the injured passenger or his descendants, over and above the options (a) to (d) can also commence an action against the carrier in the courts of the state party (e) in which at the time of the accident the passenger had his principal or permanent residence if the following requirements are fulfilled: (a) The carrier must operate to or from the territory of that state party, (b) either with his own aircraft or other carriers' aircraft on basis of commercial agreements relating to the provision of joint services, (c) from premises leased or owned by himself or by the other carrier with whom he has the mentioned agreement.

The number of options increases further if successive carriers according to Article 36 or actual carriers according to Article 39 are involved. In respect of actual carriers Article 46 avails the claimant the possibility to start an action against the contracting carrier and the jointly liable actual carrier either in the courts which have jurisdiction over the contractual carrier according to Article 33 or in the courts which have jurisdiction over the actual carrier.

In case of successive carriage, the claimant can sue the carrier in respect of personal injury and delay, at the carrier's principal place of business, who had performed the carriage during which the accident or the delay occurred (Article 36 (2)). As regards luggage or cargo, additionally, the claimant can also sue the last carrier in the courts at his principal place of business (Article 36 (3)). Different from Article 46 for involvement of actual carriers, the Convention does not avail to the claimant the possibility to sue both the first and the successive carrier in one and the same jurisdiction. For details on successive carriage please *see* above paragraph 556.

562. The Montreal Convention does not contain any own provisions on procedure. Article 33 (4) and Article 45 rather leave the procedure to the law governing the court seized of the matter.

X. Mandatory Applicability

563. Like CMR on road transport (*see* above paragraph 407) but with a different technique also the Montreal Convention addresses arbitration. Article 34 (1) allows the parties to agree on arbitration as regards disputes on the liability of the carrier. What then follows in subsections 2 and 3 are two provisions which usually would be dealt with in an arbitration clause. Article 34 (2) addresses the place where the arbitration shall take place and stipulates that this shall be a place within one of the jurisdictions referred to in Article 33. Article 34 (3) states that the arbitration tribunal shall apply the provisions of the Convention. Arbitration clauses may indeed provide this, but if they do not so, by virtue of Article 34 (4) every arbitration clause is deemed to include what is provided for in Article 34 (2) and (3). The Convention then goes on to say that any term of an arbitration agreement which would be inconsistent with what is stipulated in the two mentioned subsections is null and void.

Obviously, the Convention itself cannot prevent that arbitration clauses contain provisions which are in conflict with what is stipulated in Article 34. Such clauses may, for example, provide for a place of the arbitration different than those provided for in Article 33. Also, nothing prevents an arbitration tribunal to disregard the Montreal Convention when deciding the case. The general view in Germany is that arbitration awards rendered on basis of arbitration clauses which are in breach of Article 34 must not be declared enforceable by a German court because such arbitration clauses would be null and void according to Article 34 (4) of the Convention.

Chapter 5. Multimodal Transportation

§1. General

564. With the introduction of the container technology in transport, multimodal carriage has become more and more important in the transport sector and now probably is in use or most of the cargos carried, probably except large bulk cargos. Multimodal transport in this sense is understood to involve one contract covering the transport with different means of transport like ship, truck or aircraft. Since long international transport conventions contain provisions on multimodal transport, or, as many conventions address them, combined carriages. To the extent that Germany has ratified those international conventions, multimodal or combined transport has been a feature of German law. But it took the German lawmaker many decades until in 1998, with the General Transport Law Reform Act, for the first time statutory provisions on multimodal transport were introduced into the Commercial Code. Obviously, the phenomenon of multimodal transport was daily practice of the courts long before 1998. The Federal Court of Justice had developed a sound body of jurisprudence with principles on how to handle multimodal contracts. Much of this jurisprudence has been taken over into the statutory provisions of the Commercial Code.

§2. German Statutory Law

565. The statutory provisions on multimodal transport are part of the general transport law as contained in the Fourth Book of the *Handelsgesetzbuch* (HGB; Commercial Code). They consist of no more than four provisions, contained in §§ 452–452d HGB. § 452 HGB defines what is a multimodal contract under the HGB and declares what provisions apply to it. § 452a HGB deals with the consequences if it is known on which part of the carriage the damage occurred. § 452b HGB relates to certain statutory provisions on notice of damage and limitation periods applicable regardless of whether the place of damage is known or not. § 452c HGB contains a special provision on multimodal removal contracts and, finally, § 452d HGB deals with deviating agreements. The aforementioned provisions are explained in more detail below.

I. The Multimodal Contract of Carriage

566. § 452 HGB lays down the various requirements for a contract to qualify as a multimodal contract of carriage under German law. The first requirement is that the goods are carried on basis of a single contract of carriage. If there is not only a single contract, but a chain of contracts, in Germany this is referred to as *broken transport*. If this is the case, each of the contracts in the chain will be looked at separately and for each of the contracts the applicable law will be determined separately.

567. Next to a single contract of carriage, it is a further requirement that the goods are carried with different modes of transport. Whether the contract provides for several transport modes has to be determined on the facts of the case taking into account the customs of the trade. The most relevant distinction for daily practice obviously is the distinction between vehicles using roads, rail cars using rails, ships using rivers, and the sea and aircrafts using the air space. But also other transport means may be involved like pipelines, cranes or conveyor belts. There exist certain transport modes which have multi-functional characteristics like river-sea vessels or amphibious crafts. If they are employed, the question whether they qualify as a different mode of transport compared to other transport modes employed under the contract will depend on the particular function in which they are used. If, for example, a river-sea vessel is used for carriage of goods from an inland river port to a sea port where the goods are transshipped to an ocean-going ship, then the sea-river ship will be treated as an inland vessel, regardless of the fact that from its construction such ships are also oceangoing. Such a contract, thus, would be considered a multimodal contract under § 452 HGB because it combines transport with an inland vessel and an ocean vessel.

568. However, there is a further requirement for a contract to qualify as a multimodal contract under § 452 HGB. Even if there is a single contract only and even if this provides for carriage by different modes of transport, such a contract qualifies as a multimodal contract only if, had separate contracts been concluded between the parties for each part of the carriage involving one mode of transport (this being defined by the provision as a *transport leg*), at least two of these contracts would have been subject to different legal provisions. For determining whether this is the case, thus, the law disregards the fact that the parties had concluded one single contract of carriage. Rather the law requires taking the hypothetical view that separate contracts had been concluded for every separate transport mode and then requires the test whether different legal provisions would have applied to those hypothetical separate contracts. A multimodal contract under § 452 HGB then will only be given if the result of the hypothetical consideration leads to different legal provisions applicable.

569. In many practical cases there is no real dispute in Germany whether combinations of transport modes qualify as multimodal contracts. The reason for this is that the German general transport law as contained in § 407 HGB applies with the same legal provisions to various transport modes. The decisive statutory provision in this context is § 407 HGB which stipulates in subsection (3) that general transport law applies whenever the goods are to be carried over land, on inland waterways or by aircraft. Transport over land includes transport by road and transport by rail car. Carriage by truck, rail car, inland vessel and aircraft, thus, are all subject to the application of § 407 HGB. Nevertheless, some authors say that while always § 407 HGB may be applicable, the combination of such transport modes may nevertheless lead to different legal provisions being applicable. Examples would be the combination of a closed truck and a river pontoon because the exclusion clause of § 427 (1) No. 1 HGB for carriage on deck would only apply to the river pontoon but not to the truck. Also, in such a case the transport leg by the river pontoon would be subject to the further provisions of the Inland Navigation Act. These discussions, however, are more of dogmatic than practical value. It makes no practical difference whether to treat those modes as the same and then apply § 407 HGB directly, or to treat them as different, resulting in a multimodal transport, and, as will be seen below, end up with § 407 HGB again, but this time by virtue of the reference contained in § 452 HGB. There remain not too many combinations, thus, for which § 452 HGB genuinely leads to the application of the general transport law. These combinations are those which involve carriage on at least one transport leg on the sea. Any multimodal contract involving a sea leg would, upon hypothetical consideration of the applicable law on separate contracts, lead to the application of maritime law for the sea leg. The requirement of § 452 HGB that the hypothetical consideration leads to different legal provisions applicable then would be given because in case of combination of a sea leg with any other transport mode (truck, rail car, inland vessel, aircraft) would lead to the application of the general transport law.

570. In most cases it will not be difficult to determine whether different modes of transport are employed under the contract. There is no doubt, for example, if a truck and an ocean-going ship are involved. But it took some time until the courts have settled more subtle aspects of the law. Uncertainties had prevailed as regards cargo handling in ports and terminals. As the requirement for carriage under § 407 HGB only is that cargo is brought from one location to another (for details *see* paragraphs 408 et seq.), since long cranage, one of the most common modes of cargo handling in ports and terminals, has been considered to be a transport with the consequence that general transport law applies to such cranage. This led to the question whether a port-to-port shipment with a transshipment during the voyage from one ocean vessel to another ocean vessel qualifies as a multimodal contract under § 452 HGB, because maritime law would apply to the two ocean legs and general transport law to the cranage occurring at the transshipment port. Similarly, the question arose how to delineate different transport modes in view of cargo handling involved and necessary for taking the cargo off from one of the transport mode and loading it onto the next transport mode. This aspect, obviously, is only relevant if different legal provisions apply because otherwise everything would be subject to German general transport law anyhow. In practice, thus, this means that the question arose in cases involving ocean transport. Here, the Federal Court of Justice has held that handling of cargo, be it loading or unloading, is to be considered already and still an integral part of the ocean transport. If damage occurs during loading of cargo onto or off-loading of cargo from an ocean-going ship, thus, this damage will be considered to have occurred on the sea leg of the voyage.

571. § 452 HGB, thus, has its most, if not only, relevance in stipulating that in case of the involvement of an ocean transport in combination with any other mode of transport leads to the application not of maritime law but of general transport law. This is not at all self-explanatory. The lawmaker also could have provided that such contracts are subject to that legal regime which covers the longest part of the carriage. This principle has been followed in the delineation between maritime law and inland navigation law if under one and the same contract, without transshipment, carriage is performed both on inland waters and on the sea. For these cases § 450 HGB looks on the distance covered, and if the distance to be covered by sea is longer, then maritime law applies (for details *see* paragraph 412). This principle could have been taken over by the lawmaker also for multimodal contracts. This would have led to the application of maritime law at least in cases where the distance at sea is longer than the distance of any other transport mode. However, under § 452 HGB the distance covered is of no relevance. A contract which combines 10 km of carriage to a sea port, then 5,000 miles by ocean vessel and another 10 km from the arrival port to the final destination will not be subject to maritime law but to general transport law despite the fact that the vast majority of the transport was performed on the sea. This surprising effect is only neutralized by § 452 a HGB which provides for a different result if it is known on which leg of the transport the damage occurred (for details *see* paragraph 573).

572. There is one important proviso in § 452 HGB, however, which can block the application of the German general transport law and that is that the German law applies only if applicable international conventions do not provide otherwise. With this stipulation, the German lawmaker abides by Germany's obligations under the law of nations. Where Germany has ratified transport conventions which contain own provisions on multimodal transport, Germany had to give, and has given, preference to those provisions over the German national legislation. There are a number of conventions containing provisions on multimodal transport which will be addressed in detail below. But here it should be highlighted that the most relevant international conventions on maritime transport, the Hague Rules and the Hague-Visby Rules, do not contain multimodal provisions. Although Germany still is a Hague-Rule country, Germany was not prevented from subordinating multimodal contracts, including a sea leg, to the General Transport Law, which is in many respects very different from General Transport Law.

II. Unknown and Known Locations of Loss

573. While German law generally declares the general transport law applicable to multimodal contracts (§ 452 HGB), it provides for a special rule on the law applicable to claims for damages in respect of loss of or damage to goods or delay in delivery. Here the applicable law depends on whether it is known on which transport leg such damage was caused. The law does not contain any special rules in case this location is unknown. Such cases are simply covered by § 452 HGB with the consequence that the statutory provisions of the German general transport law as contained in §§ 425 et seq. HGB apply (for details to those provisions *see* paragraphs 442 et seq.). However, for known locations, § 452a HGB contains a special rule. This stipulates that if it has been established that the loss, damage or event which caused delay in delivery occurred on a certain transport leg, the liability of the carrier shall be determined in accordance with the legal provisions governing a contract for the carriage of goods on this transport leg. Again the law, thus, requires to identify a law which would apply to a hypothetical separate contract, had this been concluded for the respective transport leg. The first question arising is whether this is necessarily German law or can also be foreign law. This question is answered by application of the Rome I Regulation, which contains in Article 5 detailed provisions on the law applicable to a contract of carriage. The relevant parties to look on for the hypothetical contract are neither the consignor and the actual carrier of the respective transport leg nor the consignor of the hypothetical contract and the actual carrier but the actual consignor under the multimodal contract and the multimodal carrier. This is relevant when determining under Article 5 (3) Rome I Regulation whether regardless of what Article 5 (1) and (2) of the Regulation provide, the case is manifestly more closely connected with another country. On this basis, it is the general view that if a German consignor enters into a multimodal contract with a German multimodal carrier, the contract is manifestly more closely connected to Germany than to any other country, regardless of where the transport leg occurs. Even if the respective transport leg is fully performed outside Germany, thus, it will be German law applicable to such kind of transport which is relevant under § 452a HGB. Not finally settled is the question whether choice of law clauses in the multimodal contract are relevant for determining the hypothetically applicable law for the transport leg. The Hanseatic Court of Appeal of Hamburg has decided so, but there is yet a decision of the Federal Court of Justice to come.

574. As mentioned above, the relevant aspect for determining the location is causation of the loss. But it may happen that damage is caused during one transport leg but develops either partly or even completely on another transport leg. A typical example is damage to a cooling unit of a container. This will interrupt cooling of the cargo which will then gradually get warmer. It depends on the circumstances of the case whether this warming-up already occurs and leads to damage partly on the transport leg during which the defect of the cooling unit occurs, or whether this takes place only on a subsequent leg. As causation is the relevant factor in § 452a HGB, in the first place the law hypothetically applicable to a contract for the transport leg on which the cooling unit became defective has to be considered. But if the law applicable to the transport leg during which (further or all) damage to the goods occurred (but was not caused) puts the carrier under an obligation to avoid or minimize such damage (which he has not caused himself), then the claimant is entitled to pursue his claim for damages also under the law hypothetically applicable to that leg of the transport.

575. If the multimodal carrier performs all legs of the transport himself, only his own liability will be involved which then has to be determined on basis of § 452a HGB. If the multimodal carrier, however, employs subcontractors for some or all legs of the transport, it is possible, and in practice occurs often if not regularly, that the theoretically applicable law of the transport leg according to § 452a HGB is a law different from the law actually applicable to the subcontract of carriage which has been concluded between the multimodal carrier and the subcarrier. This is the necessary consequence of the German lawmaker's decision not to look on the actual contract for the respective transport leg but on a hypothetical contract. Where the liability of the subcontractor is less than that of the multimodal carrier, the multimodal carrier will not be able to obtain full indemnity for damage he has to indemnify the claimant for under the multimodal contract. For such situations, German law, thus, finally allocates a part (or in case of valid full exclusion of liability under the subcontract) all liability on the multimodal carrier. The strong German export industry has led to a strong German forwarding sector as well, and German exporters rely to a considerable extent on German forwarders, who in many cases employ non-German actual carriers on the basis of law other than German law. One maybe surprised, thus, that the German lawmaker has exposed (German) forwarders to such a liability gap. German multimodal carriers cannot avoid this situation by agreeing with their customers that the law applicable to the hypothetical contract of carriage for the transport leg shall be the law actually agreed by the multimodal carrier for such transport leg. This option is not available because § 452dHGB does not allow it (for details *see* paragraph 582). The only option left to the carrier to avoid a gap in liability is to agree with the subcarrier on German law, but the reality in international carriage of goods is that in many cases the multimodal carrier will not be able to reach such an agreement.

But there may also be cases in which the law applicable to the actual contract for the respective transport leg provides for higher liability than the hypothetical law applicable according to § 452a HGB. In those cases, thus, it may be that the liability of the multimodal carrier is lower or even excluded while the liability of the actual carrier of such transport leg under the subcontract of carriage is higher. For these scenarios it is the general view that the multimodal carrier is under an implied duty to pursue the damages suffered by the relevant party under the multimodal contract against the subcontractor if the law governing the subcontract allows this.

576. § 452a determines in its second sentence who bears the burden of proof in respect of the transport leg on which loss, damage or the event causing delay in delivery occurred. This burden is placed for all cases neither on the carrier nor on the claimant, but it is placed on the person who alleges causation on a certain transport leg. This is fully in line with the general principles on burden of proof under German law. Under these principles it is generally the party which would have an advantage out of a certain fact which has to prove this fact.

577. It cannot be overestimated that the relevance of a known place of damage is of relevance exclusively for determining the carrier's liability. All other aspects will be subject to the German general transport law.

III. Notice of Damage and Limitation Periods

578. As just explained, if it is proven on which transport leg loss, damage or delay was caused, liability for such loss, damage or delay is not determined according to the liability provisions of the general transport law as contained in §§ 425 et seq. HGB, but on basis of the liability provisions which would have been applicable if, hypothetically, a separate contract between the consignor and the multimodal carrier had been entered into for the respective transport leg. This law may, and usually will, contain provisions on notice of damage and on limitation periods. Here, § 452b HGB steps in and provides for a hybrid of respective provisions of the German general transport law and of the law governing a hypothetical contract for the respective transport leg.

579. In respect of notice of damage, § 452b (1) HGB stipulates that the respective provision in general transport law, § 438 HGB, applies regardless of whether the location of the loss is known or unknown (for details on § 438 HGB *see* paragraph 468). But for the benefit of the claimant it is further provided that in respect of compliance with form and time for the notice of damage it is also sufficient if the provisions are observed which would have been applicable to a contract for the carriage of goods for the last transport leg. This provision, thus, introduces possibly a third set of legal provisions which become relevant for determining the multimodal carrier's liability. If the location of the loss is unknown, then the liability is determined exclusively by §§ 425 et seq. HGB (cf. § 452 HGB). If a location of the loss is known, the liability is exclusively dependent on the law which would have been applicable had the parties entered into a separate contract of carriage for the respective transport leg (§ 452a HGB). As regards form and time limit for the notice of damage, form and time are protected if the claimant has observed the requirements of the last transport leg, even if this is not the transport leg on which the damage occurred. As a result, what the law governing the transport leg on which the damage was caught says in respect of form and time limit is usually irrelevant because this is governed by § 438 HGB. It can only be relevant if the damage occurred on the last transport leg, but even then it is only relevant if it is beneficial to the claimant, i.e., if the requirements in respect of form and time are less than the respective requirements of § 438 HGB.

580. In respect of limitation periods, § 452b (2) HGB deals with limitation but not with the limitation period as such. This is finally determined by § 439 HGB (one year, in case of intent or recklessness three years). The first aspect dealt with in § 452b (2) HGB is the commencement of the limitation period. Here it is provided that if the period commences at the time the goods were delivered, the relevant time of delivery shall be the time of delivery to the consignee. This stipulation has an effect only if the location of the loss is known. If it is not known, general transport law applies anyhow, and what § 452b (2) HGB intends to achieve is provided for already in § 439 (2) HGB. But if the location of the loss is known and if this loss was not caused on the last transport leg, then the law applicable to a hypothetical separate contract for this transport leg may, and usually will, provide for a commencement of the limitation period at the moment of delivery under such hypothetical contract. If this transport leg is not the last transport leg, such delivery will be delivery to a further carrier, but not to the consignee under the multimodal contract. Without § 452b (2) HGB, thus, the limitation period would commence to run before the goods were delivered, or were supposed to be delivered, to the consignee with the consequence that not the full limitation period would be available to him. By fixing the relevant time for commencement of the limitation period to delivery to a consignee this result is avoided.

A further rule laid down in § 452b (2) HGB is that regardless of what the law on liability according to § 452a HGB otherwise says, the claim for damages will only be time-barred in accordance with § 439 HGB. This gives the claimant the benefit of a suspension of the time limit by the consignee asserting his claims to the carrier (§ 439 (3) HGB). This suspension, thus, will occur even if the law governing the liability under § 452a HGB does not contain such a suspensive effect.

IV. Multimodal Removal Contracts

581. Removal contracts are in most cases concluded by consumers. This has already been the reason for the German lawmaker to include special provisions on removal contracts in the General Transport Law (§ 451–451h HGB, for details *see* above paragraph 477). This consumer protection legislation is extended to multimodal removal contracts. § 452c HGB follows the structure of § 452, 452a HGB, but with some special features. First, the multimodal removal contract is not governed by §§

407 et seq. HGB, but by the special provisions of § 451–451h HGB. Second, the provision of § 452a HGB applies only if the transport leg on which the damage was caused is subject to the provision of an international convention which binds Germany. The consequence is that absent any such international convention being applicable, § 451–451h HGB will apply regardless of at which leg of transport the damage was caused.

V. Mandatory Application

582. Mandatory application of § 452–452c HGB is dealt with in § 452d HGB. The provision is complex and follows different principles and provides for different rules on how to deviate from what provision. The general rule is that deviation from those provisions may only be made insofar as the provisions referred to therein permit deviating agreements (§ 452d (1), (2) HGB). The effect is:

- In respect of § 452: This provision refers to the German general transport law as contained in §§ 407–449 HGB. From those provisions, deviation is only possible within the limits of § 449 HGB (for details on this *see* paragraph 407). Deviations from § 452 HGB, thus, are only possible to the extent and in the way as provided for in § 449 HGB.
- § 452a HGB: In case of known location of the loss, this makes the law applicable which would govern a hypothetical contract entered into only in respect of the respective transport leg. This provision can be deviated from to the extent that deviation is possible under the respective hypothetically applicable law. As an example, suppose the damage was caused during maritime transport which is subject to German maritime law. Mandatory application of the German maritime law is dealt with in § 512 HGB (for details on this *see* paragraph 212). As a consequence, in this example the parties could deviate from what § 452a HGB stipulates only to the extent and by the ways provided by § 512 HGB.
- § 452b HGB refers to §§ 438, 439 HGB. Here the same applies as for § 452 HGB: Deviation is only possible to the extent and in the ways allowed by § 449 HGB.
- § 452c HGB: This refers to the provisions of the second sub-chapter, i.e., § 451–451h HGB. Here, deviating agreements are dealt with in § 451h HGB. Any deviation from § 452c HGB, thus, is only possible to the extent and in the way as allowed by § 451h HGB.
- International conventions: To the extent that the provisions make reference to international conventions (§ 452, 452c HGB) deviation is only possible if the conventions allow deviation.

§3. Treaty Law

583. With the exception of the Convention on International Multimodal Transport of Goods (MT Convention), which has not yet been entered into force, and, in all likelihood, never will enter into force, there does not exist a genuine multimodal transport convention. But almost all of the existing unimodal transport conventions deal with the situation that the transport mode regulated by the respective convention is not the only transport mode employed under one and the same contract of carriage. The following will introduce the various rules in a number of those conventions. As regards maritime transport, the Hamburg Rules and the Rotterdam Rules, the latter not yet being in force, will be addressed. The most widespread convention on maritime transport is the Hague/Hague-Visby Rules. They are not addressed here because they do not contain any provision on multimodal transport.

I. The Hamburg Rules

584. The Hamburg Rules are a convention governing carriage by sea. They define their scope of application in Article 2 and declare that contracts of carriage by sea are governed by the convention if a number of detailed requirements are fulfilled. The Hamburg Rules do not deal with multimodal transport in Article 2, but by way of definition of the term *contract of carriage by sea* to which the scope of application is linked in Article 2. The definition is contained in Article 1 (6). The principal meaning is that of a contract where the carrier undertakes to carry goods by sea from one port to another port. However, the definition extends to contracts which involve carriage by sea and also carriage by other transport modes. Such contracts are deemed to be contracts of carriage by sea for the purposes of the Hamburg Rules, but only so far as the contract relates to the carriage by sea. Multimodal contracts including a sea leg which is subject to the Hamburg Rules, thus, will be governed by the Hamburg Rules as far as the sea leg is concerned. For all other legs, the applicable law must be determined on basis of the applicable private international law.

II. The Rotterdam Rules

585. Also the Rotterdam Rules link their application to *contracts of carriage* if certain requirements as laid down in Article 5 are fulfilled. Like the Hamburg Rules, the Rotterdam Rules deal with the aspect of multimodal carriage by defining the term *contract of carriage*. This definition is contained in Article 1 (1) of the Convention. In the first instance it does not require shipment from port to port but rather 'from one place to another'. Maritime transport comes into play when Article 1 (1) requires in the second sentence that the contract shall provide for carriage by sea and may provide for carriage by other modes of transport in addition to the sea carriage. This is the so-called *Maritime Plus* concept of the Rotterdam Rules. They apply only if a part of the transport is made by sea, but if so they cover the whole transport, even if other modes of transport are used as well. The delineation between the Rotterdam Convention and other international transport conventions is dealt with in Article 82. Generally speaking, the Rotterdam Rules give room for the application of conventions governing the carriage of goods by air, by road, by rail and by inland waterways to the extent that they contain multimodal provisions including a sea leg.

III. The CMR Convention

586. According to Article 1 (1) the CMR Convention applies to contracts for the carriage of goods by road in vehicles. However Article 2 CMR contains an extension for cases in which the vehicle containing the goods is carried over a part of the journey by sea, by rail, by inland waterways or by air. If this occurs and if the goods are not unloaded from the vehicle, the CMR Convention applies to the whole of the carriage. But Article 2 contains an important exception. If it is proved that the loss, damage or delay in delivery of the goods occurring during the carriage by the other means of transport was not caused by an act or omission of the road carrier, but by an event which could only have occurred (a) in the course of and (b) by reason of the carriage by that other means of transport, the carrier's liability is not determined by the CMR Convention but on the basis of such provisions under which liability would have been determined if the sender of the goods had entered into a direct contract of carriage with the carrier of that other transport means.

Unfortunate enough, the wording of the two original languages French and English differ in an important aspect. While the English words provide that the respective governing law shall be determined 'in accordance with the conditions *prescribed* by law', the French wording is 'conformêment aux dispositions *imperatives* de la loi'. While the French version is understood to mean that the CMR subordinates itself only under *mandatory* provisions, the English wording is understood to mean that the CMR subordinates itself to *statutory* provisions. The difference is fundamental and tremendous if the law governing the transport leg is laid down in a statute but does not apply mandatorily. German courts had to deal with this question in respect of the fire on the RoRo vessel 'UND ADRIYATIK'. This case involved more than 180 trucks completely burnt on board of the vessel on a voyage from Turkey to Italy. The German Federal Court of Justice followed the English text and the English reasoning so that it is sufficient that the law is statutory law, even if it is not mandatory. This may seem surprising because the German official translation of Article 2 is 'zwingendes Recht', which means mandatory law. But the Federal Court recognized that the German version is a non-authoritative translation only, so that the French and the English version had to be considered. The Federal Court looked at the history of the negotiations leading to CMR and found that Article 2 CMR had been drafted by the British delegation which, in view of the geographical situation of the United Kingdom, was adamant for the CMR to provide that road carriers are exempted from liability for damage caused during sea carriage by typical perils of such sea carriage. This was enough for the Federal Court to give the English wording and its understanding preference over the French wording and its understanding.

IV. The CIM Convention

587. The CIM Convention deals with its scope of application in Article 1 which stipulates in § 1 that, subject to further requirements, the Convention shall apply to every contract of carriage of goods by rail for reward. Article 38 and Article 1 (4) address single contracts of carriage which include carriage by sea or transfrontier carriage by inland waterways as a supplement to carriage by rail. The CMI applies to such contracts if the carriage by sea or inland waterways is performed on services included in the list of services provided for in Article 24 (1) of the COTIF Convention. This means that railway law is applicable to carriage by sea or inland waterways.

However, Article 38 CIM contains further provisions on liability in respect of rail-sea traffic. They have the same purpose as Article 2 CMR, namely to avoid that a rail carrier is liable for damage caused by perils peculiar to carriage by sea or inland waterways. But the technique used by Article 38 CIM is different from the technique used in Article 2 CMR. First, it relates only to rail-sea carriage by certain rail carriers, namely services referred to in Article 24 (1) COTIF. Next, different from Article 2 CMR, Article 38 (1) CIM does not replace the provisions of CIM by provisions of maritime law, but adds additional exemptions from liability, namely (a) fire, if the carrier proves that the fire was not caused by his act or default or by that of the master, a mariner, a pilot or the carrier's servants; (b) saving or attempting to save life or property at sea; (c) loading of goods on deck with the consent of the consignor and (d) perils, dangers and accidents of the sea or other navigable waters. It is obvious that these defences were taken from the list of defences contained in the Hague Rules.

V. The CIV Convention

588. The CIV Convention defines its scope of application in Article 1 and determines in § 1 that, subject to further requirements, the Convention applies to every contract of carriage of passengers by rail. §§ 2 and 3 of Article 1 deal with two different scenarios of multimodal transport. § 2 declares the CIV Convention applicable if international carriage by rail is combined under a single contract with national carriage by road or inland waterway of a Member State. The combination of carriage by rail and carriage by inland waterway is also addressed in § 3, but here the carriage by inland waterway must be transfrontier carriage. Next to such transfrontier carriage by inland waterway, § 3 also addresses combinations of carriage by rail and carriage by sea. In both cases the CIV Convention extends also to the carriage by sea or by inland waterways if such carriage is performed by services included in the list of services provided for in Article 24 (1) COTIF. Different from the CIM Convention, the CIV Convention does not add any additional exemptions from liability for the carrier. The reason probably is that in international maritime carriage of goods the Hague/Hague-Visby Rules have a dominant and widespread relevance. International carriage of passengers by sea, in contrast, is relatively new and was first achieved by the Athens Convention. Still it is noteworthy that there is no link between the Athens Convention and the CIV Convention. It is the Athens Convention which avoids that there is a clash between the CIV Convention and the Athens Convention, as described below.

VI. The Athens Convention

589. The Athens Convention determines its application in Article 2 and declares itself applicable to any 'international carriage' which is defined in Article 1 (9) as any carriage in which, according to the contract of carriage, the place of departure and the place of destination are situated in two different states. The 'contract of carriage' is itself defined in Article 1 (2) to be a contract for the carriage by sea of a passenger and his luggage, as the case may be. Before this background, thus, Article 2 (1) applies to any contract which provides for the carriage by sea of passengers. Multimodal carriage of passengers is only indirectly addressed in Article 2 (2) according to which the Athens Convention does not apply when the carriage is subject to, under any international convention concerning the carriage of passengers or luggage by another mode of transport, a civil liability regime under the provisions of such convention, but only insofar as those provisions have mandatory application to the carriage by sea. The Athens Convention, thus, insofar subordinates itself to other mandatory international conventions.

VII. The Warsaw Convention and the Montreal Convention

590. Germany has ratified the Warsaw Convention 1929 as well as later amendments by the Hague Protocol of 1955, the Montreal Interim Agreement of 1966 and the four Montreal Protocols of 1975. However, after ratification of the Montreal Convention, according to Article 55 of the Montreal Convention, the latter prevails over the Warsaw Convention and its amendments. Due to the many ratifications of the Montreal Convention, the Warsaw Convention and its amendments are meanwhile of less relevance for Germany.

The Warsaw Convention deals with combined carriage in Article 31. There it is provided that in case of combined carriage performed partly by air and partly by any other mode of carriage, the provisions of the Warsaw Convention apply only to the carriage by air, provided this fulfils the requirements of Article 1, subsection 2. Article 31 clarifies that nothing in the Warsaw Convention prevents the parties to agree in the document of air carriage on conditions relating to other modes of carriage as long as the provisions of the Convention are observed as regards carriage by air.

Article 38 of the Montreal Convention contains an almost identical provision. The only difference is reference to Article 18 (4) of the Montreal Convention. This was necessary because Article 18 provides for a liability of the air carrier during carriage by air. Carriage by air in this meaning is not defined as the time when the cargo is on a plane, even less if the plane is in the air. Rather Article 18 (3) defines carriage by air as the period during which the cargo is in charge of the carrier. Such a definition would include into carriage by air also parts of the carriage which are not performed by aircraft. Indeed, Article 18 (4) (1) deals with carriage by land, by sea or by inland waterway and excludes such carriage from the period of carriage by air only if it is performed outside an airport. If performed inside an airport, thus, the Convention treats such transport as carriage by air and makes it subject to the Montreal Convention. But even such carriage outside an airport can ultimately be subject to the Montreal Convention because in respect of such carriage Article 18 (4) 2 of the Convention stipulates that, subject to proof to the contrary, any damage occurred is presumed to have been the result of an event which took place during the carriage by air. This means that the carrier has to prove the contrary if he wants to escape liability based on the

Montreal Convention. Finally, Article 18 (4) (3) of the Montreal Convention deals with a situation in which the carrier, contrary to the agreed carriage by air, carries out the whole or part of the carriage by another transport mode. If so, transport also by such other transport mode is subject to the Montreal Convention.

Selected Bibliography

Allstadt-Schmitz, Gisela/Boujong [Hrsg.], Karlheinz/Thomas, Carsten [Hrsg.]/Joost, Deltev [Hrsg.]/Strohn, Lutz [Hrsg.], Kommentar zum Handelsgesetzbuch, Ebenroth; Boujong; Joost, §§ 343 – 475h HGB, 3rd edn., München, 2015.

Andresen, Bernd/Bahnsen, Kay Uwe/Bydlinski, Peter/Eckardt, Tobias/Frantzioch, Fritz/Freise, Rainer/Herber, Rolf/Hesse, Peter/Jesse-Huß, Helga/Otte, Karsten/Pötschke, Jan-Erik/ Ruhwedel, Edgar/ Sager, Hartmuth/ Schmidt, Christine/ Steingröver, Wilm/ Teutsch, Christian/ Tuhme, Karl-Heinz / Schmidt, Karsten [Hrsg.], Münchener Kommentar zum Handelsgesetzbuch, §§407 – 619 HGB, 3rd edn., München, 2013.

Bergmann, Andreas/Boesche, Katharina Vera/Busche, Jan/ Kamanabrou, Sudabeh/ Koch, Robert/ Körber, Torsten/Kotzian-Marggraf, Karl/ Lieder, Jan/Martinek, Michael/ Maultzsch, Felix/ Oetker, Hartmut [Hrsg.]/Pamp, Rüdiger/ Paschke, Marian/ Preuß, Nicola/ Schlingloff, Jochen/Schubert, Claudia/ Vossler, Norbert/ Wedemann, Frauke, Handelsgesetzbuch, Kommentar, 5th edn., München, 2017.

Bremke, Nils, Handbuch Transportrecht : Fachinformationen der deutschen Transportversicherer, 1st edn., Berlin, 2008.

Czerwenka, Beate, Das Gesetz zur Reform des Seehandelsrechts : Einleitung – Erläuterung – Synopse, Köln, 2014.

Czerwenka, Beate, Die geplante Reform des Seehandelsrechts : Einführung – Referentenentwurf – Sachverständigenbericht – Synopse, Köln, 2011.

Giemulla, Elmar/ Schmid, Ronald/Müller-Rostin, Wolf, Kommentar zum Montrealer Übereinkommen : Internationales Lufttransportrecht, 41st edn., Neuwied, 2016.

Giemulla, Elmar/Schmid, Ronald/Müller-Rostin, Wolf, Frankfurter Kommentar zum Luftverkehrsgesetz : mit den luftverkehrsrechtlichen Vorschriften des Strafgesetzbuches, 77th edn., Frankfurt am Main, 2017.

Hartenstein, Olaf/Reuschle, Fabian, Handbuch des Fachanwalts : Transport- und Speditionsrecht, 3rd edn., Köln, 2015.

Herber, Rolf, Seehandelsrecht : systematische Darstellung, 2nd edn., Berlin, 2016.

Hofmann, Max/Grabherr, Erwin/Reidt, Olaf/Wysk, Peter [Hrsg.], Kommentar zum Luftverkehrsgesetz, 19th edn., München, 2017.

Koller, Ingo, Transportrecht : Kommentar zu Spedition, Gütertransport und Lagergeschäft, 9th edn., München, 2016.

Lommatzsch, Jutta, Transportrecht, 1st edn., Stuttgart, 2012.

Ovie, Talke, Praxishandbuch Transport : Logistik, Versicherung, Zoll, Exportkontrolle, Steuern, 1st edn., Köln, 2014.

Paschke, Marian/Furnell, Winfried, Transportrecht, 1st edn., München, 2011.

Rabe, Hans-Jürgen [Hrsg.]/Bahnsen, Kay Uwe [Hrsg.]/Rittmeister, Sabine, Seehandelsrecht : fünftes Buch des Handelsgesetzbuches mit Nebenvorschriften und Internationalen Übereinkommen, 5th edn., München, 2018.

Ramming, Klaus, Hamburger Handbuch zum Binnenschifffahrtsrecht, 1st edn., München, 2009.

Ramming, Klaus, Hamburger Handbuch multimodaler Transport : das Recht des Gütertransports mit unterschiedlichen Beförderungsmitteln einschließlich Seestrecke, 1st edn., München, 2011.

Reuschle, Fabian, Montrealer Übereinkommen unter Berücksichtigung der aktuellen Anhebung der Haftungshöchbeträge, 2nd edn., Berlin, 2011.

Schladebach, Marcus, Luftrecht, 1st edn., Tübingen, 2007.

Schwenk, Walter/Giemulla, Elmar/Schyndel, Heiko van, Handbuch des Luftverkehrsrechts, 3rd edn., Köln, 2005.

Index

The numbers here refer to paragraph numbers.

Index

Index

Index

Index

Made in the USA
Monee, IL
13 September 2026

62974267R00149